WRITERS, CRITICS, AND CHILDREN

WRITERS, CRITICS, AND CHILDREN

Articles from
Children's literature in education

Edited by
Geoff Fox
Graham Hammond
Terry Jones
Frederic Smith
Kenneth Sterck

AGATHON PRESS
New York

HEINEMANN EDUCATIONAL BOOKS
London

Selection and arrangement
© 1976 by Geoff Fox
'Myth and Education' © 1976 by Ted Hughes

First published in the United States, 1976, by

AGATHON PRESS, INC.
150 Fifth Avenue
New York, N.Y. 10011

ISBN (U.S.A.) 0-87586-054-0

First published in Great Britain, 1976, by

HEINEMANN EDUCATIONAL BOOKS LTD.
48 Charles Street, London W1X 8AH
and Edinburgh Melbourne Auckland
Hong Kong Singapore Kuala Lumpur
Ibadan Nairobi Johannesburg
Lusaka New Delhi Kingston

ISBN (UK, cloth) 0 435 18302 8
     (UK, paper) 0 435 18303 6

Library of Congress Cataloging In Publication Data
Main entry under title:

Writers, critics, and children.

    1 Children's literature--History and criticism--
Addresses, essays, lectures. I. Fox, Geoffrey Percival.
II. Children's literature in education.
PN1009.A1W7   809'.89282   76-5418
ISBN 0-87586-054-0

Printed in the United States

In Memory of
SIDNEY ROBBINS

Contents

Preface

IN 1969 the late Sidney Robbins, Senior Lecturer at Saint Luke's College, Exeter, brought together children's writers, teachers, lecturers and librarians at the first Exeter Conference on *Recent Children's Fiction and Its Role in Education*. His intention was both to make outstanding postwar books more widely known and to encourage the keener consideration of the books and the responses of young readers.

One immediate consequence of that conference was the journal *Children's literature in education** devoted to the discussion of children's books, in the belief that those interested in writing about them needed sufficient space to develop their subject.

Small, specialist journals are often short-lived. We felt that six years of publication, an increasing readership and the growth from three to four issues a year were worth celebrating. More important, we felt that many contributions—more than we have been able to include—deserved the more accessible form which this book provides.

In Part One of this collection, individual writers consider some of the challenges and choices implicit in writing for children. Part Two is concerned with evaluation and critical discussion of children's fiction. Part Three deals with books and young readers themselves, suggesting methods of presentation and deepening both enjoyment and appreciation.

The Editors

*First published in Great Britain and, since 1972, by APS Publications, Inc., 150 Fifth Avenue, New York, N.Y. 10011.

Part One
WRITERS

A Dead Pig and My Father

Nina Bawden

Nina Bawden is well known as the author of several adult novels and as a writer for children. Four of her children's books (The Witch's Daughter, Carrie's War, The Runaway Summer and A Handful of Thieves) have been made into television serials.

ONE OF MY earliest memories is standing in the London Docks looking at a dead pig in the water. It was floating belly upwards, a tight yellowish balloon, veined with blue. It was surrounded by several planks of wood that were being pushed into the side by a passenger liner that was coming into dock. When these planks crowded together and bumped the swollen-bellied pig, it bobbed in the water and squeaked.

I was four years old. I know how old I was because my mother was standing beside me, holding my baby brother. He was wrapped in a shawl and he had a face like a wet, wrinkled prune. He was two months old and he had been born just after my fourth birthday.

We were standing on the dockside, my mother and my baby brother and me, because my father's ship was coming in. He was a marine engineer, coming home from Australia after a long time away and he hadn't seen my baby brother so this was an important occasion. My mother said, 'Look at the big ship, Nina. See if you can see Daddy.'

But I was more interested in the dead pig. I went on watching it as it bobbed and squeaked in the water.

Children don't always feel what adults expect them to feel, nor see what adults expect them to see. They inhabit the same world but they look at it so differently. This is why they are so rewarding to write about, so *useful* to the novelist. Novelists have always used children, as Henry James used his little heroine in *What Maisie Knew*, to comment on the hypocrisies and follies of society. They move, as it were, in the undergrowth; they have their ears to the ground, and their eyes are unclouded. They are detached, attentive and sometimes quite cruel observers of what goes on in the adult world because, although it is their world too, their interests in it are basically quite different. A dead pig, to a four-year-old, can be more interesting than the father she has not seen for years and has almost forgotten.

Of course, this small personal anecdote is really a bit disingenuous. I was perfectly well aware that my father was coming home and that this was an important occasion. I knew to some extent how my mother felt—and what she wanted from me. She wanted to present him with a charming picture of a happy, welcoming family. She wanted me to smile and be nice, jump up and down, shout, 'Hallo Daddy'. I couldn't do it, that was all. It was true that I was fascinated by the dead pig, but I was also paralysed by embarrassment at this dreadful role she was expecting me to play. And the more she coaxed and persuaded, the more impossible it was for me to do what she wanted. We were bellowing to each other across an unbridgeable gulf.

We were both there together, caught up in the same highly charged, emotional situation, but we each saw it quite differently. And the important difference between writing for adults and writing for children is not style or subject matter, though those things come into it, but the point of view you're looking from.

I should say, before I go on, that by writing for children I mean writing for pre-adolescents from about ten to thirteen or so. The child I am writing for is, I suppose, the child I used to be, and since my childhood came to an end, more or less, when the war broke out and I left home for the first time, I have a fairly clear, fixed picture of that child and her emotions and preoccupations in my mind. I do not write for older children—although any literate teenager could read my adult novels—and I do not think there is any point in writing specifically for them. I believe, indeed, that the growing tendency in children's fiction to give more critical attention to books for adolescents than to those written for a younger audience is a slightly pernicious one.

Of course, a statement like that must be qualified. There are some novels that are especially suitable for teenagers, some fantasies, some historical stories, and there are occasional books, like that marvellous, stylized comedy, *The Strange Affair of Adelaide Harris*, that appeal enormously to them. But in general, it seems to me that most modern novels aimed deliberately at this older age group are often watered down adult fiction; thin gruel, rather foolishly served to people who not only should be cutting their adult teeth on more solid food, but, given the choice, would prefer to. Dr Johnson may not have been right when he said that babies do not want to read about other babies, but I am quite sure that most adolescents don't want to read about other adolescents, or at least not in a selectively limited way. They may read children's books, consciously slipping back into childhood from time to time for a number of reasons and no harm in that, but once they've crossed the bridge—so to speak—emerged from childhood, what they want to read about is the new world they've just entered. They are concerned with their own position in it, of course, but *not* in the way in which it is being presented in those novels that are written about what are presumed to be exclusively teenage problems. We all know the story about the mother who went to the library to get a suitable novel for her fifteen-year-old and was asked by the librarian, 'What's his problem?'

Literature has a function in education, obviously—we all learn about the world and our place in it through story—but it is not a branch of the social services, supplying advice about drugs or sex, what to do about VD or where to get an abortion, which is the sort of subject that seems to appeal to the writers who have decided to cash in on this particular market, or work out their own emotional hangups by passing them on to the young. As a view of adolescence this seems not only unpleasantly prurient, but as curiously unrealistic as the romantic Victorian view of childhood as a state of innocence from which we have all fallen. And even when good novelists write for adolescents they tend to give a narrower picture than they should, write over-sensitively about 'growing up' as an exercise in nostalgia, or as an escape perhaps from the spiritual and emotional confusion of being really grown up. Which is not to say one should not write *about* adolescence, only that one should do so in the mainstream of fiction for adults, from an adult point of view, so that the book is there on the shelves along with Tolstoy and Salinger and Graham Greene and Kurt Vonnegut and can be judged beside them.

Now, having cleared that bit of ground, let's turn to the children. When I started to write it never occurred to me to write for them. Why should I? I was grown up. I wrote three books before I even used a child as a fictional character and when I did, in *Devil by the Sea*, it was only, initially, to give an extra turn of the screw to a thriller. But as I wrote that book the child in it, a fat, unattractive nine-year-old who became hopelessly involved with a murderer, began to fascinate me. She was a liar as well as being fat and plain, and when she tried to explain to her parents what was happening to her—which she only half understood anyway—they either misinterpreted what she told them or assumed she was lying as usual. She was locked in her small, nightmarish world as they were locked in theirs, and there was no communication between them.

That child was part of me, of my own remembered past, far more so than any adult character I had invented up to that time, and, as I developed her, I began to see clearly for the first time, for *myself*, how true it is that the child is father to the man. This is something Wordsworth knew long before Freud. Writing about children you have to hold in your head what they will become when they are grown. Writing about adults, you must be able to see what they once were. You go back to the beginning so you can see how things became as they are. This is why I write as I do, alternately for adults and for children. I find the one kind of book feeds the other.

But to begin with, although I wrote several novels after *Devil by the Sea* with children in them—*Tortoise by Candlelight, A Little Love, a Little Learning*—the story was always told from the adult standpoint. That is, the adult looking back and using the child's innocence and fresh sensibilities as a way of commenting on the accepted assumptions of society and so getting a double view of what seems to be going on. We, the writer and reader, think we know what the adults are up to. The child will only partly know. To him, criminal actions, say, or gross sexual misconduct, may only appear as lying or cheating, unkindness, thoughtlessness—cruelty of one kind or another towards other people. I say 'only'. What, in truth, could be worse? Hurting people is a greater crime than robbing banks. The very fact that the child has a partial view and is ignorant of some more trivially nasty aspects of adult behaviour, serves to put them in perspective and so makes an important moral point.

Writing *for* children is not easier than writing for adults: it is different. The storyline, clearly, has to be stronger. Children may say, if asked, that they have enjoyed a highly praised book without much of a plot, but then children will often give the answer they think is expected. They are naturally courteous in this way like some primitive tribes. The clue to what they really enjoy is what they reread, what they go back to, and this is almost always a book with a strong narrative line.

Not that they are unsubtle. Most of the subjects I write about for adults I write about for children, too: personal relationships, emotions, motives—the extraordinary gulf between what people say and what they really mean. The only real difference—or so it seems to me—between writing for children and writing for adults is the difference of viewpoints. When I wrote my first children's novel I just became eleven years old again.

And that wasn't so difficult. Time travel is not simply a device dreamed up by science fiction writers. We can all travel backwards, whenever we fancy, inside our own heads. You remember the physical sensation of, say, a stocking stuck on the blood of a grazed knee, the smell of dog dirt on the path by the railway line, and the emotional memories follow at once . . . .

Writing for children I remembered, too, the kind of books I had enjoyed as a child. Adventure stories, of course. All children like adventure, and not just for the excitement of what happens next. You don't have to read Anna Freud to know that children enjoy Jack killing the giant. But more important than that basic fantasy is the fact that children are, by and large, singularly helpless. In real life they can't make anything happen. All they can do is stand by and watch. In adventure stories they can see themselves taking part in the action and not only that. They can also test themselves, measure themselves against the characters in the book. Would *they* be brave in such a situation, or would they run away? Would they be honest, or would they lie?

Remembering what I had enjoyed when I was young, I remembered what I had missed in children's books, too. The grown-ups, apart from a wicked stepmother or uncle, were always flat, peripheral figures with no emotions and no function. The books offered to me in my childhood left out the adult world, and even when they didn't, entirely, they never presented adults as children really see them. Parents and teachers were usually shown as kind, loving, distant figures— emotionally hygienic, you might say. Not only were they never beastly to children except in a stereotyped, fairy tale way, but they were never beastly to anyone. They were never the uncertain, awkward, quirky, *dangerous* creatures that I knew adults to be. Since it was the adults who had written these books, it was reasonable to assume that they didn't want to give themselves away; show themselves to us children, to their *enemies*, as they really were. I think, when I started writing for children, I wanted to put this right. To include the grown-ups as solid characters whose roles were as important in a child's life as I knew them to be, and also to *expose* them. And of course, recognizable meanness in adults is something children do enjoy reading about. A boy wrote to me about *A Handful of Thieves* and said, 'I liked that book because Fred's Mum is sometimes nasty to his Gran the way my Mum is sometimes nasty to my Gran. I made my Mum read the book.'

Not that children are perfect, either. But what they do have, however they behave, is a strong sense of right and wrong, an awareness, if you like, of good and evil. They are often aware of their own badness in a way adults sometimes forget. When I was young, I often felt very bad and wicked. All children do—I know this now, but I didn't know it then. The children in the books I had read never seemed to have the kind of dark, angry feelings that worried me. They were often naughty in a jolly way, but they were never bad. None of them felt as I did when I was nine years old, no one in the world.

When I was nine, I went to stay with my grandmother for the summer. She lived in Swaffham, in Norfolk. My grandfather had just died and I was to keep her company. She had been born in 1860, married a coach painter, had four children —an ordinary life, but it didn't seem ordinary to me. That summer I stayed with her she told me stories, about her girlhood and young womanhood—about her whole life. Reliving it, perhaps, to comfort herself as well as amuse me, but because she was a natural storyteller she made a great tale of it, a kind of celebration. And as a result, although I have my own memories of Swaffham, the town I saw then and still see now was the one she told me about which was more real and more vivid than anything I could see with my own eyes. The Sunday School treat, the Harvest Fair, the gipsy carts, the booth where you could have a tooth pulled for sixpence with a brass band to drown your screams, the Toffee Woman's stall. The Toffee Woman used to pick up a lump of sticky brown toffee, throw it over a nail, moisten her hands with spit, and then draw it out in a long skein until it was as smooth as pale glass.

It was at the Harvest Fair that one of my grandmother's suitors came after her with a shotgun. He pointed it at her and said that if she wouldn't marry him, he'd shoot her and himself after. She looked coldly down the barrel and said, 'Go and put your father's gun back before he misses it, Willy Hollis. I wouldn't have you if you were stuffed with gold.'

My grandmother was often the heroine of her own stories

but she peopled the world she told about with a great host of minor characters. Some were eccentric, to say the least, like the farmer who shut his wife in the sty at night and drove the pigs up to the best bedroom. Some were sad, some were comic—and there was a certain amount of half-pleasurable horror, like the tale of the woman down Tank Lane who had a baby every year. Only one had survived, little Johnny, who had a permanently snotty nose and was a bit weak in the head, I suspect like his mother. The rest died mysteriously soon after birth and were buried in the back garden. The doctor was reported as saying, 'If the next one goes it'll be prison, so watch out.' The next one did live, thanks to my grandmother, who kept a neighbourly eye, but eleven months later she was passing the house and saw a dead, newborn baby lying on the window sill in full view of the street. When she knocked on the door she was told, 'I did put it on the chest behind the looking glass but Johnny would play with it.'

Not a very suitable tale for children, perhaps. But it did me no harm. I was fascinated by my grandmother's stories, by the glimpses they gave me of an adult world which was rather different from anything I had been shown before. I would not, all the same, put that kind of story in a children's novel. There is all the difference in the world between hearing something at your grandmother's knee and reading it in print. Writing for children, you should never pretend things are other than they are, but you can, and should, leave out things that are beyond their comprehension. Answering their questions, their doubts and fears, is one thing. Clobbering them over the head with the facts of life, quite another.

A good book for children, like a good book for adults, should hold an honest mirror up to life; reflect the emotional landscape they move in, tell them what they want to know. And what they want to know, what they want to understand, is their own situation. What they see from their point of view, not what the adult sees, looking back. And their view is necessarily limited. They cannot understand, for example, the desperate anxiety, the helpless love, that parents feel for them. My novel, *The Birds on the Trees*, is about the family of a boy who takes drugs. It is an adult novel because although the central character is a boy of eighteen with a younger brother and sister, the theme of the book is the parents' helplessness, their bitter sense of failure. The boy takes LSD and goes mad. His father and mother try to explain to their eleven-year-old daughter what has happened to him but she cannot understand it. She understands that her brother is ill because he has gone to hospital. People go to hospital because they have appendicitis, or something like that. She explains his illness this way because the real situation is beyond her comprehension. She is aware of her parents' fear and the fact that they are so engrossed with her brother that they no longer seem to care about her. So, since appendicitis is not very dreadful, and people recover from it, the real reason they have ceased to love her must be something they have not told her. They love Toby more than they love her because she is, quite probably, adopted.

Children relate what happens about them to themselves. Blame themselves. If you include an adult situation in a children's book, you must look at it from their side. The child, Mary, in *The Runaway Summer,* sees her parents' divorce as her fault. They are getting divorced because she is so horrible that they no longer love her. You could write an adult novel as Henry James did, around this subject. I chose to write about Mary for children, an adventure story, in which she finds an immigrant boy on the beach and hides him from the uncertain, dangerous world where no adult can be trusted. She doesn't want to know, or be told, how her parents feel; all she wants to know is how the divorce will affect her.

There is no other way she can look at it. The central fact of a child's life is that everything that happens to her depends on the uncertain whims of the adults. As Mary shouts at her Aunt Alice, 'Children don't have any say; they just have to do what they're told. They have to wear what they're told and eat what they're given and live where they're *put*. It's not fair. . . .'

It's not fair. The old childhood cry—and we should listen to it, because it tells us something important. Children inhabit, as few adults do, a morally structured universe. Things are right or they are wrong, or unfair, black or white. You can show them a few shades in between if you are cunning, but not too many or you will confuse them, disturb their sense of moral judgment which they have to develop, slowly, for themselves, or they will never judge soundly later.

In writing for children, if you take your role seriously and believe who you are writing for is important, you must remember this. My children's novel, *Squib*, is about a battered child, a neglected, pale little boy that four other children meet in the local playground. But it is not about Squib himself but about the children who rescue him and the fantasies that they pin on him. The littlest ones think he is being fattened up by a wicked witch for her supper, an older boy thinks he has been kidnapped and held for ransom, a girl pretends he is her young, drowned brother come back. To have written the truth about Squib would not only have been too horrifying—and I do not think one should deliberately horrify children—but also too complicated. It would have meant considering the ignorant people who had ill-treated him and admitting that they might be pitiable, too. And I think that would have been too morally confusing for children, who need to feel the ground is firm under their feet. As Chesterton said, 'Children are innocent and love justice, while adults are wicked and naturally prefer mercy.'

I used the same theme in my next adult novel. When I had finished *Squib*, I found myself wondering what would have happened to a child like that when he grew up. However carefully he was tended later there would still have been this gap, this terrible space in his life, when normal emotional growth had been suspended. I thought of the war, when I had been evacuated to Wales. Suppose there had been a little girl, treated as Squib had been . . . .

And so I wrote *Anna Apparent*, about a child who is treated by her foster parents like an animal—thrown scraps of bread, forced to sleep, like a dog, in a barn. She is rescued and brought up by a silly but well-intentioned woman, appearing to grow and develop quite normally, but there is always this gap in her life which affects not only her but all those about her.

Writing the same story for adults, you see, but looking at

it from a different point of view; trying to understand what happens later, when the same child is grown. The final effect, not just the immediate one. The long view, for which you need an adult perspective, both in writer and reader. It is possible, occasionally of course, for the two views to come fairly close. When I finished *Anna Apparent*, in the way that one thing leads to another, I found I was still thinking about the war and my own experiences as an evacuee, a child far from home, suffering in some ways but still surviving, adapting, learning about other people.

I started *Carrie's War* with a mother going back to the mining valley where she had lived during the war and telling her children what happened to her there. It was the first time, starting a novel, that I had actually wondered whether this was a story for adults or for children. But I didn't wonder long because I soon discovered that although Carrie appears to be telling it to her own children, she is not really telling it from the point of view of a grown woman looking back over her shoulder, but from the point of view of the child she was when it happened, a twelve-year-old girl putting her own interpretation, which is still a child's interpretation, on what goes on around her. She and her young brother are living with a mean, difficult man with a huge chip on his shoulder. The little boy sees him, quite simply, as an ogre. He learns to keep out of his way and has no interest in why he behaves as he does. Nor has Carrie, really. She sees that he tries to be nice, in his way and is, up to a point, sorry for him, but although she is told that he had a harsh, cold, early life, she does not really relate this to his present behaviour.

Quite simply, he does not really concern her. What does concern her are her own feelings about her small brother and about the kind woman, Hepzibah Green, who lives in a house called Druid's Bottom. Hepzibah may or may not be a witch. She feeds the children vast, comforting meals and tells them wonderful stories. One of the stories is about the screaming skull that belongs to the house. If it is ever removed, the walls of the house will crumble . . . .

Carrie half believes this. Towards the end of the book, for what seems to her a very good reason, she throws the skull into the horse pond. That night the house catches fire and she blames herself for it until thirty years later when she comes back to the valley and understands fully what happened.

If I had been a grown-up writing that story, I suppose I might have used the episode of the skull in some other way, as a symbol for some deep, inadmissible feeling of guilt. And perhaps it was, too. But since it wasn't a grown-up telling it, but the twelve-year-old girl that still lurks inside me, it was just the terrible thing Carrie did that she couldn't tell anyone about, but that she knows will haunt her for ever.

There you have it. My secret is out, as they say. As far as I am concerned, the only real difference between writing for adults or for children is whose eyes I am looking through. My mother's—standing on the dockside and wishing her wretched child would smile and be nice. Or the little girl's, standing beside her and watching a dead pig in the water, instead of her father's ship coming in.

From *Children's literature in education*, No. 14, May 1974

Writing for Enjoyment

Joan Aiken

Joan Aiken has written about thirty books: children's fiction, adult novels and plays. In 1969 she won The Guardian *award for children's fiction and was a runner-up for the Carnegie Medal. This extract is from an article in which she described her own childhood reading which gave her a preoccupation with the past and a taste for mystery.*

FOR SOME time I'd been wanting to do a full-length children's book—one that was really my own, not modelled on somebody else's. I wanted it to have a lot of hardship and danger, and yet be funny too—by that time I had children of my own and knew about the hazards and boredoms of reading aloud. What happened then was, I suppose, a sort of coming together of all the forces that had influenced me when I was very young. It's simple enough to trace now.

Obviously the yearning to link up with a lost Golden Age before one was born is not peculiar to me. It is universal, probably connected with pre-natal memories, with half-heard, half-understood fragments of parent's conversation, with the collective unconscious, with race memory, with whatever you believe in. I believe in the lot, particularly pre-natal memories. I'm also pretty sure that anyone from an immigrant family, or anyone with elder brothers and sisters, has an extra sense of this strangely close but unreachable past, because damn it, there are one's coevals, one's own generation, remembering and talking about a time before oneself existed—and that is so extraordinary.

Has it ever struck you how much more beautiful Eden is than

Paradise? Paradise is a sort of tuppence-coloured Sunday School treat, a lowest common denominator version of Happily Ever After, but Eden is absolute nostalgia, because it is still remembered, and yet gone beyond recall.

So I think what happened was that my subconscious, called on to produce ideas for a children's book, let out a shout of joy and instantly came up with a plan for a historical tale set in a period of history that never was, that anybody could claim for their own, a nineteenth century—not too long ago, still within reach, but turned upside down with Stuarts on the throne instead of Queen Victoria, and Hanoverians plotting to bring back Bonnie Prince Georgie from over the water. (The whole Bonnie Prince Charlie myth, if you think about it, depends on the glamour of failure. If he had gone on from Derby and actually won it would have been a very different kettle of fish.)

Of course the book, *The Wolves of Willoughby Chase*, was tremendously enjoyable to write. Have you ever noticed how peculiarly liberating it is to follow a conventional pattern in nearly all respects, but to include one odd factor? One notices this over and over in every department of art or life. It must, for instance, have been the motivation for carnival masks. Almost any out of the ordinary bit of behaviour has the same effect. I've seen it happen at advertising market-research sessions in which one housewife is asked to sit on another's lap and pretend she is in a car—a lot of mental blocks are suddenly demolished. At a sticky children's party, if you simply paint a blue nose on every guest the effect is very uninhibiting. One step aside from the normal and you're away. This was what I found with my period piece—having a Stuart king and a few wolves in the middle of the nineteenth century somehow set me free to enjoy myself. I wrote a straightforward rags-to-riches-to-rags-to-riches nineteenth-century tale, and had tremendous fun filling in my own details.

Details—if I may diverge from my main track for a moment—are crucially important in children's writing. I remember my daughter once picking up a woman's magazine and starting to read a serial in it by an extremely well-known writer. It was laid in the south of France and after a few paragraphs the heroine narrator said, 'We went into the chateau and were served with wine and little cakes.' My daughter flung down the magazine in utter scorn exclaiming, 'Wine and little cakes indeed! What's the use of that, if she doesn't tell you what sort of wine and little cakes?' She has had the lowest opinion of that particular writer ever since and the phrase 'wine and little cakes' has come, in our family, to typify a lazy indifference to detail. It doesn't necessarily follow that because a children's book has lively detail it is first class, but I do think that poverty of detail instantly stamps a book as second rate. Details, after all, are what one chiefly remembers of many books. Think of Elnora's lunchboxes in *A Girl of the Limberlost* or those little sharp tacks with which the Indian servant fixed bright, strange, foreign embroideries to the wall in Frances Hodgson Burnett's *Little Princess*: 'tacks so sharp they could be pressed into the wood and plaster without hammering.' They were a touch of inspiration those tacks, instantly instilling belief in the whole transformation scene, because if there is one thing that every child knows, it is that the sound of hammering will fetch any parent at the double to find out what mayhem is going on.

And think of little Ellen's workbox in *The Wide Wide World*:

> The box was of satinwood, beautifully finished and lined with crimson silk. Mrs Montgomery had taken good care it should want nothing that Ellen might need to keep her clothes in good order.
>
> 'O Mamma, how beautiful! Here is more cotton than I can use up in a good while—every number I do think—and needles, oh, the needles! what a parcel of them, and Mamma! what lovely scissors—and here's a thimble—fits me exactly; and an emergy bag—how pretty! and a bodkin—this is a great deal nicer than yours Mamma, yours is decidedly the worse for wear—and what's this? Oh, to make eyelet holes with, I know. And here are tapes, and buttons, and hooks and eyes, and darning cotton, and silk winders, and pins—what's this for, Mamma?'
>
> 'That's a scissors to cut button holes with. Try it on that piece of paper and you will see how it works.'

'Oh I see,' said Ellen, 'How very nice that is. Well, I shall take great pains now to make my button holes very handsomely.'

The description of Ellen's desk in the same book is done even more lovingly, but that goes on for pages—I couldn't possibly quote it all.

I'm very fond of details myself—I probably tend to get carried away by them—but it's a tremendous pleasure when, as occasionally happens, someone says, 'I particularly like the bowl of radishes—or whatever it was—that you had in such and such a story.' Details, after all, are the material of fiction—the plot is just the skeleton.

Anyway, back for a moment to *The Wolves of Willoughby*, the first book I wrote on this period-that-never-was thesis. Another thing I found enjoyable about writing it was that it involved all the fun and invention of fantasy without the need to bring in the supernatural or any impossibilities. Don't think I'm opposed to the use of the supernatural—far from it—I use it myself a lot in my short stories, but I'm fussy about this. I feel the supernatural is fine in a short story but I think it takes a very special kind of talent of a very, very high order to keep it going successfully in a full length book. Tolkien can do it, Alan Garner can, William Mayne can, but I'm doubtful whether I can. I've avoided it so far anyway. In my last full length children's book, *The Whispering Mountain*, there is, to be sure, an ancient prophecy about a harp which is fulfilled, but in fact everything that happened can be accounted for by natural causes. I do like to keep one foot on the ground. It's a kind of game making sure that it's all just feasible. With this end in view I like to get as many facts as I can as accurate as I can—stuff about Roman goldmines and whaling vessels and topography and dialect and so forth.

Another benefit of inventing one's own period is that it is a very good means of giving one's readers an in-feeling. You know what I mean. There is a sort of trick about inventing a world and making readers free of it which is very agreeable for all concerned. Josephine Tey did it with great economy; she would nonchalantly refer in one book to a quite irrelevant character who appeared in another, secure in the knowledge that her readers would pick up the clue. It creates a privileged atmosphere right away. But that is a piece of rather sinful know-how which I didn't consciously apply at the time I was writing *The Wolves of Willoughby* and its sequels.

So I wrote *The Wolves of Willoughby* and that was fun. I had to break off in the middle of writing it for personal reasons, and in fact I wasn't able to take it up again for about seven years, but when I did there was not the slightest difficulty about starting again, the gap might have been no more than a day. So then I did a sequel to it, *Black Hearts in Battersea*, and that was even more fun. With *Black Hearts* I applied more consciously my theory that it enriches a book to have had a lot of relevant action take place before the story opens. (This happened even more successfully than I intended, as it turned out to be about ten thousand words longer than was economic to publish so I had to chop a whole slab out of the beginning.) I also gave it an elaborate kind of Dickensian plot because I think children like complicated plots. It is part of their general passion for rules and games, and ramifications, and organization. (It's interesting that plots are no longer considered truly grown-up. They are all right for children's books and for thrillers and historical novels, but not for real adult fiction. Is this because our lives are now so unfree, so exceedingly organized that we can't bear to have them organized for us in novels as well? My trouble is that I have a simple nature and enjoy plots, as I enjoy tunes in music. Obviously the more sophisticated you are, the more you want harmonic complications and for the tune to be developed, rather than just more and more of it. I personally love the music of Handel, who has almost unlimited fertility in tunes, and I take comfort from the fact that Beethoven thought Handel was the greatest composer and I sometimes indulge in the sour-grapes theory that people who disapprove of plots do so because they can't produce them. If I could write a children's book with a story as clear and inventive and beautiful as a Handel tune I would feel I had done a good job.)

There was a second reason for my giving *Black Hearts* a complicated Dickensian plot. Children carry on the physical process of reading in several different ways and in a way that is totally different from that of adults. I've seen different forms in my own two children. My daughter was the quick kind of voracious reader who would finish a book at a sitting and read comics, textbooks, anything, rather than be stuck without reading matter. My son was a slow, conservative reader, inching his way through a book, marking the place with a grassblade and going back next day for another stint. But both of them, like me, like all the other children I know, didn't just read a book once if it established a place in their affections. They went back and read it again and again and again. I came across a psychological explanation recently for this demand in a child to have a story retold, or a book reread, over and over. It is a wish for security, a wish to be sure that the story still exists, is still there. This seems quite reasonable. Furthermore, this rereading doesn't necessarily take place consecutively. Children may read the whole book backwards, or the whole book skipping about, or the whole book in a special sequence—all the Cloister bits first, then all the Hearth bits—or not the whole book at all, just their favourite passages. If you look at the children's books in our house you find things stuck in specially loved passages— a feather in the packing scene in *Three Men in a Boat*, biscuit crumbs in Thurber's *French Travel Guide*, tomato ketchup smears in the spontaneous combustion scene in *Bleak House*, a squashed daisy in the marvellous underground scene with Gollum in *The Hobbit*. I'm afraid our books get treated with love rather than respect—most of them were second-hand to begin with anyway.

Obviously when you bear in mind the fact that children read back to front and upside down and sideways and very slowly and very fast, it becomes plain that the actual texture of the writing is terribly important. It ought to have a kind of quadruple, quintuple richness, so as to be able to take all this extra wear and tear—quite different from that of the adult books which are simply intended to be read once and tossed out. Furthermore since so many children go on reading and rereading the same book over what may easily be a span of ten years or so, a book ought ideally to have something new to offer them at every reading—a sort of graded series of concepts, graspable at each stage of development. Satire—or anyway a kind of subterranean humour—is another possibility. Think of Beatrix Potter. 'Will not the string be very indigestible, Anna Maria?' said Samuel Whiskers. 'I do not think this will be a good pudding.' Or 'Tiddly, widdly, widdly, Mrs Tittlemouse,' said the smiling Mr Jackson, 'I can smell the honey.' Very often children miss this kind of humour at the first reading; intent on the plot they go plunging along to the end, but come back and pick it up and enjoy it later. I still find my eighteen-year-old daughter grinning over 'Tiddly, widdly, widdly, Mrs Tittlemouse.' So in my books I tried, when I thought about it, to enrich the mixture with a sort of entertainment which might be picked up on a second or third reading if not a first—such as the fact that it is always the Duchess's bit of embroidered tapestry that saves everybody's lives in *Black Hearts*, or the revolting priggish knowledgeability of the boy Owen in *The Whispering Mountain*. This sort of thing also, I hope, keeps the adult reader-aloud from going frantic with boredom. Mind you I think it is extremely dangerous to write with the adult reader-aloud in mind. It is a thing I try to avoid because it can lead to an awful tongue-in-cheek coyness, one adult talking to another over the heads of the kiddies, which is patronizing and offensive. Just occasionally E. Nesbit fell into this error though in general her books can't be faulted. But when one has done a great deal of reading to children, and been faced with their demands to have some dearly loved book over again for the umpteenth time, it is impossible not to have sympathy for the potential reader-aloud. And in fact all my children's books are written to be read aloud in that they were all read serially to my children as written, and anything that didn't flow as it should, or that sounded silly, was changed on the spot.

This is where I get back to mystery again. Mystery is another essential element in the operation of making a book rereadable. Mystery of language first. I wage a constant battle with my American publishers who are under the impression that if children can't understand every single word, every single term in a book, they will instantly reject it and cast it aside. Furthermore American publishers seem to have a very low estimate of the kind of language that children will understand—anything over two syllables, any unfamiliar phrase, seems to them an almost indefensible risk. However I hope I am gradually getting my lot out of these ways, because that really is such a non-sensical point of view. In my recollection, and this is borne out by endless corroboration from children and friends, unfamiliar words are a tremendously important feature of reading, an active pleasure. Children naturally don't bother to stop and look words up; they make a guess at the meaning and float past, and the unknown term remains embedded like a rock in memory.

Presently one meets it again in a different context and the meaning suddenly becomes clear, forming a link with the previous passage: 'Oh, *that's* what it meant. . .' I can remember having this with the word 'urn' which I first came across when my mother read me *Lycidas*. Familiar only with 'to earn' used as a verb, I was utterly baffled by the sentence 'So may some gentle Muse favour my destined urn,' and puzzled over it vaguely for some months before by chance I discovered that an urn was also a receptacle for putting ashes in. Needless to say it didn't occur to me to ask about it. Often in this random way, something which might have been forgotten is kept actively in mind and may have an extra glamour and luminosity. I found this with a lot of terms in American books: 'pickled limes' in *Little Women*, the candle that they stuck on a 'shingle' in *Tom Sawyer*, mysterious creatures called 'patter-rollers' in *Uncle Remus*. And quite apart from the interest and mystery of unknown words, children find them beautiful. It was the lavish language, expressions such as 'cynical immorality' and 'blatant indecency' that I relished in *Stalky & Co.*

When I was writing *The Whispering Mountain* I ran slightly amok with language. As the scene was set in Wales I necessarily put in some Welsh. Then it happened that I had, shortly before starting to write it, been reading a splendid book, *The Elizabethan Underworld* by A.V. Judges, which is full of the texts of broadsheets and examples of thieves' cant from the sixteenth century. Thieves' cant is fairly conservative philologically, a lot of Elizabethan expressions like *scarper* are still in use, so it seemed reasonable to let my two nineteenth-century thieves,

Bilk and Prigman, use some of these Elizabethan words. I also dipped pretty freely into Shakespeare, because it has always seemed to me a terrible shame not to make more extensive use of his vocabulary. Just consider these words: *frampold*, ill-natured; *brabble*, to quarrel; *slubber*, to make a mess of something; *probal*, reasonable; *drumble*, sluggish; *fustilarian*, tiresome; *nook-shotten*, remote; *whoobub*, a loud noise; *garboil*, another kind of loud noise; *cockshut time*, twilight; *libbege*, a bed; *dews-a-vill*, the country; *aswame*, fainting; *doddypol*, fool; *imbraid*, to scold; *mandilion*, an overcoat; *to be on one's pantofles*, to stand on one's dignity; *stigmatical*, infamous; *diddering and doddering*, shivering. Aren't they beautiful? It seems a sin not to bring them back into everyday use. And moreover they are just the kind of words that children enjoy—garboil, whoobub, drumble-head, fustilarian—I probably used too many of them, especially from the point of view of the unfortunate reader-aloud, but I still think that is a better fault than having a vocabulary that is too familiar, like a threadbare carpet.

Obscurity of vocabulary is one way to look after the repetitive *da capo* reader. I don't go for complicated sentence construction for fear of slowing down the action. And of course obscurity of theme and character are two other ways. I do not think that young children find meanings very important necessarily. If they can get some value out of a text, some vision or flavour or satisfying sound, they are often quite content to leave the meaning on one side for the time being. If you think about it, to a young child the whole of life is pretty much of a mystery. People behave in thoroughly unaccountable ways—or at least they do not always trouble to explain their behaviour to their children. Life is insecure and arbitrary and often utterly unexpected. To young children their dreams are often almost as real as their daytime existence, which adds yet another incomprehensible layer to experience. Naturally they do not expect to have their dreams explained and, though of course they may ask, they are used to not having explanations for a lot of what goes on in the daytime too. It is only adults who feel they have a right to an explanation for everything. I'm sure that this view is fairly recent and very regrettable—it probably drifted in during the nineteenth century along with the theory of progress and the awful impression that there is an intrinsic virtue in work.

I expect by now I have made fairly plain my view that, on the whole, the less explanation the better. Things not understood have a radiance of their own. It is a challenge to go back to them, to puzzle and puzzle. De la Mare, of course, has obscurity of every kind—theme and behaviour as well as language. I used to go back and back to some of his short stories, *The Almond Tree*, *The Snow Mountains*, *Broomsticks*, and that terrifying *Seaton's Aunt*, trying to worry out the meanings and what had really happened. And Kipling's characters behaved in baffling ways. *Kim* and *Captains Courageous* were full of minor puzzles, and his collections of short stories, *Plain Tales from the Hills* and the rest, a positive forest of major ones, to be hacked through as best one could, from clearing to clearing.

In my own writing I don't try to make my characters inexplicable, since I think children also enjoy simple morality-type figures who behave in fairly predictable ways, however odd the circumstances in which they find themselves. This gives a feeling of security. I try to give my characters some solidity though, and I try to differentiate sharply between them by giving each one as individual a manner of speech as possible, because I think it important, especially if a book is being read aloud, that the different speakers should be readily recognizable. So Dido Twite, my own favourite heroine, has a sort of cockney dialect, and Captain Casket on the whaler used the Quaker thee and thou, and the oriental potentate, the Seljuk of Rum, speaks like a thesaurus, and the Prince of Wales, being a Stuart, naturally speaks lowland Scots. I have had complaints that there was altogether too much of this sort of thing in *The Whispering Mountain*—which is worrying, as I've just come across a marvellous dictionary of Sussex dialect which I was planning to use extensively in my next children's book. I expect I shall use it just the same. One could hardly resist expressions like *to nurt*, to entice away; *tossicated*, drunk; *Bishop Barnaby*, a ladybird; *snotty-gog*, a yewberry.

I also try to introduce the fact of death, and the fact that parents are not infallible, are often indeed extremely silly and unreliable, in a matter-of-fact way, buttressed by anticlimax and the sort of comic relief which, thank heaven, life is full of anyway. And I try to provide a sense of mystery by references to things outside the orbit of the book which the reader can pursue or ignore as he pleases. And I take pains to know a great deal more about the action and background than I put down, so that what is actually written is like the tip of the iceberg. My three books *Wolves*, *Black Hearts*, and *Night Birds on Nantucket*, follow one another chronologically and link up, though each is concerned with a different set of characters. But *The Whispering Mountain*, set in the same period, is parallel with *Night Birds* in time, and I am now going to link them together with a fifth book, *The Cuckoo Tree*, which follows on from the end of both. I felt it would provide an interesting complication, for me anyway, and give me another dimension to my home-made period of history.

I've been talking about my full-length children's books which are, as you'll have gathered, quite carefully planned. I work them out very thoroughly beforehand, with charts and time-schemes, and before I start writing I know just about what is going to happen in each chapter. The fairy tales or fantasies in my four collections of short stories are written quite differently. The process of writing them is, I suppose, much closer to that of writing poetry. Often an idea hits me and I just sit down and write it straight off. Or I try to get into direct touch with my subconscious and let it do most of the work, either by using a dream as basis, or thinking out a story the instant I wake in the morning—always a very fertile time—or producing one by a short free-association method, slapping down a little very quickly, then drawing out two or three apparently dissociated, random ideas, and then somehow linking them all up. Often I hardly know what the end will be till I get there but—if I can draw the distinction—I know that there is an end already decided below the level of consciousness, and that I shall recognize it when I get there. This method of writing is exhausting as it is almost always fatal to stop in the middle. One has to do the whole story in one burst, at full pitch, flat out, or the mood, the transmission, is broken. It often does seem almost like automatic writing, getting a message from the Holy Ghost. One sometimes reads it afterwards in a kind of daze, thinking 'How did I know that?' When I was young I used to do all my writing this way; it took me years to learn that one could proceed as it were in gear, with a hand on the steering wheel and a foot on the brake. And I still feel that the more consciously directed kind of writing is on a lower level, not so pure. I don't know if unconsciously directed writing is better for children though—it may even not be so good. Children, after all, are in touch with their own subconscious and can tap their own store of myths whenever they like. It is adults, I find, who seem to enjoy this kind of quick plunge into the underworld. And of course it is a marvellously exhilarating way to write.

This brings me to my last point. I really take a very humble view of my own writing; I don't feel it is worth a lot of analysis. On the other hand, I certainly don't want to denigrate the importance of writing for children. I can see that in such an increasingly threatened and frightening world as ours now is, children, probably more than ever before, need to be given real values and sustaining ideas and memories that they can hold on to and cherish. But I must confess straight out that I don't write my children's books with this kind of moral purpose in mind—or even because I think children ought to have good books, though I *do* think so—I just write children's books because that is what I happen to love doing. If I have any moral purpose at all, it is simply perhaps the wish to give the same sort of pleasure that I had from my childhood reading.

From *Children's literature in education*, No. 2, July 1970

A Sense of Audience—1

An Rutgers van der Loeff

*An Rutgers van der Loeff has had most of her books trans-
lated into a number of languages, and they have won awards
in Holland, Britain, Germany and America.*

WRITING for children is as far as I am concerned a social
engagement. If at the same time my work has some literary
merit, that is simply because I do the best I can. This must
seem far too simple a statement, but for me it involves a great
deal. It involves the background of my upbringing, the obliga-
tions towards everything I got in the course of my life—from
my parental home and school to my family life now, the
thousands of books I read, the people I had the privilege to
meet and the many children I learned to know and respect.
Owing so much to so many I should feel unhappy if I did not
do the best I could. If that results in more or less literary work,
I am grateful.

But what interests me far more than the *way* I write is the
substance of my work, the material I want to pass on to children. Certain subjects fascinate me, and I want children to share
that fascination with me.

Children are eager and inquisitive; that is why I write mostly
and most wholeheartedly for *them*. I want to try to satisfy
part of their eagerness and inquisitiveness. I feel we owe this
to them. They are put into this chaotic, raging mad world and
they have to find their way. Can we give them guidance? Scarcely. Moreover they do not want any guidance; they want to find
out for themselves. But can we give them information? I think
so—and I think this is what they want.

I do not refer to the fragmentary information you may find

27

in encyclopedias and reference books. I mean information woven into a *pattern of human relationships* against social backgrounds, in such a way that while they are reading the children are living in a new world—and I really mean *living*. They can absorb it and this may help them; eventually they may use it to find their way and to find a certain balance and their own personal order in chaos.

For children, to live is to discover. To discover means to find out about things vaguely known or completely new. They will discover new opinions and possibilities, new values and new doubts. Perhaps surprises and doubts—even anguish and terror —are the essence of life: we cannot withhold them from our children. If we do, we fail, because we deceive them. Deceit is often so easy and cosy for them and their grown-ups: but only for the moment, not in the long run. If we work along the easy way, I feel that we deceive them as well as ourselves, and having disappointed them we shall lose their confidence and spoil the relationship.

It is not by withholding things from children that we help them. And surprises can be wonderful as well as ugly; doubts find their counterbalance in hope and belief; anguish and terror in courage, patience and something of that fine human tenacity that is called integrity. All of this we can find in real life, which we can draw upon for our books, and all of this we can find in our imagination reinforced by our experience, both of which help us along while writing our stories. We arm children by helping them build up critical minds; we can help them to develop the scope of their imagination. I often wonder if I perhaps fool myself in thinking that I feel such a social engagement and obligation towards children. Perhaps it is nothing but my own eagerness, inquisitiveness and uncertainty I want to still and satisfy through this job of writing. Perhaps I could not do without the fun and tension of finding out and digging into things, exploring backgrounds and the motivations in human beings. But if so I still want children to have this fun too, the tension of the adventure into what they do not yet know, the satisfaction of discovering new grounds, having climbed out of windows thrown open wide.

Why is my choice of material mostly related to some social

issue? I am intrigued by the way in which human beings—children and grown-ups—can react and perform surprisingly while under a certain pressure either from within or without. The circumstances they live in may change, suddenly or gradually —how do they then face problems that arise, how do they struggle with themselves and/or others to survive, to adapt themselves, seemingly or really? How do they find their own identity and aim? I am attracted by subjects which give me the chance to find out about these things. Let me give two examples.

Children on the Oregon Trail was my first children's book and was written at the instigation of my publisher, after he had handed me some material and spoken some encouraging words. But the real motivation was that I could not stop wondering how these seven children, roaming through America's wilderness in 1843, had managed to stay alive and reach their goal. I began reading, looking for facts. I found extremely little as far as these children were concerned; but the social background and the central phenomenon of the emigration from the eastern states of North America to the far west kept me reading for two long years before writing the book in a few weeks. By that time I was so totally involved that it was urgent for me to write. I wanted to pass on this thrilling stuff. I wanted present-day children to be involved too, to know how on another continent in another century people—children of their own age—had struggled, and had laughed and cried as they do.

Avalanche was a similar enquiry: how does the population of a Swiss mountain village react when an avalanche destroys their homes, their way of life and the lives of some of them? What is the interplay between children and grown-ups when stricken by disaster? In those circumstances both must play their negative and positive roles. In the avalanche-stricken region where I lived for some time, I found that the selfishness and cowardice were counterbalanced by a surprising and taken-for-granted heroism in a most matter-of-fact way. Building a plot around this theme seemed fascinating. But I must confess that it took a long time for my motor to warm up before I could begin to write the story. When it was written the material proved to be fascinating to the readers in exactly the way it had been fascinating to me. Surprisingly the book itself became an avalanche of copies and there were translations in sixteen countries.

*   *   *   *   *

Am I too serious? Why do I not simply give children amusement? My answer is that certainly they need amusement—relaxation and pure amusement; but lots of other writers take care of that. In any case I do not try to feed them solely on problems: I give them laughs too. I try to give them a whole range of feelings; if I did not, my books would be cold affairs.

In the course of the last ten years I have had requests to write about all sorts of subjects. I have accepted the invitation whenever I felt interested and challenged. Thus I came to write about blind children, children in wartime, war and peace in general, poverty in vast parts of the world and the problem of race. And I do this for *children*. And I cannot complain about their receptiveness—on the contrary. The fine intuition and receptiveness of many children is surprising. It is worthwhile to work for them. It is work I love—a job I cannot leave undone. To explore the world, explore things far and near, amassing the data and then, after the process of sifting and selecting, to pass on the essence of what I have found to children—because their ears, eyes and minds are still open, not yet sealed up by prejudices and stale opinions—this is what I feel urged to do.

From *Children's literature in education*, No. 5, July 1971

A Sense of Audience—2

Gillian Avery

Gillian Avery has written a number of novels for children set in the Victorian period, and is the author of Nineteenth-Century Children—Heroes and Heroines in English Children's Stories, *and* Childhood's Pattern, *a study of the ethics of children's stories, 1770-1950.*

IT SEEMS sad. Childhood is so short, a seventh of one's life perhaps, and only five years of one's reading life. Surely there is a case for leaving them alone just for those five years with the books they like? Dr Johnson, speaking of the dedicated horde of late Georgian women like 'Mrs Lovechild' and 'Arabella Argus' who poured out moral fables for the young, said, 'Babies do not like to hear stories of babies like themselves, they require to have their imaginations raised by tales of giants and fairies, and castles of enchantment.'

To which that arch-theorist, Richard Lovell Edgeworth, retorted sharply, 'The fact remains to be proved, but supposing they do prefer such tales, is this a reason why they should be indulged in reading them?'

I feel that it is a reason. Not just giants and fairies (works of high imagination are the 'in' thing now anyway) but the stories of children that do things better than themselves, like ballet, or riding ponies, where you can retire into a dream world and pretend that you are Damaris dancing at Covent Garden or Rebecca winning the Badminton dressage event. Or Noddy, who makes the younger children feel big and comfortable and superior. You can't enjoy this sort of thing for long, so let the young

31

have them undisturbed for those few brief years. Why should they leave their cosy corners until they have to? Pretty soon the adult world is going to be all about them and they will have to take notice of it. It's already thrust on them at a woefully early age—in the 1930s we were left in peace much longer. I was told recently of a twelve-year-old who burst into tears at his music lesson when asked to repeat a phrase. 'Everything's gone wrong today. I didn't pass my arithmetic test, and I can't play the oboe and I'll never be able to get a job when I leave school.' Of course, if they *want* to read about the emotional problems of the deprived child, or world hunger, encourage them—but at least let it not be turned into a moral issue.

*   *   *   *   *

The first book I ever wrote was begun in Manchester in 1955 in a fit of longing for Oxford where I had just spent four happy years. Its successors were written in the same spirit. I would settle down in February in the bitterly cold study of the tall semi-detached Victorian house in the decaying Victorian suburb, look with distaste at the lowering grey skies outside and the shrivelled wallflowers in the garden dejectedly drooping their leaves, and write to drive them out of my mind. The beginning was a delightful escape, the middle was more of a struggle, and by the end I felt as though I was rowing the Boat Race course—if *only* I could keep afloat until I reached Mortlake. But basically, I write to please myself, and it is still a matter of faint surprise to me that I should actually be *paid* for this. It is even more of a surprise that anybody, except myself, reads them, and I certainly give no thought to the tastes or the welfare of any particular age group. I can remember pretty well what I liked when I was ten and what I disliked, and when I come to thrash out the final shape of the book I have this in mind.

Re-reading my earlier books I realize that the central characters are mostly projections of what I remember as aspects of my own personality as a child. Romanticized, hopefully, in the case of the first, *The Warden's Niece*. ('My God, Gill,' said my youngest brother when he read that one, 'I suppose you think you were like Maria. But you weren't you know. Oh no.') In books that succeeded I tried to atone for the awful child I knew I had been by showing myself up: the officious older sister, the self-conscious prig, the ill-tempered, self-pitying adolescent, the clumsy and awkward outsider longing to be accepted—I had been all of those in my time. I added comedy, because comedy is what I enjoyed as a child and what I enjoy now.

But what occurs to me amid the welter of theory that has always gone on about what a child should read is the encouraging thought that you never know what he is going to make of the material with which you confront him. He has his own defence against what he doesn't like or doesn't understand in the book that is put in front of him. He ignores it, subconsciously perhaps, or he makes something different from it. There was a famous book of the evangelical sort by Mrs O.F. Walton called *A Peep Behind the Scenes*. It sets out to show the misery behind the tinsel of circus life. It is also written in an ardent missionary spirit; the little heroine approaches every adult with the guileless question 'Has the Good Shepherd found *you*?' The author must have felt satisfied that her message would get across to everybody. But my mother who read it and re-read it as a child missed the message completely; she remembered it as a happy book about a circus. And a child to whom I recently gave the harrowing story of *Froggy's Little Brother* ignored all the horrors of slum life which 'Brenda' was trying to convey to the more privileged child, the death of Froggy's parents and then of the little brother, and she wept for the death of the pet mouse. Another child who could not be tempted out of her cosy corner.

Children have always resisted improvement; they extract what they want from a book and no more. As long ago as 1798 a Quaker writer, Priscilla Wakefield, who wrote a number of books for the young popular in her day, realized something of this:

The objection that I have frequently heard children raise against the influence of moral tales on their own conduct, that they were not true, but merely fictions to entertain, induced me to believe, that real anecdotes of characters of their own ages and dispositions . . . would probably reach their hearts with peculiar force.

She accordingly produced a *Juvenile Anecdotes* which told among others of industrious Ambrose, and Edward Seymour—a model for little boys to imitate, but I don't suppose these had the slightest effect on anybody's behaviour. Remembering my own attitude to books, I imagine the Georgian child would have picked out the plummy bits—what Ambrose had to eat, and what Edward wore when he went out with his mother—and ignored the rest. I read *The Fairchild Family* in this spirit, I recall, savouring the hot buttered toast and the crumbs it made, and the behaviour of the pet hare and the magpie, not bothering myself with the brimstone and hellfire.

And if further proof is needed of the wholly unpredictable selectiveness of a child's memory, let me conclude with the story of the distinguished general who was asked on the occasion of some city book festival to name, along with a lot of other distinguished people, the children's book that had meant most to him. He said that he had long ago lost sight of the one he had really treasured, and all he could remember of it now was the couplet

Pingo sat in the wood of Pottle
With strawberry juice in a thermos bottle.

So much for all the earnest writers who were at work on *him* during his childhood!

From *Children's literature in education*, No. 6, November 1971

A Sense of Audience—3

Roger Collinson

Roger Collinson is the author of A Boat and Bax, Butch and Bax *and* Four-Eyes. *His teaching experience has been in secondary modern, grammar and primary schools. He was a founder member of the Federation of Children's Book Groups.*

Gingerly his Lordship took the gaudy red and blue book. First his Lordship fumbled in his breast pocket for some seconds before he pulled forth an eyeglass attached to a long gold chain, which he screwed into one eye. Then lowering a ginger eyebrow over it and holding out the book at arm's length, he scrutinized the cover. Willy looked at it too, for he had not examined it before. There was a picture of a burly tough with a mask over his face, kneeling beside a heap of jewels. His Lordship gave it long consideration. Then he picked open the yellowed pages and drew in his cheeks as if in pain.

'Do you know what I would have done if I had found one of my own sons reading this gallows literature? I would have made him wash out his eyes with soap, yes soap, to cleanse him of the filth contained within it! Do you know what gallows literature is, boy?'

Dazed by the completely unexpected turn that things had taken, Willy shook his head.

'It is reading-matter like this that drives boys into crime, men to the gallows! It is poison, the rankest poison. Better that you had never learned to read than that you polluted yourself with this.'   *A Likely Lad*—Gillian Avery

CLEARLY his Lordship exaggerates the perils that threaten the reader of that cheap thriller, which he was condemning on such a cursory inspection. The wonder is that Willy wasn't consumed with curiosity about the confiscated book. All my own reluctant readers would part with hard cash to get hold of any book I had so rashly anathematized.

But for all that we find his Lordship a comic figure, we do not disagree with him about the importance of what children read. Books can and do influence outlook, belief, and conduct. This isn't to suggest that every book a child reads is in itself going to determine his destiny. No *one* book, nor even all books on their own, will ever do that. But if a writer has succeeded in getting any imaginative engagement with his young reader, then he has made some small contribution to that child's development. For this reason, the writer for children will weigh his words carefully.

Didacticism in children's books is quite rightly frowned upon, for the harmful thing about didacticism is not that the writer has some clear convictions himself and is anxious to communicate them, but that he does not help you to discover that truth for yourself, he doesn't stimulate your imagination in such a way that you exclaim, 'Yes, *of course,* that's it!' Rather, instead of taking the reader on a quest for the living truth, he presents him with a formula into which he must fit experience rather than offer him some points of the compass by which he may explore and interpret his own unique experience. I recall Alan Garner a couple of years ago telling his audience that the writer's task was 'not that' (pointing an admonitory finger) 'but this' (opening his hands in display). You don't tell your young reader what's what, you demonstrate what life's about.

The author who does not take an overtly didactic approach may well seem a much safer, more neutral and less philosophically objectionable fellow than your out-and-out propagandist. But it is arguable that he—the man with the obvious axe to grind—is less effective (or dangerous) than the *apparently* uncommitted writer, for we are aware of what he is up to. Unless he is a powerful writer, he is not going to achieve any deep imaginative involvement with his reader. Morals in any case are such a bore: many an otherwise interesting Sunday School yarn has been overcast by the certain knowledge that it would finally be interred in a moral grave. On the other hand, the 'this-is-how-it-is-kids' author may simply be confirming them in their prejudices or impressing them with his untroubled confidence. Moreover, I cannot as a writer for children escape the fact that whatever I write is presenting a picture of life as *I* see it. In the most low-pitched and unsensational story my prose will betray my beliefs and values.

The first essential of a book for children is that it must be a truthful book, using language honestly. The difficulties arise because we ourselves are often uncertain of what the truth is, or will disagree with the philosophy of an author. The writer of children's books, and by this I mean the writer who intends, hopes, or expects that if published his book will be on a children's list, cannot ignore his readers or afford to keep them at any distance further than the back of his mind. For the duration of his book he will be engaging a child's mind, and, by the nature of a book, in a singularly exclusive way. He owes it to the child to share with him as far as possible for him in the telling of his story, the truth and his honest pursuit of the truth. In this, of course, the writing of books is no different from the rest of living. A writer is as much his brother's keeper in his writing as a baker is in his breadmaking, except that the book is more durable and assumes an independent life. If later on we decide our book is a bad one, we cannot prevent its being read.

I maintain, then, the author's duty of truth to his child reader. But, and here we begin to distinguish between the real writer for children and the writer whose books for one reason or another just happen to get published for children, the real writer for children is going to have to decide first *what* of the truth of living he is going to share with the child, and, secondly, *how* he is going to do it.

In their book *School Libraries: Theory and Practice,* Dyer, Brown and Goldstein quote Mandy Brook and Nancy Martin, who say: '. . . the children's author who boasts that he doesn't think of his audience but writes for himself is showing that he has no real claim to understanding what his readers are struggling with . . . he might think twice about being an author for children.'[1] And 'If he cannot evolve a style based on a careful study of the growing language of a child, then he has no claim to be a specialized author and is, in all probability, merely an adult author whom adults find childish'.[2]

To treat children just as adults is to reveal that one has no understanding of or concern for how children develop, emotionally, conceptually and linguistically. I am not suggesting that one needs a diploma before one may write for children, but if the writer is not concerned about what children read books for and does not subordinate his talents to the needs of his readers, he may produce a book which could prove a damaging experience, or, more probably, one which the child will simply find unreadable.

This degree of self-denial makes the task of the writer for children a hard one. But I would not have it thought that I think writing for children is just a matter of following an academic formula, or that the author will not find any personal satisfaction and fulfilment in his work. On the contrary, I am quite sure that the author must want to tell his story for its own sake if it is going to have any success as a children's book. But it is surely indefensible for an author to work out his own *adult* problems and hang-ups in a book for children. This would be unacceptable self-indulgence. But at the other extreme, experience suggests that books written in cold blood to meet an educational requirement have none of that life and sparkle which go to making 'a good read'.

From *Children's literature in education*, No. 10, March 1973

[1] Christopher Dyer et al., *School Libraries: Theory and Practice,* Bingley.
[2] *Ibid.*

The Historical Novelist at Work

Geoffrey Trease

Geoffrey Trease has written over sixty children's books and a critical survey of juvenile fiction, Tales Out of School. *His life's work in this field is described in his autobiographical* Whiff of Burnt Boats *and* Laughter at the Door.

WHEN I began writing historical fiction, right back in 1933, I think the common attitude of the reader was expressed by a schoolgirl named Gillian Hansard. She said, and I quote, because her comments appeared in print: 'Though the details of Scott's novels are not always correct they give one a very good idea of the period, and though they are rather painful to read they always give benefit.' The phrase 'the giving of benefit'—as understood at that date—has a rather depressing sound. In those days, children showed a stubborn and pardonable resistance to historical stories which had to be broken down before the storyteller could get anywhere. I would like to think that it is nothing like so strong or so widespread today.

The author has to be clear from the start what *kind* of historical fiction he is going to write. I am not thinking so much of the differences between the adult novel and what I like to call the junior novel rather than the children's story; apart from length, and the possible use of illustrations, those differences become fewer and fewer as the scope and depth of so-called juvenile fiction are enlarged. Those of us who write for both age groups know how little conscious we are of what Rosemary Sutcliff has called 'the quite small gear change' when we turn from one type of work to the other, and most of what I want to say applies to both. The distinction I have in mind concerns first of all the attitude one adopts to the past. I think that most readers of historical fiction—adult readers anyhow—tend to fall into one of two categories. They are concerned with, fascinated by, either the differences between bygone times and their own, or the similarities. Broadly speaking, the former category read to escape from real life; the latter to illuminate it by comparison and recognition of unchanging human characteristics.

The authors in their turn fall into the same two categories. If they belong to the first they are likely to produce the 'costume' novel as I prefer to call it, to distinguish it from the true 'historical' novel. They may do an impressive amount of research. We can be pretty sure today that they will get all their dates right and that every button will be in the proper place, though not necessarily fastened, for of late years the old 'cloak and sword' school of fiction has rather given place to what we might term 'bed and bawd'. But as we were long ago taught by the Hollywood film producers, the greatest possible accuracy of isolated detail can still add up to a total effect of psychological falsehood, and that is what happens all too often with a novel conceived in this spirit. Everything has to be larger than life—more colourful, more violent, more passionate, more romantic. Wit, subtlety, understatement, have little place in such novels. They lower the temperature; the reader feels let down. That is why, I think, historical novels in general are intellectually suspect and despised by a sophisticated public which has not examined them closely enough to discern that quite another type exists.

This type is the product of the other category of writers. It is the true 'historical novel', seeking not only authenticity of fact but—so far as it is humanly discoverable—a faithful re-creation of minds and motives. In the last analysis a good historical novel is a good novel, neither more nor less, whose story happens to be laid outside the time limits of living memory. You can subdivide it again if you like. There is the novel which closely follows historical events and introduces famous characters. And there is the novel which we could distinguish as the 'period novel', in which every event and every character is as imaginary as in a contemporary story, but in which the author's aim is to re-create some historical period. But both subdivisions stem from the same approach to history, both can claim in turn the interest of the same writer.

In fact it is often a pleasant relief to turn from one method to another. My own motives in writing have sometimes impelled me towards the great subjects that I wanted to tell children about—the French Revolution, the Russian Revolution, Garibaldi. In such cases the chronology of well known events imposes a ready-made framework on the fictitious plot—I found this particularly with my two Garibaldi stories. It is all very labour saving but can also be inhibiting. Although grateful for the splendid material history hands over ready-made—the colourful characters, the dramatic incidents—one sometimes experiences a wonderful sense of liberation when planning the next book as what I have called a 'period novel' in which one admittedly has to do all the work—all the invention of plot and character—but one also has complete liberty of action.

Whichever of these two kinds of novel an author is planning to write, I think it is important that he or she should be in love with the period. Some authors are so deeply, so inexhaustibly, in love with a single century that the affair goes on throughout their working lives and they never feel the need to look elsewhere for inspiration. I myself have to admit not perhaps to promiscuity but certainly to polygamy. So many aspects of history attract me that I have never been able to confine my attention to one. I have flitted widely between the Athens of Socrates, the fifth century BC, and St. Petersburg of AD 1917. But it would be quite easy to lay a finger on the single common factor occurring in every period I have chosen between these extremes in time—the period has to be *literate*, or at least someone in the story has to be literate. I once did a book about the Danes. I could not possibly have emulated the primitive gusto with which Henry Treece so splendidly handled that kind of subject. It's not the splitting of skulls with battle axes that inspires me; it's the opening of minds in a gentler sense. I could only bother with Guthrum because of Alfred.

That particular book, *Mist Over Athelney*, will serve to illustrate another consideration that affects my choice of theme. I like sometimes to get two themes into the one story. It's not just economy of effort—two statements for the effort of one; it's not just the growing consciousness that I shan't have time to write all the books I'd like to. It is rather that the interplay of

two themes, as in a piece of music, helps to give the story an extra depth and texture. Sometimes those two themes are conveniently embodied in the same historical period. Many years ago,
waiting in India for my release from the army, I filled in my
time writing a story about the Glorious Revolution which interested the political side of me. But just about that time I had
been learning a little about Purcell, and John Blow, and Jere-
miah Clarke, and I was full of another enthusiasm to tell English
children that there had been a time in history when England
had been the most musical country in Europe. Any fellow
writer may imagine my glee when I discovered that dates coin-
cided and would fuse my two story lines into one. William of
Orange entered London in January 1689, and February saw the
performance of the first English opera, Purcell's *Dido and
Aeneas*. When I add that the performance took place at a girls'
school in Chelsea—which meant that my fictitious heroine could
sing in it—you will appreciate that it was truly, in a different
sense from usual, 'a turn-up for the book'. *My* book, *Trumpets
in the West,* was quickly written in the East and posted home to
my wife four foolscap pages at a time. That was as much as
would go post free by Forces Air Mail.

It is not often that two suitably interlacing themes emerge so
neatly from the period itself. The second theme may be a general one. I wanted for years to write a story of the French
Revolution to counteract the aristocratic bias of the romantic
novelists. I also wanted to use a character who was to develop
into a painter. *He* could have gone into a dozen other historical
stories. As it happened, he went into *Thunder of Valmy*. Sometimes the second theme can be modern and highly topical, but
suitably transmuted and transferred to another period it helps
to give the emotional vitality the story needs. To refer again to
my story about the Danes, *Mist Over Athelney,* the first
—the obvious initial inspiration—was the rich, underestimated
civilization of those who used to be dismissed as 'our rude
Anglo-Saxon forefathers'. But the second theme came straight
from the atmosphere of the time when it was written in 1957.
We were then experiencing one of our monotonously recurrent
economic crises. Each evening the newsreels showed us the
queues of would-be emigrants outside Canada House and Aus-

tralia House. The usual cry was going up, 'England's finished, there's no future here.' And I realized that in the winter of 878 people had been saying just the same—doubtless in the rudest Anglo-Saxon. People in Hampshire and Dorset actually *were* emigrating—packing into ships and crossing the Channel to settle on the other side. They thought it was all over; Alfred was dead, and it was just a matter of months before the Danes over-ran the last southwestern corner of England. People had been wrong then, they could be wrong again. The emotion of 1957 came out in the story of 878.

So the author picks his period. He knows it or he couldn't love it, but the knowledge at this stage can be very superficial. You can fall in love with an unknown girl in a railway carriage, as my father did with my mother, but he had to put in a lot of patient study afterwards.

Authors today need to do a great deal of research. I suppose the standard of sheer accuracy attained by the average historical novelist today has never been equalled in earlier generations. He is writing, of course, for a much better educated public, alert for the slightest mistake. I believe that Victor Hugo once referred to James II of England as 'a jovial monarch', and in another passage somewhere appeared to imply that a 'wapen-take' was a kind of Anglo-Saxon policeman. Such casualness would be inadvisable today. Some nineteenth-century writers were more conscientious. George Eliot tore up the first draft of *Romola* when she realized how many mistakes she had made, and writing that book is said to have 'changed her from a young woman into an old'. I sympathize with her, though I have never been in quite the same danger. When I look round my own study shelves, full of handy illustrated volumes on every aspect of everyday life in different historical periods, I wonder how on earth people like Scott and George Eliot managed to get as many details right as they did.

On the other hand sometimes I reflect that ignorance could be bliss. There are just too many books now. Somewhere, in some book, someone has recorded everything (if only one knew where to look) and that realization is paralyzing.

I recall a moment of utter despair one evening, walking down the Herefordshire lanes near my house. I was in the middle of

Thunder of Valmy. I had read, or at least skimmed, about fifty
books on the French Revolution. I thought I had got all my
facts at my fingertips. I had just finished writing about that his-
toric June morning in 1789 when the deputies were locked out
of the hall at Versailles and had to move into the tennis court.
I'd imagined a June morning at Versailles—sunshine, sparkle,
splendour. And then in the public library I'd come across the
fifty-first book, the one I hadn't seen before, the memoirs of
the American ambassador at that time, and he'd noted what a
miserable wet morning it had been. It changed the feeling so
completely that I had to rewrite the whole passage. And I said
to myself, if this is going to happen all through the story, I'm
going to give it up. I'll switch to a period where there aren't so
many damn documents.

Does it matter? Would anyone spot it? You never know. In
Mist Over Athelney, when I realized that my adventurous young
people would have to eat sooner or later, I let them encounter a
hermit and share his campfire supper of rabbit stew. That detail
passed my learned publishers without comment; it passed the
Times Literary Supplement and a host of other reviewers. But it
didn't pass an eleven-year-old boy in Aberdeen, who wrote to
tell me that there were no rabbits in England before the
Norman Conquest.

Even if no one else is going to pounce on a mistake, one hates
to make them. They're like a secret burning shame inside, if you
only discover them in the published book and it's too late to do
anything. But you can't go on researching and checking for-
ever. You have to ask yourself—as the girl in some historical
novels should ask herself but too seldom does nowadays—'How
far ought I to go?' You do your best to get things right. You
can do no more.

Now I have to admit, and I do so with some reluctance, that
many a book with unsound history is far better literature than
one in which the details are impeccably researched. What's
worse, I could go further and concede that some old favourites
of bygone ages which are no great shakes either as literature or
as history have done far more to stimulate an enthusiasm for
the past than many books which are their superiors in both
respects. They are bad or mediocre books with, in general, good

lasting effects. I would put the works of Henty and Harrison Ainsworth into that category. But surely the success of those books lay not in their shortcomings but in their virtues—they won their public in spite of their faults, not because of them. Falsifying history just to make a better story is to me a confession of artistic laziness and imaginative poverty. The elder Dumas justified it if it led to a good book, not otherwise. He expressed it in a characteristically earthy Gallic way: 'One can violate History only if one has a child by her.' I may be thought prudish and pedantic, but I still prefer my own literary off-spring to be legitimate.

You have to work at it. Strict adherence to truth can present baffling problems. An example occurred in my own book about ancient Athens, *The Crown of Violet.* I had a boy character and a girl. For the plot to be possible the girl needed a certain free-dom of movement to come and go in the city. This is an oft-recurring problem in historical fiction. In the Athens of that date I was up against the blunt fact that no respectable Athen-ian girl—no citizen's daughter, that is—could possibly have gone around like my Corinna; she would have lived a life of almost Asiatic seclusion. I could overcome this difficulty quite simply by making her one of the numerous resident aliens, who were less fettered by conventions. But this solution merely created a new difficulty. I wished to imply, at the end of the story, that the boy and girl would later marry. Yet the law of Athens for-bade marriage between citizens and non-citizens. It seemed an insoluble problem. Of course it wasn't. Few problems are if you think long enough. A solution presented itself, and it was a solu-tion supported, though not consciously suggested, by one of the traditional plot situations and denouements of classical comedy. I think the book was improved by sticking to historical truth rather than by taking the quick and easy way out and falsifying it.

Of course none of us can say, with his hand on his heart, that he has never bent the documented record in some trivial detail, for example, by telescoping some period of time and combining two unimportant episodes into one in the interests of dramatic unity. But speaking for myself, I always make even the most minute adjustment of this kind with a feeling of reluctance. One would like to manage without it, but sometimes one just can't. The overall authenticity is what matters. Also the fiction writer has got to produce a picture which *looks* right as well as *being* right. Paradoxically, it can happen that the documented truth sounds false, and the fiction writer, unlike the straight historian, cannot slip in a footnote reference to justify himself. I remember once using the phrase 'What the dickens' in that story of the Glorious Revolution. My publishers challenged it. I replied that Shakespeare had used it in *The Merry Wives of Windsor*. Historically I was right. Artistically I was wrong. The average reader winced at what he thought was an anachronism. You shouldn't make your readers wince. There has to be a measure of compromise.

And there has to be compromise, I fear, on other and more important points. There is the question of what is acceptable to the modern taste, and by that phrase I don't mean anything to do with sexual outspokenness, where indeed the 'modern taste' seems to be for highly spiced dishes. No, I mean quite simply how can the author hold his reader's sympathy, how can the reader identify wholeheartedly with the historical character—all of which is absolutely vital, especially when we are dealing with *young* readers—when so much that was authentic and unavoidable, or at least socially acceptable, in the period of the story repels the reader today?

One's Elizabethan heroine probably had black teeth and anything but a sweet breath. The one atmosphere which was probably authentic in most historical eras was of human bodies too little washed and too heavily clothed. It was not only the villains who smelt. Or take our changed attitude to cruelty. What happens to our readers' sympathy if our debonair Regency hero goes, as well he might, straight from partnering the heroine at an elegant ball to the enjoyment of a public execution at dawn? With the young public I should think that the treatment of animals would be one of the worst stumbling blocks, if we represented it with complete historical accuracy. The old squire dies. He may have included in his last wishes—I believe it was commonly done—that all his dogs should be hanged. It would be a foolhardy author who let his hero carry out that sort of instruction. One can think of countless such difficulties where the author is compelled to present something less than the complete historical picture.

Not every awkwardness is so charged with potential emotion and disgust. There are many little genuine period touches which merely seem odd and may distract the reader, again especially the young reader, such as the way seventeenth-century men sat about indoors with their immense hats on. Then there are the things which may strike a modern reader as ambiguous when at the time they were innocent and commonplace, such as the way men used to share a bed. Some of Pepys's most enjoyable conversations on music, careers and life in general seem to have been conducted in this setting, but it is open to misunderstanding if it is used by a novelist.

Psychological authenticity is the great problem. Anyone can find out what people wore and ate. We know how a portcullis worked, and a ballista, and a kitchen spit. But do we know how people's *minds* worked?

I remember as a very young man going up to Naomi Mitchison after a lecture and shyly telling her what her books about the ancient Greeks and Romans had meant to me, *Cloud Cuckoo Land, The Conquered, The Corn King and the Spring Queen*, and I can still recall vividly my utter dismay when she told me she wasn't going to write any more books like that. She had come to the conclusion that she had got the ancient Greeks and Romans all wrong, they hadn't really been a bit like that. I still regret her decision, but I think now that I can understand why she made it. To imagine the *internal* and not just the *external* reality of historical characters is a most daunting enterprise.

Stop and imagine the simplest things. The significance of nightfall when there was no good artificial light; the misery of winter for the same reason, as well as many others; conversely the tremendous liberation of May Day and the lengthening days. Imagine the bodily sensation of cluttering clothes; wet weather before the invention of rubber and plastics. Think of the different sense of time before we had watches with minute hands. There was no really practicable watch, I believe, before Robert Hook invented the balance spring about 1675. Stop and consider how this affects our description of suspense. An officer might conceivably count the minutes before battle was joined at Blenheim; he couldn't really have done so at Naseby. So too with slow communications and consequent anxieties. The invaders might have landed days ago, a man's son might have been born to his wife on the other side of England, a new king might already be on the throne—and there was nothing faster than a galloping horse to bring you the news. It *must* have affected the way people thought and felt.

These, as I say, are the simplest things. Add a few of the complications—taboos, superstitions, religious certainty, medical ignorance. My lord collapses, writhing in agony, and is quickly dead. Today any doctor can tell us various natural conditions which, if not quickly treated with all our modern resources, could prove fatal in such a situation. Our historical characters have no notion of such things, any more than they know malaria is carried by mosquitoes and mental illness is not induced by evil spirits. How many hapless cooks and courtiers must have died horrible deaths for supposedly poisoning their masters who really died of, say, a burst appendix? Spells, astrology, hell fire and horoscopes—these were just some of the things that shaped the thoughts of our ancestors. On the other hand, they were spared the brainwashing of the advertisers and they knew nothing of opinion polls.

Is it any wonder that sometimes the conscientious novelist despairs of being able to think himself inside the skin of someone living in an earlier century, when he wonders if he hasn't merely achieved the result he so much despises in other people's books—to create what are really only modern characters decked up in fancy dress? In such moments of depression it is salutary to turn to contemporary writings of some other age—to Byron's letters or the Pastons', Pepys's Diary or Evelyn's, Lucy Hutchinson's memoirs or Boswell's journals, even to some passages from Plato or Aristophanes, Pliny or Petronius or Martial. At once you sense their common humanity—what I meant when I emphasized at the beginning of this article the *similarities* in history, which to some of us make a deeper appeal than the differences, however picturesque. And sensing that common, continuing humanity you take heart again.

So you get your characters, you costume them correctly, you

set them in action against a background as accurate as you can make it, you do your imaginative best to endue them with an authentic inner life of thought and feeling. All you have to do now is *write* the book!

Most of the problems now are those common to any kind of fiction. Most of the differences that emerge at this stage are, I think, those between the adult and the junior novel. Making every allowance for the great development in breadth of theme, in maturity, in sophistication, of the junior novel in recent years, and making every allowance for changes in the juvenile audience—their conditioning, for example, by television and other media to a quick-witted grasp of techniques, such as the flashback which would have puzzled an older generation of children—making every allowance for all this, I think it is still fair to say that plot and incident retain all their old importance, and that the younger reader, unlike some of his elders, likes a story to have a beginning, a middle and an end—and in that order. And if the adult writer feels bored doing it this way, he might be wiser to work in another field.

We all know that a worthwhile children's book of any type has more than one level. Each reader penetrates as deeply as his years, his sensitivity, his emotional maturity allow. What really inspires the author may be what lies at the deepest level. But he must be prepared for many children to love his book for what he himself regards as the superficial qualities. What I think is vital is that he should never privately despise those superficial qualities and think of them as synthetic decoration—put on, in a calculating spirit, to make the book attractive to the young. It must be a genuine book at all levels. When he is choosing his theme and doing his research his standards can be as adult, indeed as academic, as he likes. When he is writing—when emotion and art begin to take over from intellect—then he must let the child in himself dictate much of the form. I say very deliberately 'the child in *himself*'. Some writers acknowledge the influence of their sons and daughters or other individual children they have specially studied to please. But on the whole a writer should please himself, and a children's writer should not worry and scheme to study children's interests and cater for their demands. He should be a children's writer because he still retains inside himself, perhaps more vividly than the average adult, the vestigial child he once was, and can still enjoy some of the same things that he did then. He may plan his book, as I planned *The Crown of Violet,* with an adult motive—indeed a didactic motive—to inform children about classical Athens and to communicate my own interest and enthusiasm. But in the telling he must, at another level, enjoy the action as genuinely as he wants his readers to enjoy it. To paddle up the shallow river in its gorge, to find a cave with a mysterious girl playing a flute, and then later to get caught up in a plot to overthrow the government—the author himself has got to love every minute of it himself. He is not 'putting it in because the children like it'. He is living it, in imagination, because it is a fantasy which after forty or fifty years still satisfies a hunger of his own.

There is one special problem for the historical novelist, and this applies whatever the age group he is primarily addressing. It is the problem of the vocabulary he should use for his dialogue.

When I came into this field of writing, right back in 1933, the historical adventure story for children was bogged down in tushery. People shouted, 'Quotha!' and 'Ha, we are beset!' and a quotation I specially cherish is ' "Yonder sight is enough to make a man eschew lance and sword for ever, and take to hot-cockles and cherry pit," exclaimed the Earl of Pembroke, adding an oath which the sacred character of the building did not in the least restrain.' One of the reasons why historical fiction was then in the doldrums was, I am sure, that even in the leisurely 1930s the child could not be bothered to fight his way through such verbiage.

Should dialogue attempt an authentic period flavour? It is of course possible to construct pastiche conversations for an English story that goes no further back than the eighteenth century and use no single word that has not contemporary authority. It is possible. It is debatable whether such an exercise is worth the effort, or whether it can fully convey what the characters mean, as well as what they are saying. For we can never afford to forget the way in which words have changed their meanings while preserving their appearance. Today, I imagine, a bishop welcomes any sign of 'enthusiasm' among his clergy. He would not have done so in the eighteenth century.

In any case, if we go back to earlier periods, we cannot attempt a faithful reproduction of speech without becoming almost unintelligible. And the effect is to push the characters further and further back into the past, to raise more and more barriers between them and ourselves.

From the moment I planned my very first book I was in no doubt as to my own way of dealing with the problem. The answer had really been given me (I didn't realize it consciously but it was there all right, submerged in my mind) about seven years earlier, when as a schoolboy I had read Naomi Mitchison's story of Caesar and the Gauls. It was only long afterwards, when I dipped into *The Conquered* again, and read Ernest Barker's introduction to my pocket edition, that I knew my debt to Naomi Mitchison. *I* had made Robin Hood speak modern English, without tushery or archaisms, because I felt it was the only way he could speak to the modern child. But it was Naomi Mitchison—even before Robert Graves with his *I, Claudius* in the same style, which I had not heard of then—who blazed the trail. As Ernest Barker said in his introduction:

> If the novelist of classical times were to make the speech, dress and other appurtenances true to the text of a classical dictionary, he would hardly make his puppets live or his action move. These ancient figures must break into modern speech if they are to touch us.

They must indeed. Obviously they must not break into modern slang or jarring anachronisms. I believe there was once a Hollywood film showing Henry VIII at the Field of the Cloth of Gold, and one courtier was made to say to another, 'I do hate parties, don't you?' There must be artistic compromise. The ear must be the final judge. A line may be historically right and still sound wrong and if it sounds wrong, it must go as remorselessly as any other kind of blemish. At every moment of the story the reader has got to be simultaneously convinced of two separate things: first that these characters are alive and warm and tangible, as if they were in the room with him; second that they are *not* modern people in this room, but are in another time and place whose atmosphere they have thrown around him and themselves, like some magic pavilion. The achievement of that illusion is really the whole craft of the historical storyteller.

From *Children's literature in education*, No. 7, March 1972

Part Two
CRITICS

Jorinda and Jorindel and Other Stories

Penelope Farmer

Penelope Farmer has written six novels for children, one of which, The Summer Birds, *was runner-up for the Carnegie Medal in 1962. She has also written a number of scripts for B.B.C Schools radio.*

I USED TO be surprised that adult readers should sometimes try to distinguish fantasy from fairy tale, myth and legend, because all seemed to me to have roughly the same function: to interpret human and imaginative experience in terms of symbol or image. Fantasy and fairy tale in any case are usually hopelessly confused, so that any short story tends to be called fairy tale while the longer ones are called fantasy. Yet the more I think about it, the more I begin to find one clear distinction. Myth, fairy tales and legend all relate to general experience and come from the mass subconscious—myths, obviously, dealing with much grander matters than fairy tales, concerns of a more universal kind—yet the difference being of degree not kind, since both relate to the minds of a people rather than of an individual. Fantasy, on the other hand, though it may use universal symbols, springs from purely private experiences—it is psychological image, coloured and transformed by the workings of a single mind. This does not mean that a modern fairy story from some particular modern writer cannot, *per se,* be a fairy story, or that it cannot be told in an individual idiom or style; only that the writer has to maintain some distance from the material, to let the feeling of the story come from his interpretation and re-working of themes within the fairy tale convention, even if in a fairly original way, rather than from unknown recesses of his own mind. Robert Nye, for instance, though a highly idiosyn-cratic writer, still produces fairy stories in the genuine tradition; whereas Hans Andersen, usually classed as a writer of fairy tales, is to my mind anything but. On the face of it he appears to have done what Robert Nye does now—either retelling stories from sources such as Grimm, or else inventing his own—yet I would call him a writer of fantasy because all his stories are so deeply coloured by the curious, obviously unhappy workings of his subconscious mind. I shall return to this later but at this stage I wish to make two other points.

In an article in a short-lived newspaper called *Play*, Helen Cresswell made a distinction between phantasy in the psycho-logical sense spelt with a 'ph' and fantasy in the literary sense spelt with an 'f'. I regard this more often than not as an entirely false distinction. Many kinds of literary fantasy are just psycho-logical phantasy given form, narrative and coherence; the staple themes are, after all, the stuff of dreams—witches, ogres, time shifts, flying, changes of shape or size. The same thing, of course, is true of myth and fairy tale, though there the phantasy (with a 'ph') is of a more general kind. In one sense, though, myth here is the reverse of fantasy. The more sophisticated a culture, the more coherent are its myths. In the primitive myths of the Australian aborigines, for instance, it is hard to find or to follow any story line; they have a totally dreamlike incoher-ence, compared with the strong narrative lines of, say, the Greek myths. Conversely, the more sophisticated an audience, the less does the creator have to disguise the subconscious of his fantasy; it can, even should, retain that kind of incoherence, or at least appear to do so, as with Kurt Vonnegut, whose brilliant fantasies, particularly *Slaughterhouse Five,* have this surface incoherence—or rather perhaps illogicality, like the process of consciousness or of dream—but an enormously strong and con-scious structure underlying them. (This says more about war in a hundred pages than Norman Mailer does in a thousand, and should disabuse anyone of the idea that fantasy has only some-thing to say to children. Probably only in film, though, has the thing been taken to its logical extent, as in Fellini's *Satyricon,* which abandons narrative entirely in favour of the incoherence of the subconscious and the dream.)

Jonathan Miller's television version of *Alice* brought home to me the fluid, illogical, totally dreamlike shiftings of Lewis Carroll's narrative—so that almost for the first time I saw what *Alice* was really about: not only a dream but having the struc-ture of dream itself.

As a child, though, I read *Alice* straight. For children are not a sophisticated audience, and therefore—and this is my second point—if you write fantasy for children, whatever its origins, you must provide or, as Lewis Carroll did, appear to provide, a strong narrative line. You must create a beginning, a middle and an end; a process which can, I think, make it much clearer to yourself from where your ideas spring, even if disguising it from the audience. It is not that you cannot or must not play with form. Event does not have to be extrovert, it can go on in people's heads, or within the most simple domestic situation. But the form must be there and be seen to be there, otherwise children will not read you.

Here I must make a distinction. Up till now I have been con-sidering fantasy as an introvert form, but it does not necessarily have to be.

Roughly, extrovert fantasies rely more on surface mechanics, or machinery. They may use the themes and devices of introvert fantasy, yet the source and consequence of event is basically ex-terior to both the author and his or her characters. And though the failings of the characters, such as stupidity, cowardice, idleness or overenthusiasm, may land them in danger or embar-rassment, there is not so much a sense of terror below terror, joy below joy as you will find in fantasy of the other sort. For instance, I would say that both Philippa Pearce's *A Dog So Small* and Catherine Storr's *Marianne Dreams* are examples of introvert fantasy: the first about a boy who becomes so pas-sionately involved with an imaginary, or almost imaginary, dog that he loses almost all contact with reality, with nearly fatal results; the second about a ten-year-old girl confined to bed with a severe illness and dreaming as she convalesces a series of increasingly terrifying dreams, which gradually, through actions in her waking life, she learns to control.

Most of E. Nesbit's fantasies on the other hand I should call extrovert fantasies—which is not belittlement, because she was and undoubtedly is, one of the best, certainly the most inventive and imaginative of all writers for children. In *The Phoenix and the Carpet* and *Five Children and It* the magic arises from the chance discovery of the phoenix in the one, and of the psammead in the other: the phoenix able to transport children anywhere on the inevitably magic carpet, the psammead able to grant a wish a day; both of which gifts turn out to be more problematical than they appear. For instance, the day Anthea and company wish for wings, the magic wears off when they are sitting on a church tower with no means of getting down; the day they wish for boundless wealth, it arrives in the form of golden coins which none of the local shopkeepers will accept.

You can learn plenty about Mrs Nesbit herself from her books—her passionate Fabianism, her deep interest in and knowledge of archaeology (e.g. in *The Story of the Amulet*) her wit, inventiveness, and intelligence—but this is all on the level of the intellect; there are no apparent undercurrents, as you get in more introverted writers—except perhaps in one of her less known, and certainly less admired books, *The Enchanted Castle*. Though this is certainly less sure, more uneven than her other books, for me it still contains examples of her most powerful writing—precisely because its terrors have echoes, are more than terrifying. I am thinking of the Uglies, people made out of bolsters and walking sticks as an audience for a play. Here they are when we first meet them:

> The seven members of the audience seated among the wilderness of chairs had, indeed, no insides to speak of. Their bodies were bolsters and rolled up blankets, their spines were hockey sticks and umbrellas . . . and their faces were the paper masks painted in the afternoon by the untutored brush of Gerald. . . . The faces were really rather dreadful. Gerald had done his best, but even after his best had been done you would hardly have known they were faces, some of them, if

they hadn't been in the position which faces usually occupy, between the collar and the hat.

And now here are the Uglies alive:

> The hall was crowded with live things, strange things—all horribly short as broomsticks and umbrellas are short. A limp hand gesticulated. A pointed white face with red cheeks looked up at him, and wide red lips said something, he could not tell what . . . These creatures had no roofs to their mouths, of course—they had no—
> 'Aa oo re o me me oo a oo ho el?' said the voice again. And it had said it four times before Gerald could collect himself sufficiently to understand that this horror—alive and most likely uncontrollable—was saying, with a dreadful calm, polite persistence:
> 'Can you recommend me to a good hotel?'

I find this terror reaches below consciousness. The only way of getting rid of the Uglies is to turn them back into collections of inanimate objects. But even then, you are left with the feeling that having come alive once, they could come alive again. The terror can never be wholly eliminated—like all the domestic terrors, deep cupboards, dark shadowy corners on a staircase, it is always somewhere there.

Once you make categories of course it is hard to find anything that fits them exactly. Tentatively, though, I would call Joan Aiken's fantasies extrovert rather than introvert (especially her short stories). Perhaps it is no coincidence that she is probably also one of the most inventive and fertile of present children's writers. Do the writers of introvert fantasies have to go deeper into smaller areas precisely because they are less inventive, even if no less imaginative?

Lewis Carroll, Alan Garner, Lucy Boston, Russell Hoban I would call introvert fantasists. Mary Norton is harder to categorize but I think I would put her among the introverts, especially in her first two Borrower books. The sense of human littleness in an enormous universe is a basic human fear or feeling—even more literally true for children—and the Borrowers' shifts and artifices to turn objects from the giant human world to their own use go beyond invention; they have a quirkiness, an oddity, which makes them precisely right, which moves an imagination on, as well as satisfying it.

I need not make any too high claims for my books when I say that they tend to fall into the same category, because I find myself dealing with the same interior kinds of subjects—often, unknowingly—and quite often again touch on problems of my own, even if I do not always recognize this and certainly do not know how or why. For instance, halfway through *Charlotte Sometimes* I realized that I was writing a book about identity. I am a twin, a non-identical one, and apparently one of the chief problems of non-identical twins is always the establishment of a genuine and separate sense of identity. Looking back I can see this has in fact been an obsession with me, since the age of twelve or so at least. Margery Fisher has said that *Emma in Winter* is also about a search for identity, which is interesting because it is quite certainly something that I did not recognize at any stage while writing it. And it is true, if you write this kind of book, that though some of its concerns may become apparent to you as you write, some never do, unless they are brought to your attention when other people comment on what you have written. One reviewer for instance, talking about *Charlotte Sometimes*, said it was full of images suggesting the gap between appearance and reality—an acorn which didn't quite fit its cup, a huge bell which was cracked and so only made a small sound, marbles which looked huge in water and smaller outside. I still do not know myself if, subconsciously, this was for me an underlying concern.

I wonder if other writers too have experienced, in the middle of some emotional or nervous crisis, a totally blinding and startling sense of *déja-vu*. Or again, have had some curious emotion, say an enormous feeling of elation, or again, of terror, when reading or describing some passage from an earlier book which is much more powerful than the feeling that at the time appeared to generate the passage? It almost seems as if what you write previews some future state of crisis, or alternatively previews its resolution. (On a much larger and wider scale the same thing happens perhaps with a major writer, composer or painter whose work is rejected by his contemporaries because it, or the feelings and ideas expressed by it, appear meaningless to them— e.g. Beethoven's last quartets and practically everything William Blake wrote or painted—but which is taken up by later genera- tions who feel it understands or states their own mood and feel- ing precisely.)

In fact these decidedly personal origins of my kind of fantasy make it very hard to discuss. To say much more about what appears to be the genesis of one or other of my books would involve revelations which I have no intention of making. Equal- ly, to investigate the origins of books written by other writers could well lead one into exceedingly impertinent assumptions— unless they are safely dead, that is. Most people are acquainted with the psychological repressions and oddities that underlay Lewis Carroll. However I shall have to take the risk of being impertinent in order to go on to discuss a little further Cath- erine Storr's *Marianne Dreams* and her later book *Rufus.*

Now the fear in *Marianne Dreams* is elemental. The ring of stones round the house in which Marianne and Mark are trapped in their dream grows progressively more threatening; they have eyes, they start to whisper; later they move. It is nightmare incarnate, the more so because Marianne herself has created them through her drawing. This is the essential nature of depres- sive illness which often involves a high degree of aggression turned in against the self. A friend of mine going through a breakdown recently drew obsessively, endlessly, rows of hills with eyes and mouths, herself a pin figure screaming in a corner in front of them. She said she felt totally alone in an empty landscape, yet the landscape itself had developed personality, was advancing on her threateningly. This image progressively tightened till it became eventually, an enormous eye, its iris a lake, with a whirlpool in the centre in which a screaming figure drowned. It was herself drowning, she said. The eye was every- thing and everybody else. It is a succinct and precise image, which I envy, and it says pretty much the same thing as Cather- ine Storr is saying. But I wonder where in *Marianne Dreams* she got it from. Mrs. Storr is, I think, a psychiatrist and must know clinically the symptoms and effects of breakdown and depres- sion—the latter something that can affect children as much as adults. She must know the kind of images produced by patients in these conditions. But *Marianne* is no case history. I do not believe it would be possible for anything so felt, so powerful, to come only from clinical knowledge—it must have had its roots basically in herself. You can see this even more if you take later books—*Marianne and Mark* and *Rufus*—because they seem so much more detached and conscious.

The theme of *Rufus* is similar in some ways to that of *Marianne Dreams*. Rufus is an orphan and lives in a children's home, where he is bullied by another boy, and just as Marianne draws herself a dream world, Rufus, in an agony of longing, carves himself a dream mother. This little figure does indeed take him back in dreams to a prehistoric world, in which he has a mother and a place of his own to fill, instead of being an outsider as he feels in the home. In the end, like Marianne, he resolves his own life through what he learns in the dream and comes to terms both with it and himself.

Catherine Storr is a gifted writer and has a clarity, precision and elegance which I envy. *Rufus* is fluently, tightly, exactly written. It is convincing too. But it is much too cool to my mind. Perhaps in a way the problems are too extreme. Marianne was more of a sick child than a maladjusted child, while Rufus is a case history which in its outline anyway could have come from the files of a psychologist, even though it has been imaginatively reconstructed here. If you like, it is an extrovert fantasy on an introvert subject, as if E. Nesbit had turned herself out and made her intellectual patterns with the materials of her own, or someone else's mind. Some passages from both *Rufus* and *Marianne Dreams* may make this clear.

Marianne looked round the side of the window. From where she stood she could see five—six—seven of the great stones standing immovable outside. As she looked there was a movement in all of them. The great eyelids dropped; there was a moment when each figure was nothing but a hunk of stone, motionless and harmless. Then, together, the pale eyelids lifted and seven great eyeballs swivelled in their stone sockets and fixed themselves on the house.

Marianne screamed. She felt that she was screaming with the full power of her lungs, screaming like a siren; but no

The Stones (ill. by Marjorie-Ann Watts, from *Marianne Dreams* by Catherine Storr. Faber, 1958; Penguin, 1964). Reprinted by permission of Faber & Faber Ltd.

sound came out at all. She wanted to warn Mark, but she could not utter a word.

In her struggle she woke.

By contrast, here is a climactic passage from *Rufus:*

In the instant that this happened Rufus had a hundred thoughts and knowledges. He thought that Erek would kill them. He, a man, even a weak man, was a match for them all. He thought that if he, Rufus, attempted to fight him he would be killed. He felt the knife sink deep into his flesh, letting out his blood and his love and his guilt. He thought that Gurya's screams would call no one. They were still too far from the huts. He thought that he might take Gurya and run for help, while at the same time he knew that with the child in his arms, he could not run swiftly enough to fetch help. . . . He thought too of running alone. His body longed to go, to escape from danger and death. His traitor mind told him that this was right, it was better to save himself than to risk all, and in this moment he knew, as he had never done before, that it was the lying, stealing Rufus who thought this, that this was what Nicky would have done, cheating himself into believing that by flying alone he had just a chance of reaching the huts in time to fetch help for the woman and the child, while the truth was that to do this would be to save only himself.

I should now like to turn to the effect of fantasy on its audience. But perhaps I had better start briefly, and I fear grandiosely, by talking more generally about the function of art, and of images in art. For me, chiefly, their function is to communicate, and particularly to communicate the almost incommunicable; that is feelings and experience of every kind—emotional, spiritual, intellectual, aesthetic; all of which helps to lessen the huge distances between ourselves and other people, so making us feel less isolated, less alone. This can be done more effectively often by symbol or image—even by abstract image—than by direct statement, precisely because images are so much more powerful. They can be almost limitless in their reverberations. For instance, if my friend with the breakdown had simply said, 'I feel that everyone around me is threatening and attacking me', it would not have communicated her fear and desperation one quarter as effectively as that single eye with the figure drowning in it. Art, through images, analysed and began to comprehend the states of the human mind long before there was any science available to do it. I think of those fantastic nightmare pictures by Hieronymus Bosch. Some of his images appear spontaneously in the paintings of mental patients now. I think of *Hamlet,* a complete portrait of a manic depressive, long before there were psychologists, let alone a clinical recognition of manic depression; and of Blake whose prophetic books set out almost precisely the same fourfold analysis of the mind of man as Freud did a century later.

Poetry, via images, compresses the deepest and most complex ideas into the space of a few lines. Here is part of a poem by Sylvia Plath which says much the same kind of things about internalized threat and fear as Catherine Storr does in *Marianne Dreams*, and is, I think, the most terrifying description of paranoia that I know—paranoia seen from right inside. It is called *The Arrival of the Bee Box*.

> I ordered this, this clean wood box
> Square as a chair and almost too heavy to lift.
> I would say it was the coffin of a midget
> Or a square baby
> Were there not such a din in it.
>
> The box is locked, it is dangerous.
> I have to live with it overnight
> And I can't keep away from it.
> There are no windows, so I can't see what is in there.
> There is only a little grid, no exit.
>
> I put my eye to the grid,
> It is dark, dark,
> With the swarmy feeling of African hands
> Minute and shrunk for export,
> Black on black, angrily clambering.
>
> How can I let them out?
> It is the noise that appals me most of all,
> The unintelligible syllables.
> It is like a Roman mob,
> Small, taken one by one, but my god, together!

There are three more verses but these say enough I think. It is the 'swarmy feeling of African hands' which shows the fear at its most basic, instinctive, primitive—even more primitive really than Catherine Storr's stones with eyes. The point is that fantasy does precisely what poetry does, but in a way which children can take. Poetic images, except of the simplest kind, are too compressed and elliptical—while fantasy images are extended through narrative and character and are, therefore, more approachable. Children need such images quite as much as adults do, because so much of what goes on around them, and even more what goes on in their minds and the minds of other people, is totally inexplicable intellectually; because explanation would involve terms and concepts way beyond their grasp. Only through images, therefore, can they begin to recognize and understand many of their own feelings and much of their emotional experience, or at least to recognize that they are not alone in it. You might say the images I have chosen to illustrate this point—images of fear—are not ones you ought to give to children at all, that you frighten them unnecessarily. This is, I think, why *Marianne Dreams* has never been read on children's television—it is considered too frightening; and this was the reason why some people were dubious about Maurice Sendak's picture book *Where the Wild Things Are* when it first came out. But the point is that what goes on in children's heads—hate, fear, aggression—is just as frightening, if not more so, and needs to be externalized in some intuitively recognizable form. The importance of both *Marianne* and *The Wild Things* is that the fears are both examined and resolved—or overcome for the time being—in a satisfying and logically convincing way. Max arrives home to find his supper waiting, and still hot; and Marianne draws bicycles and so eventually reaches the lighthouse, daylight, the open cliff top.

Even where children might be able to accept a more direct intellectual explanation, through imagery they can be given a great deal more; the idea can be taken a great deal further. In *Charlotte Sometimes* I did not immediately realize I was writing a book about a search for identity; but by taking a literal situation—an extended image if you like—making Charlotte take the place of Clare who had lived fifty years earlier—I could take the matter, both consciously and unconsciously, a good deal further than if I had just made the schoolgirl sit down and debate to herself 'Who am I?' Apart from anything else, if she had debated it for a hundred and fifty pages or so, what child would have read it? In the same way Lewis Carroll put Alice into a dream and then made her ask:

'I wonder if I've changed in the night? Let me think: *was* I the same when I got up this morning? I almost think I can remember feeling a little different. But if I'm not the same, the next question is, who in the world am I? Ah that's the great puzzle.' And she began thinking over all the children she knew. . . to see if she could have been changed with any of them.

'I'm sure I'm not Ada,' she said, 'for her hair goes in such long ringlets and mine doesn't go in ringlets at all: and I'm sure I can't be Mabel, for I know all sorts of things and she, oh, she knows such a very little. Besides *she's* she, and *I'm* I, and oh dear how puzzling it all is.'

Now Alice could not have asked these questions if she had simply gone for a walk down the street. Any child would simply think, how silly, of course she's the same person. But suggested like this the question 'Who am I?' may occur to them later if not sooner, will lodge in a corner of their minds as a valid question, one they themselves one day will need to ask.

To take another example, Philippa Pearce's *Tom's Midnight Garden* examines in depth problems of time, of human growth and change that would be way beyond children in any other form. And again, I doubt if you could find any piece of realistic fiction for adolescents that says a quarter as much about adolescence as Alan Garner's *The Owl Service*. You could extend such a list indefinitely.

The point is perhaps that all good writing for children has to be highly selective and precise, but with a sense of underlying richness, of immensity left out, as in some lyric poetry. You do not forget adult consciousness or adult experience as a writer for children, you rather push it underground, so that it is like a stream making the ground above more fertile, though remaining unseen. But in fantasy particularly you can use fully your own feelings as an adult because you are not using them directly, but working around them; in a way you can, in the fullest sense, write for yourself, indeed I think you must. William Mayne has said that he writes for himself as a boy, but I do not find it possible myself to differentiate so sharply between adulthood and childhood. Most of the time in memory one state melts into the other; they are inextricable.

But now I return to the question of the audience. For though the origins and functions of fantasy may in some sense be constant, its effect on the audience varies greatly, particularly when that audience is made up of children, whose reading is much more related to psychological need than that of most adults. A child does not read a book making cool assessments of its aesthetic qualities (though he may, of course without knowing it, gain aesthetic pleasure). He takes from the book what he most needs, from wish fulfilment at the lowest level, upwards to the pointing and even partial resolving of the most complex of subconscious dilemmas. Sometimes a child recognizes the need quite consciously. I can remember myself that as a child, if I needed comfort or security, if I was depressed, I went straight off and read either the cooking chapter of *Little Men*—when Daisy gets given a stove and has a gloriously cosy, domestic day; or else Rat and Mole's long stay in Badger's den in *Wind in the Willows*. But unconsciously, in other ways, books can trigger off sets of the most powerful psychological responses, fear, uncertainty or joy, without anyone quite knowing why.

Fairy tale, as I suggested earlier, arouses these responses in a fairly ritualistic way and is therefore often easier for a child to take, because he sees precisely what frightens him and what makes him sad. And there is no doubt that a child, like an adult, likes both to be frightened and made sad sometimes. How do we otherwise explain the continuing popularity of books like *Black Beauty* or the stories of Edgar Allan Poe? As an adult I read Grimm, horrified by the sadism, the gougings and stickings, the tearing out of eyes, the cutting off of heads and limbs—all of which must have gone straight over my head as a child because I don't particularly remember them, though I knew Grimm almost by heart.

Fairy tales resolve themselves so neatly, too. Goodies are happy and cruelties perpetrated on them avenged; the baddies die miserably. Perhaps if anything they are almost too predictable, as my six-year-old daughter suggested when she said in a bored voice, 'I don't want to hear *any more* of those stories when the woodcutter's son has to do three tasks before he's allowed to marry the princess.' Probably fairy tales are only really disturbing to a child if they touch on some very particular but hidden fear; which is where, in case you were wondering, Jorinda and Jorindel come in.

Jorinda, if you remember, is stolen away by a witch and turned into a nightingale, and when her friend Jorindel goes to look for her, he finds a whole roomful of nightingales in cages, Jorinda quite indistinguishable from the rest. If he can pick her out, the witch promises, he shall have his Jorinda back. The task is impossible—it is only because the witch herself loses courage and sneaks away with Jorinda's cage, that Jorindel guesses right- ly and chooses that one.

I read this story again recently and found nothing in it to alarm me now, yet a kind of indefinable depression came over me as I thought about it, which I can trace back to a similar feeling I had about that story as a child, and which I can proba- bly relate to my own difficulty in establishing a separate identi- ty. Because it is, of course, the ultimate story about loss of identity—to become one nightingale among so many, all of them alike.

I did not usually get such feelings from traditional stories though. I got them more—and again the memory of the feeling revives itself when I read them again—from Hans Andersen's fairy stories, which as I said earlier I would call fantasy rather than fairy story. Mainly they depressed me, these stories, the more so because often there was no obvious reason for my depression even when they had unhappy endings. (The death of Beth, for instance, in *Little Women* never depressed me in that sort of way.) And depression, I think, is much more disturbing for a child than fear or grief, because its origins are less defina- ble, are harder to isolate and understand.

With Hans Andersen this feeling must have arisen from the severely disturbed mind behind the stories. *The Red Shoes* for instance, can only have been written by someone very sick in- deed. I regard it as one of the most revolting stories that I know, with its mixture of sickly religious sentiment and sadism.

You could say Walt Disney is a twentieth-century equivalent —think of the beastliness of the witch in Snow White, and the appearance of the enormous, looming yellow-eyed devil towards the end of *Fantasia*. It is brilliant, riveting stuff, but horrific in the extreme. Then think of the pastel-coloured heroines and those babycham fairies sprinkling pixie dust. Straightforward horror stories where the avowed and deliberate intention is to terrify are much healthier, much less disturbing, I believe.

Alice in Wonderland used to disturb me too, and much as I

love it now, the unease remains. Though the violence is more implied, less actual than in Hans Andersen, it has, at a guess, one of the highest aggression levels in English literature. It is interesting that *Through the Looking Glass* is so much gentler, basically melancholic. Even as a child I used to find it easier to take and still do now. Perhaps Lewis Carroll had exorcized something in writing the first book. Equally, and this is interesting too, he spares us here the sentimental conclusions with which he ended *Alice in Wonderland*—sentiment following violence just as in Hans Andersen.

I don't think overt sadism worries children so much—just as it did not worry me in Grimm. They tend not to notice it, any more than they notice or are sickened by the sentimentality. What might disturb them is being shown, if only subconsciously, that all is not straightforward in the adult world; that growing up solves nothing, but merely introduces more intractable problems, more moral subtleties and endless emotional shades of grey. This unresolved, unfocused fear and anxiety, unlike that in *Marianne Dreams* and *The Wild Things*, is too complex for a child to face.

Not all children are worried by this. Many will reject a book like *Alice* as boring, just as they will reject some more recent book such as Russell Hoban's *The Mouse and His Child*. I read this, of course, as an adult, not as a child, but it has a lot in common with other books I have discussed, and its effects on me were totally different from its effects on a friend of mine—which may illustrate how a book can also affect two children quite differently.

The Mouse and His Child distressed me almost as much as any book I've read. Indeed at times I had to stop reading it because I could not bear the continuing images of cruelty and decay. Such images might well have gone straight over a child's head. The dynamic of the book, as with Andersen, Disney and Carroll, seems to me to be impermanence, decay, cruelty. It is like Beckett for children and no one will say that Beckett is an optimistic writer.

Indeed the more I consider *The Mouse and His Child*, the more similarities I can see with Andersen. I am reminded of *The Little Fir Tree* left mouldering in the attic after its Christmas glory, just as the mouse and his child, new and shiny in the toyshop at the beginning of the book, find their way to the rubbish dump. I am also reminded of *The Steadfast Tin Soldier*. Indeed there are a great many Andersen stories involving inanimate objects, toys and ornaments, in which the more elaborate despise lesser ones. Usually they point the moral that 'pride comes before a fall' or 'golden lads and lasses must as chimney sweepers come to dust'.

I am not sure that Russell Hoban does not share Andersen's sweetness as well as his bitterness. Of course he is much too modern and sophisticated to show the kind of overt sentimentality that Andersen does, but for me the ending of *The Mouse and His Child* is just as fundamentally soft-centered as anything in Andersen. The conversion of Manny Rat, the rehabilitation of the toys and of the doll's house seem a convention, as if the heart is not really in the writing any more. For me, cruelty and decay are what the book is really about. But I stress again, this is a purely personal reaction, which might well have arisen as much from my own state of mind at the time of reading as from the book itself.

For I am someone defeated by breakages and disorder. A toy once broken is lost to me because I am incapable of mending it or at least defeated by the effort involved in doing so. By contrast, a friend of mine who will always mend things, indeed spends a great deal of her time doing so, came away from *The Mouse and His Child* with an entirely different impression from mine. She was wholly reassured by the ending. And what for her came through this book was not the cruelty or the destruction but the quite indomitable spirit of the increasingly decrepit mice. The responses of children will differ just as radically, with many as likely to be reassured by the ending, as I, unhappily, was not.

I do not have any conclusion. Introvert fantasy may well be a dangerous affair but no one can legislate for everyone, so heaven forfend that we should try to keep the more uncomfortable writers from the children they write for. If you did get rid of Hans Andersen you would still be left with children frightened by Beatrix Potter (as well they might be— *The Tale of Samuel Whiskers* gives me a goodly chill to this day). You certainly cannot submit writers to psychological tests before letting them loose to write children's books, though you might well think that many of us need them.

Children need this kind of writing. They need fantasy of all kinds. It is up to the adults round them to mediate, if necessary to explain and reassure. They should know something about children's literature, if for no other reason, in order to judge its effects on children in their care, and to mediate between child and book where this seems necessary.

From *Children's literature in education*, No. 7, March 1972

A Defence of Rubbish

Peter Dickinson

Peter Dickinson was educated at Eton and Cambridge. His adult crime novels have twice won the Crime Writers' 'Golden Dagger Award'. He has written six novels for children. The 'Weathermonger' trilogy has been serialized on B.B.C. Television under the title The Changes.

The danger of living in a golden age of children's literature is that not enough rubbish is being produced.

* * *

Nobody who has not spent a whole sunny afternoon under his bed rereading a pile of comics left over from the previous holidays has any real idea of the meaning of intellectual freedom.

* * *

Nobody who has not written comic strips can really understand the phrase, economy of words. It's like trying to write *Paradise Lost* in haiku.

* * *

THE ABOVE remarks, and a few more like them, have now haunted me for five years. They were part of a digression in a talk I gave to the 1970 Exeter conference on children's literature, and if I'd realised then what a powder-keg I was throwing my fag-end of thought into I would have kept my trap shut. I've no wish to be type-cast as the man who likes rubbish. On the other hand I did (and do) believe what I said then, and what follows is a more serious attempt to formulate my ideas.

I have always believed that children ought to be allowed to

read a certain amount of rubbish. Sometimes quite a high proportion of their reading matter can healthfully consist of things
that no sane adult would actually encourage them to read. But
I had not, until people started asking me what I really meant,
attempted to defend my position or to think it out in any detail.

Definition: by rubbish I mean all forms of reading matter
which contain to the adult eye no visible value, either aesthetic
or educational.

First, I believe that it is very important that a child, or anybody for that matter, should have a whole culture—at least one
whole culture—at his fingertips. We make no objection now to
those adults who spent their youth going two or three times a
week to the cinema regardless of the merit of the films shown.
They have the whole of the Golden Age of the flicks at their
fingertips down to the last most trivial B film and it has immensely enriched their lives and their outlook in a way which a
diet which consisted solely of plums could not possibly do.
Nowadays one can say the same about the pop song culture.
There is good stuff on the discs, mixed in with an enormous
amount of trash, but both of these are necessary to a child who
is taking a serious interest in pop. The child may not realize that
the interest is serious but when he grows up he will then find,
with luck, that it has been and that he is the better for it. As
one teacher expressed it to me at the conference, it is vital that
children should have 'all that stuff churning around in there',
and he rubbed his belly.

Second it is also especially important that a child should belong, and feel he belongs, to the group of children among whom
he finds himself and he should feel that he shares in their culture. Inevitably the group interest will be mostly rubbish. For
instance, my son at the moment reads two football comics a
week. I love comics, but by the standard of comics these are
not much cop. Even so I do not discourage him because this
gives him that essential sense of belonging to a group. To remove these comics or to attempt to discourage their reading
in any way would be a socially divisive move. A child should
feel that he is an individual; but he must not, if possible, feel
that he is somehow set apart, especially by family taboos
which are not shared by the families of the group to which he

belongs. Obviously one can carry this point too far, but in the case of things like football comics I am sure that laissez-faire is the only sensible attitude.

Third I am convinced of the importance of children discovering things for themselves. However tactfully an adult may push them towards discoveries in literature, these do not have quite the treasure trove value of the books picked up wholly by accident. This can only be done by random sampling on the part of the children, and it is inevitable that a high proportion of what they read will be rubbish, by any standard. But in the process they will learn the art of comparison and subconsciously acquire critical standards, so that in the world they are discovering—even in the world of football comics— they will begin to work out why one strip is 'better' than another and seems more fascinating and is more eagerly looked forward to than another. They may even argue about this with their friends and so make the beginning of an effort at rationalizing their appreciation or dislike of cultural objects.

Fourth comes a psychological point. Children have a very varying need of security, but almost all children feel the need of security and reassurance sometime. For instance, in those families where boys are sent away to boarding school it is often very noticeable that, in the first week of the holidays, the boys do not read just the books they read last holidays, but books off their younger brother's bookshelves. One can often tell how happy or insecure a child is feeling simply by what he is reading. And sometimes he may need to reread something well known but which makes absolutely no intellectual or emotional demand. Rubbish has this negative virtue, and I would be very chary of interfering with a child who felt an obvious need of rubbish.

My fifth point is more nebulous. There is no proof, or even arguing about it. But I am fairly sure in my own mind that a diet of plums is bad for you, and that any rational reading system needs to include a considerable amount of pap or roughage—call it what you will. I know very few adults who do not have some secret cultural vice, and they are all the better for it. I would instantly suspect an adult all of whose cultural activities were high, remote and perfect.

Sixth, it may not be rubbish after all. The adult eye is not necessarily a perfect instrument for discerning certain sorts of values. Elements—and this particularly applies to science fiction —may be so obviously rubbishy that one is tempted to dismiss the whole product as rubbish. But among those elements there may be something new and strange to which one is not accustomed, and which one may not be able to assimilate oneself, as an adult, because of the sheer awfulness of the rest of the stuff; but the innocence—I suppose there is no other word— of the child's eye can take or leave in a way that I feel an adult cannot, and can acquire valuable stimuli from things which appear otherwise overgrown with a mass of weeds and nonsense.

I am not of course advocating a total lack of censorship. I have no doubt in my own mind that there are certain sorts of reading which are deleterious, and from which a child should be discouraged. Rubbish does not have this quality. It has absolutely no quality. It is neutral.

Nor am I advocating that children should be *encouraged* to read rubbish. None of the ones I know need much encouragement. All I am asking is that they should not be discouraged from reading it.

The question remains of the children whose diet appears to consist solely of rubbish. Obviously, as far as possible, they should be slightly weaned. But not totally weaned. And besides, if they did not have this diet they would not be reading at all, and in a verbal culture I think it is better that the child should read something than read nothing. And perhaps, long after the child is out of the hands of parents or teachers, the habit of reading—even the habit of reading rubbish—may somehow evoke a tendency to read things which are not rubbish. I know two or three of my contemporaries who were, by cultural standards, total philistines in their boyhood, but they used to read a considerable amount of rubbish and have now, from the habit of reading, become considerably more literate than I.

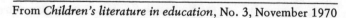

From *Children's literature in education*, No. 3, November 1970

Myth and Education

Ted Hughes

Ted Hughes was born in 1930. His books of verse include
The Hawk in the Rain, Lupercal, Wodwo, *and* Crow, *published
by Faber & Faber in England and Harper and Row in the
United States. He has written a number of books for children
and a series of educational broadcasts. In the essay that follows,
written specially for this collection, Ted Hughes discusses
afresh a topic he explored in the first issue of* Children's literature in education *(March 1970).*

SOMEWHERE in *The Republic*, where he describes the con-
stitution of his ideal State, Plato talks a little about the education of the people who will live in it. He makes the famous
point that quite advanced mathematical truths can be drawn
from children when they are asked the right questions in the
right order, and his own philosophical method, in his dialogues, is very like this. He treats his interlocutors as children
and by small, simple, logical, stealthy questions gradually
draws out of them some part of the Platonic system of ideas
—a system which has in one way or another dominated the
mental life of the Western world ever since. Nevertheless he goes
on to say that a formal education—by which he means a mathematical, philosophical and ethical education—is not for children. The proper education for his future ideal citizens, he
suggests, is something quite different: it is to be found in the
traditional myths and tales of which Greece possessed such a
huge abundance.
  Plato was nothing if not an educationalist. His writings can
be seen as a prolonged and many-sided debate on just how the
ideal citizen is to be shaped. It seemed to him quite possible

77

to create an elite of philosophers who would also be wise and responsible rulers, with a perfect apprehension of the Good. Yet he proposed to start their training with the incredible fantasies of these myths. Everyone knows that the first lessons, with human beings just as with dogs, are the most important of all. So what would be the effect of laying at the foundations of their mental life this mass of supernatural figures and their impossible antics? Later philosophers, throughout history, who have come near often enough to worshipping Plato, have dismissed these tales as absurdities. So how did he come to recommend them?

They were the material of the Greek poets. Many of them had been recreated by poets into works that have been the model and despair of later writers. Yet we know what Plato thought about poets. He wanted them suppressed—much as it is said he suppressed his own poems when he first encountered Socrates. If he wanted nothing of the poets, why was he so respectful of the myths and tales which formed the imaginative world of the poets?

He had no religious motives. For Plato, those Gods and Goddesses were hardly more serious, as religious symbols, than they are for us. Yet they evidently did contain something important. What exactly was it, then, that made them in his opinion the best possible grounding for his future enlightened, realistic, perfectly adjusted citizen?

Let us suppose he thought about it as carefully as he thought about everything else. What did he have in mind? Trying to answer that question leads us in interesting directions.

Plato was preceded in Greece by more shadowy figures. They are a unique collection. Even what fragments remain of their writings reveal a cauldron of titanic ideas, from which Plato drew only a spoonful. Wherever we look around us now, in the modern world, it is not easy to find anything that was not somehow prefigured in the conceptions of those early Greeks. And nothing is more striking about their ideas than the strange, visionary atmosphere from which they emerge. Plato is human and familiar; he invented that careful, logical step-by-step style of investigation, in which all his great dialogues are conducted, and which almost all later philosophers developed, until it evolved finally into the scientific method itself. But his predecessors stand in a different world. By comparison they seem like mythical figures, living in myth, dreaming mythical dreams.

And so they were. We find them embedded in myth. Their vast powerful notions are emerging, like figures in half-relief, from the massif of myth, which in turn is lifting from the human/animal darkness of early Greece.

Why did they rise in Greece and not somewhere else? What was so special about early Greece? The various peoples of Greece had created their own religions and mythologies, more or less related but with differences. Further abroad, other nations had created theirs, again often borrowing from common sources, but evolving separate systems, sometimes gigantic systems. Those supernatural seeming dreams, full of conflict and authority and unearthly states of feeling, were projections of man's inner and outer world. They developed their ritual, their dogma, their hierarchy of spiritual values in a particular way in each separated group. Then at the beginning of the first millennium they began to converge, by one means or another, on Greece. They came from Africa via Egypt, from Asia via Persia and the Middle East, from Europe and from all the shores of the Mediterranean. Meeting in Greece, they mingled with those rising from the soil of Greece itself. Wherever two cultures with their religious ideas are brought sharply together, there is an inner explosion. Greece had become the battle-ground of the religious and mythological inspirations of much of the archaic world. The conflict was severe, and the effort to find solutions and make peace among all those contradictory elements was correspondingly great. And the heroes of the struggle were those early philosophers. The struggle created them, it opened the depths of spirit and imagination to them, and they made sense of it. What was religious passion in the religions became in them a special sense of the holiness and seriousness of existence. What was obscure symbolic mystery in the mythologies became in them a bright, manifold per-ception of universal and human truths. In their works we see the transformation from one to the other taking place. And the great age which immediately followed them, in the fifth cen-tury BC, was the culmination of the activity.

It seems proper, then, that the fantastic dimension of those tales should have appeared to Plato as something very much other than frivolous or absurd. We can begin to guess, maybe, at what he wanted, in familiarizing children with as much as possible of that teeming repertoire.

To begin with, we can say that an education of the sort Plato proposes would work on a child in the following way.

A child takes possession of a story as what might be called a unit of imagination. A story which engages, say, earth and the underworld is a unit correspondingly flexible. It contains not merely the space and in some form or other the contents of those two places; it reconciles their contradictions in a workable fashion and holds open the way between them. The child can re-enter the story at will, look around him, find all those things and consider them at his leisure. In attending to the world of such a story there is the beginning of imaginative and mental control. There is the beginning of a form of contemplation. And to begin with, each story is separate from every other story. Each unit of imagination is like a whole separate imagination, no matter how many the head holds.

If the story is learned well, so that all its parts can be seen at a glance, as if we looked through a window into it, then that story has become like the complicated hinterland of a single word. It has become a word. Any fragment of the story serves as the 'word' by which the whole story's electrical circuit is switched into consciousness, and all its light and power brought to bear. As a rather extreme example, take the story of Christ. No matter what point of that story we touch, the whole story hits us. If we mention the Nativity, or the miracle of the loaves and fishes, or Lazarus, or the Crucifixion, the voltage and inner brightness of the whole story is instantly there. A single word of reference is enough—just as you need to touch a power-line with only the tip of your finger.

The story itself is an acquisition, a kind of wealth. We only have to imagine for a moment an individual who knows nothing of it at all. His ignorance would shock us, and, in a real way, he would be outside our society. How would he even begin to understand most of the ideas which are at the roots of our culture and appear everywhere among the branches? To follow the meanings behind the one word Crucifixion would take us through most of European history, and much of Roman and Middle Eastern too. It would take us into every corner of our private life. And before long, it would compel us to acknowledge much more important meanings than merely informative ones. Openings of spiritual experience, a dedication to final realities which might well stop us dead in our tracks and demand of us personally a sacrifice which we could never otherwise have conceived. A word of that sort has magnetized our life into a special pattern. And behind it stands not just the crowded breadth of the world, but all the depths and intensities of it too. Those things have been raised out of chaos and brought into our ken by the story in a word. The word holds them all there, like a constellation, floating and shining, and though we may draw back from tangling with them too closely, nevertheless they are present. And they remain, part of the head that lives our life, and they grow as we grow. A story can wield so much! And a word wields the story.

Imagine hearing, somewhere in the middle of a poem being recited, the phrase 'The Crucifixion of Hitler'. The word 'Hitler' is as much of a hieroglyph as the word 'Crucifixion'. Individually, those two words bear the consciousness of much of our civilization. But they are meaningless hieroglyphs, unless the stories behind the words are known. We could almost say it is only by possessing these stories that we possess that consciousness. And in those who possess both stories, the collision of those two words, in that phrase, cannot fail to detonate a psychic depth-charge. Whether we like it or not, a huge inner working starts up. How can Hitler and Crucifixion exist together in that way? Can they or can't they? The struggle to sort it out throws up ethical and philosophical implications which could absorb our attention for a very long time. All our static and maybe dormant understanding of good and evil and what opens beyond good and evil is shocked into activity. Many unconscious assumptions and intuitions come up into the light to declare themselves and explain themselves and reassess each other. For some temperaments, those two words twinned in that way might well point to wholly fresh appraisals of good and evil and the underground psychological or even actual connections between them. Yet the visible combatants here are two stories.

Without those stories, how could we have grasped those meanings? Without those stories, how could we have reduced those meanings to two words? The stories have gathered up huge charges of reality, and illuminated us with them, and given us their energy, just as those colliding worlds in early Greece roused the philosophers and the poets. If we argue that a grasp of good and evil has nothing to do with a knowledge of historical anecdotes, we have only to compare what we felt of Hitler's particular evil when our knowledge of his story was only general with what we felt when we learned more details. It is just those details of Hitler's story that have changed the consciousness of modern man. The story hasn't stuck onto us something that was never there before. It has revealed to us something that was always there. And no other story, no other anything, ever did it so powerfully. Just as it needed the story of Christ to change the consciousness of our ancestors. The better we know these stories as stories, the more of ourselves and the world is revealed to us through them.

The story of Christ came to us first of all as two or three sentences. That tiny seed held all the rest in potential form. Like the blueprint of a city. Once we laid it down firmly in imagination, it became the foundation for everything that could subsequently build and live there. Just the same with the story of Hitler.

Are those two stories extreme examples? They would not have appeared so for the early Greeks, who had several Christs and several Bibles and quite a few Hitlers to deal with. Are Aesop's fables more to our scale? They operate in exactly the same way. Grimm's tales are similar oracles.

But what these two stories show very clearly is how stories think for themselves, once we know them. They not only attract and light up everything relevant in our own experience, they are also in continual private meditation, as it were, on their own implications. They are little factories of understanding. New revelations of meaning open out of their images and patterns continually, stirred into reach by our own growth and changing circumstances.

Then at a certain point in our lives, they begin to combine. What happened forcibly between Hitler and the Crucifixion in that phrase, begins to happen naturally. The head that holds many stories becomes a small early Greece.

It does not matter, either, how old the stories are. Stories are old the way human biology is old. No matter how much they have produced in the past in the way of fruitful inspirations, they are never exhausted. The story of Christ, to stick to our example, can never be diminished by the seemingly infinite mass of theological agonizing and insipid homilies which have attempted to translate it into something more manageable. It remains, like any other genuine story, irreducible, a lump of the world, like the body of a new-born child. There is little doubt that if the world lasts pretty soon someone will come along and understand the story as if for the first time. He will look back and see two thousand years of somnolent fumbling with the theme. Out of that, and the collision of other things, he will produce, very likely, something totally new and overwhelming, some whole new direction for human life. The same possibility holds for the ancient stories of many another deity. Why not? History is really no older than that new-born baby. And every story is still the original cauldron of wisdom, full of new visions and new life.

What do we mean by 'imagination'? There are obviously many degrees of it. Are there different kinds?

The word 'imagination' usually denotes not much more than the faculty of creating a picture of something in our heads and holding it there while we think about it. Since this is the basis of nearly everything we do, clearly it's very important that our imagination should be strong rather than weak. Education neglects this faculty completely. How is the imagination to be strengthened and trained? A student has imagination, we seem to suppose, much as he has a face, and nothing can be done about it. We use what we've got.

We do realize that it can vary enormously from one person to the next, and from almost non-existent upwards. Of a person who simply cannot think what will happen if he does such and such a thing, we say he has no imagination. He has to work on principles, or orders, or by precedent, and he will always be marked by extreme rigidity, because he is after all moving in the dark. We all know such people, and we all recognize that they are dangerous, since if they have strong temperaments in other respects they end up by destroying their environment and everybody near them. The terrible thing is that they are the planners, and ruthless slaves to the plan—which substitutes for the faculty they do not possess. And they have the will of desperation: where others see alternative courses, they see only a gulf.

Of the person who imagines vividly what will happen if he acts in a certain way, and then turns out to be wrong, we say he is dealing with an unpredictable situation or else, just as likely, he has an inaccurate imagination. Lively, maybe, but inaccurate. There is no innate law that makes a very real-seeming picture of things an accurate picture. That person will be a great nuisance, and as destructive as the other, because he will be full of confident schemes and solutions, which will seem to him foolproof, but which will simply be false, because somehow his sense of reality is defective. In other words, his ordinary perception of reality, by which the imagination regulates all its images, overlooks too much, or misinterprets too much. Many disturbances can account for some of this, but simple sloppiness of attention accounts for most of it.

Those two classes of people contain the majority of us for much of the time. The third class of people is quite rare. Or our own moments of belonging to that class are rare. Imagination which is both accurate and strong is so rare, that when somebody appears in possession of it they are regarded as something more than human. We see that with the few great generals. Normally, it occurs patchily. It is usually no more than patchy because accurate perceptions are rarely more than patchy. We have only to make the simplest test on ourselves to reconfirm this. And where our perceptions are blind, our speculations are pure invention.

This basic type of imagination, with its delicate wiring of perceptions, is our most valuable piece of practical equipment. It is the control panel for everything we think and do, so it ought to be education's first concern. Yet whoever spent half an hour in any classroom trying to strengthen it in any way? Even

in the sciences, where accurate perception is recognizably crucial, is this faculty ever deliberately trained?

Sharpness, clarity and scope of the mental eye are all-
important in our dealings with the outer world, and that is
plenty. And if we were machines it would be enough. But the
outer world is only one of the worlds we live in. For better or
worse we have another, and that is the inner world of our bodies and everything pertaining. It is closer than the outer world,
more decisive, and utterly different. So here are two worlds,
which we have to live in simultaneously. And because they are
intricately interdependent at every moment, we can't ignore
one and concentrate on the other without accidents. Probably
fatal accidents.

But why can't this inner world of the body be regarded as an
extension of the outer world—in other words why isn't the
sharp, clear, objective eye of the mind as adequate for this
world as it is for the other more obviously outer world? And if
it isn't, why isn't it?

The inner world is not so easily talked about because nobody
has ever come near to understanding it. Though it is the closest
thing to us—though it is, indeed, us—we live in it as on an unex-
plored planet in space. It is not so much a place, either, as a
region of events. And the first thing we have to confess is that it
cannot be seen objectively. How does the biological craving for
water turn into the precise notion that it is water that we want?
How do we 'see' the make-up of an emotion that we do not
even feel—though electrodes on our skin will register its presence? The word 'subjective' was invented for a good reason
—but under that vaguest of general terms lies the most important half of our experience.

After all, what exactly is going on in there? It is quite frightening, how little we know about it. We can't say there's nothing—that 'nothing' is merely the shutness of the shut door. And
if we say there's something—how much more specific can you
get?

We quickly realize that the inner world is indescribable, im-
penetrable, and invisible. We try to grapple with it, and all we
meet is one provisional dream after another. It dawns on us
that in order to look at the inner world 'objectively' we have

had to separate ourselves from what is an exclusively 'subjective' world, and it has vanished. In the end, we acknowledge that the objective imagination, and the objective perceptions, those sharp clear instruments which cope so well with the outer world, are of very little use here.

By speculating backwards from effects, we can possibly make out a rough plan of what ought to be in there. The incessant bombardment of raw perceptions must land somewhere. And we have been able to notice that any one perception can stir up a host of small feelings, which excite further feelings not necessarily so small, in a turmoil of memory and association. And we do get some evidence, we think, that our emotional and instinctive life, which seems to be on a somewhat bigger scale and not so tied to momentary perceptions, is mustering and regrouping in response to outer circumstances. But these bigger and more dramatic energies are also occasionally yoked to the pettiest of those perceptions, and driven off on some journey. And now and again we are made aware of what seems to be an even larger drama of moods and energies which it is hard to name—psychic, spiritual, cosmic. Any name we give them seems metaphorical, since in that world everything is relative, and we are never sure of the scale of magnification or miniaturization of the signals. We can guess, with a fair sense of confidence, that all these intervolved processes, which seem like the electrical fields of our body's electrical installations—our glands, organs, chemical transmutations and so on—are striving to tell about themselves. They are all trying to make their needs known, much as thirst imparts its sharp request for water. They are talking incessantly, in a dumb radiating way, about themselves, about their relationships with each other, about the situation of the moment in the main overall drama of the living and growing and dying body in which they are assembled, and also about the outer world, because all these *dramatis personae* are really striving to live, in some way or other, in the outer world. That is the world for which they have been created. That is the world which created them. And so they are highly concerned about the doings of the individual behind whose face they hide. Because they are him. And they want him to live in the way that will give them the greatest satisfaction.

This description is bald enough, but it is as much as the objective eye can be reasonably sure of. And then only in a detached way, the way we think we are sure of the workings of an electrical circuit. But for more intimate negotiations with that world, for genuine contact with its powers and genuine exploration of its regions, it turns out that the eye of the objective imagination is blind.

We solve the problem by never looking inward. We identify ourselves and all that is wakeful and intelligent with our objective eye, saying, 'Let's be objective'. That is really no more than saying 'Let's be happy'. But we sit, closely cramped in the cockpit behind the eyes, steering through the brilliantly crowded landscape beyond the lenses, focussed on details and distinctions. In the end, since all our attention from birth has been narrowed into that outward beam, we come to regard our body as no more than a somewhat stupid vehicle. All the urgent information coming towards us from that inner world sounds to us like a blank, or at best the occasional grunt, or a twinge. Because we have no equipment to receive it and decode it. The body, with its spirits, is the antennae of all perceptions, the receiving aerial for all wavelengths. But we are disconnected. The exclusiveness of our objective eye, the very strength and brilliance of our objective intelligence, suddenly turns into stupidity—of the most rigid and suicidal kind.

That condition certainly sounds extreme, yet most of the people we know, particularly older people, are likely to regard it as ideal. It is a modern ideal. The educational tendencies of the last three hundred years, and especially of the last fifty, corresponding to the rising prestige of scientific objectivity and the lowering prestige of religious awareness, have combined to make it so. It is a scientific ideal. And it is a powerful ideal, it has created the modern world. And without it, the modern world would fall to pieces: infinite misery would result. The disaster is, that it is heading straight towards infinite misery, because it has persuaded human beings to identify themselves with what is no more than a narrow mode of perception. And the more rigorously the ideal is achieved, the more likely it is to be disastrous. A bright, intelligent eye, full of exact images, set in a head of the most frightful stupidity.

The drive towards this ideal is so strong that it has materialized in the outer world. A perfect mechanism of objective perception has been precipitated: the camera. Scientific objectivity, as we all know, has its own morality, which has nothing to do with human morality. It is the morality of the camera. And this is the prevailing morality of our time. It is a morality utterly devoid of any awareness of the requirements of the inner world. It is contemptuous of the 'human element'. That is its purity and its strength. The prevailing philosophies and political ideologies of our time subscribe to this contempt, with a nearly religious fanaticism, just as science itself does.

Some years ago in an American picture magazine I saw a collection of photographs which showed the process of a tiger killing a woman. The story behind this was as follows. The tiger, a tame tiger, belonged to the woman. A professional photographer had wanted to take photographs of her strolling with her tiger. Something—maybe his incessant camera—had upset the tiger, the woman had tried to pacify it, whereupon it attacked her and started to kill her. So what did that hero of the objective attitude do then? Among Jim Corbett's wonderful stories about man-eating tigers and leopards there are occasions when some man-eater, with a terrifying reputation, was driven off its victim by some other person. On one occasion by a girl who beat the animal over the head with a digging stick. But this photographer—we can easily understand him because we all belong to this modern world—had become his camera. What were his thoughts? 'Now that the tiger has started in on her it would be cruelty to save her and prolong her sufferings', or 'If I just stand here making the minimum noise it might leave her, whereas if I interfere it will certainly give her the death bite, just as a cat does when you try to rescue its mouse', or 'If I get involved, who knows what will happen, then I might miss my plane,' or 'I can't affect the outcome of this in any way. And who am I to interfere with the cycles of nature? This has happened countless millions of times and always will happen while there are tigers and women,' or did he just think 'Oh my God, Oh my God, what a chance!'? Whatever his thoughts were he went on taking photographs of the whole procedure while the tiger killed the woman, because the pictures were there in the magazine. And the story was told as if the photographer had indeed been absent. As if the camera had simply gone on doing what any camera would be expected to do, being a mere mechanical device for registering outer appearances. I may be doing the photographer an injustice. It may be I have forgotten some mention that eventually when he had enough pictures he ran in and hit the tiger with his camera or something else. Or maybe he was just wisely cowardly as many another of us might be. Whatever it was, he got his pictures.

The same paralysis comes to many of us when we watch television. After the interesting bit is over, what keeps us mesmerized by that bright little eye? It can't be the horrors and inanities and killings that jog along there between the curtains and the mantelpiece after supper. Why can't we move? Reality has been removed beyond our participation, behind that very tough screen, and into another dimension. Our inner world, of natural impulsive response, is safely in neutral. Like broiler killers, we are reduced to a state of pure observation. Everything that passes in front of our eyes is equally important, equally unimportant. As far as what we see is concerned, and in a truly practical way, we are paralyzed. Even people who profess to dislike television fall under the same spell of passivity. They can only free themselves by a convulsive effort of will. The precious tool of objective imagination has taken control of us there. Materialized in the camera, it has imprisoned us in the lens.

In England, not very long ago, the inner world and Christianity were closely identified. Even the conflicts within Christianity only revealed and consolidated more inner world. When religious knowledge lost the last rags of its credibility, earlier this century, psychoanalysis appeared as if to fill the gap. Both attempt to give form to the inner world. But with a difference.

When it came the turn of the Christian Church to embody the laws of the inner world, it made the mistake of claiming that they were objective laws. That might have passed, if Science had not come along, whose laws were so demonstrably objective that it was able to impose them on the whole world. As the mistaken claims of Christianity became scientifically meaningless, the inner world which it had clothed became incomprehensible, absurd and finally invisible. Objective imagination, in the light of science, rejected religion as charlatanism, and the inner world as a bundle of fairy tales, a relic of primeval superstition. People rushed towards the idea of living without any religion or any inner life whatsoever as if towards some great new freedom. A great final awakening. The most energetic intellectual and political movements of this century wrote the manifestos of the new liberation. The great artistic statements have recorded the true emptiness of the new prison.

The inner world, of course, could not evaporate, just because it no longer had a religion to give it a visible body. A person's own inner world cannot fold up its spirit wings, and shut down all its tuned circuits, and become a mechanical business of nuts and bolts, just because a political or intellectual ideology requires it to. As the religion was stripped away, the defrocked inner world became a waif, an outcast, a tramp. And denied its one great health—acceptance into life—it fell into a huge sickness. A huge collection of deprivation sicknesses. And this is how psychoanalysis found it.

The small piloting consciousness of the bright-eyed objective intelligence had steered its body and soul into a hell. Religious negotiations had formerly embraced and humanized the archaic energies of instinct and feeling. They had conversed in simple but profound terms with the forces struggling inside people, and had civilized them, or attempted to. Without religion, those powers have become dehumanized. The whole inner world has become elemental, chaotic, continually more primitive and beyond our control. It has become a place of demons. But of course, insofar as we are disconnected anyway from that world, and lack the equipment to pick up its signals, we are not aware of it. All we register is the vast absence, the emptiness, the sterility, the meaninglessness, the loneliness. If we do manage to catch a glimpse of our inner selves, by some contraption of mirrors, we recognize it with horror—it is an animal crawling and decomposing in a hell. We refuse to own it.

In the last decade or two, the imprisonment of the camera lens has begun to crack. The demonized state of our inner world has made itself felt in a million ways. How is it that children are so attracted towards it? Every new child is nature's chance to correct culture's error. Children are most sensitive to it, because they are the least conditioned by scientific objectivity to life in the camera lens. They have a double motive, in attempting to break from the lens. They want to escape the ugliness of the despiritualized world in which they see their parents imprisoned. And they are aware that this inner world we have rejected is not merely an inferno of depraved impulses and crazy explosions of embittered energy. Our real selves lie down there. Down there, mixed up among all the madness, is everything that once made life worth living. All the lost awareness and powers and allegiances of our biological and spiritual being. The attempt to re-enter that lost inheritance takes many forms, but it is the chief business of the swarming cults.

Drugs cannot take us there. If we cite the lofty religions in which drugs did take the initiates to where they needed to go, we ought to remember that here again the mythology was crucial. The journey was undertaken as part of an elaborately mythologized ritual. It was the mythology which consolidated the inner world, gave human form to its experiences, and connected them to daily life. Without that preparation a drug carries its user to a prison in the inner world as passive and isolated and meaningless as the camera's eye from which he escaped.

Objective imagination, then, important as it is, is not enough. What about a 'subjective' imagination? It is only logical to suppose that a faculty developed specially for peering into the inner world might end up as specialized and destructive as the faculty for peering into the outer one. Besides, the real problem comes from the fact that outer world and inner world are interdependent at every moment. We are simply the locus of their collision. Two worlds, with mutually contradictory laws, or laws that seem to us to be so, colliding afresh every second, struggling for peaceful coexistence. And whether we like it or not our life is what we are able to make of that collision and struggle.

So what we need, evidently, is a faculty that embraces both worlds simultaneously. A large, flexible grasp, an inner vision which holds wide open, like a great theatre, the arena of contention, and which pays equal respects to both sides. Which keeps faith, as Goethe says, with the world of things and the world of spirits equally.

This really is imagination. This is the faculty we mean when we talk about the imagination of the great artists. The character of great works is exactly this: that in them the full presence of the inner world combines with and is reconciled to the full presence of the outer world. And in them we see that the laws of these two worlds are not contradictory at all; they are one all-inclusive system; they are laws that somehow we find it all but impossible to keep, laws that only the greatest artists are able to restate. They are the laws, simply, of human nature. And men have recognized all through history that the restating of these laws, in one medium or another, in great works of art, are the greatest human acts. They are the greatest acts and they are the most human. We recognize these works because we are all struggling to find those laws, as a man on a tightrope struggles for balance, because they are the formula that reconciles everything, and balances every imbalance.

So it comes about that once we recognize their terms, these works seem to heal us. More important, it is in these works that humanity is truly formed. And it has to be done again and again, as circumstances change, and the balance of power between outer and inner world shifts, showing everybody the gulf. The inner world, separated from the outer world, is a place of demons. The outer world, separated from the inner world, is a place of meaningless objects and machines. The faculty that makes the human being out of these two worlds is called divine. That is only a way of saying that it is the faculty without which humanity cannot really exist. It can be called religious or visionary. More essentially, it is imagination which embraces both outer and inner worlds in a creative spirit.

Laying down blueprints for imagination of that sort is a matter of education, as Plato divined.

The myths and legends, which Plato proposed as the ideal educational material for his young citizens, can be seen as large-scale accounts of negotiations between the powers of the inner world and the stubborn conditions of the outer world, under which ordinary men and women have to live. They are immense and at the same time highly detailed sketches for the possibilities of understanding and reconciling the two. They are, in other words, an archive of draft plans for the kind of imagination we have been discussing.

Their accuracy and usefulness, in this sense, depend on the fact that they were originally the genuine projections of genuine understanding. They were tribal dreams of the highest order of inspiration and truth, at their best. They gave a true account of what really happens in that inner region where the two worlds collide. This has been attested over and over again by the way in which the imaginative men of every subsequent age have had recourse to their basic patterns and images.

But the Greek myths were not the only true myths. The unspoken definition of myth is that it carries truth of this sort. These big dreams only become the treasured property of a people when they express the real state of affairs. Priests continually elaborate the myths, but what is not true is forgotten again. So every real people has its true myths. One of the first surprises of mythographers was to find how uncannily similar these myths are all over the world. They are as alike as the lines on the palm of the human hand.

But Plato implied that all traditional stories, big and small, were part of his syllabus. And indeed the smaller stories come from the same place. If a tale can last, in oral tradition, for two or three generations, then it has either come from the real place, or it has found its way there. And these small tales are just as vigorous educational devices as the big myths.

There is a long tradition of using stories as educational implements in a far more deliberate way than Plato seems to propose. Steiner has a great deal to say about the method. In his many publications of Sufi literature, Idries Shah indicates how central to the training of the sages and saints of Islam are the traditional tales. Sometimes no more than small anecdotes, sometimes lengthy and involved adventures such as were collected into the Arabian Nights.

As I pointed out, using the example of the Christ story, the first step is to learn the story, as if it were laying down the foundation. The next phase rests with the natural process of the imagination.

The story is, as it were, a kit. Apart from its own major subject—obvious enough in the case of the Christ story—it contains two separable elements: its pattern and its images. Together they make that story and no other. Separately they set out on new lives of their own.

The roads they travel are determined by the brain's fundamental genius for metaphor. Automatically, it uses the pattern of one set of images to organize quite a different set. It uses one image, with slight variations, as an image for related and yet different and otherwise imageless meanings.

In this way, the simple tale of the beggar and the princess begins to transmit intuitions of psychological, perhaps spiritual, states and relationships. What began as an idle reading of a fairy tale ends, by simple natural activity of the imagination, as a rich perception of values of feeling, emotion and spirit which would otherwise have remained unconscious and languageless. The inner struggle of worlds, which is not necessarily a violent and terrible affair, though at bottom it often is, is suddenly given the perfect formula for the terms of a truce. A simple tale, told at the right moment, transforms a person's life with the order its pattern brings to incoherent energies.

And while its pattern proliferates in every direction through all levels of consciousness, its images are working too. The image of Lazarus is not easily detached by a child from its striking place in the story of Christ. But once it begins to migrate, there is no limiting its importance. In all Dostoevsky's searching adventures, the basic image, radiating energies that he seems never able to exhaust, is Lazarus.

The image does not need to be so central to a prestigious religion for it to become so important. At the heart of King Lear is a very simple Fairy Tale King in a very simple little tale— the Story of Salt. In both these we see how a simple image in a simple story has somehow focussed all the pressures of an age—collisions of spirit and nature and good and evil and a majesty of existence that seemed uncontainable. But it has brought all that into a human pattern, and made it part of our understanding.

Thoughts on a Shirtless Cyclist, Robin Hood and One or Two Other Things

Russell Hoban

Russell Hoban's children's books include the Frances *series,* The Mouse and His Child, The Sea-Thing Child, *and the award-winning* How Tom Beat Captain Najork and His Hired Sportsmen. *His adults novels are:* The Lion of Boaz-Jachin and Jachin-Boaz; Kleinzeit; *and* Turtle Diary.

THE OTHER DAY when I was going to my office in the morning I saw a man without a shirt riding a bicycle in circles at a traffic light and shouting unintelligibly. It was a chilly morning, so he must have been uncomfortable without a shirt on, and he wasn't a hippy. He looked like a workman, and he didn't look drunk. So it seemed to me that he must be having a mental breakdown of some sort.

I thought about it for a while, and then it occurred to me that maybe the man's mind wasn't breaking down. Maybe what had broken down was the system of restraints and conventions inside him that ordinarily made him keep his shirt on and not shout. That system, I think, is part of what could be called an inner society. The inner society has its ballrooms and bedrooms and kitchens, its shops and offices, its narrow alleys and its open places, its figures of authority and rebellion, of usage and surprise, love and hate, should and should not, is and isn't. As in the outer society, some things are done and some are not.

When I had thought that far, my next thought was that on that particular day that particular man's inner society was rioting. The windows of the shops were being smashed, the offices were being deserted, and he was doing what he was doing.

My next thought was that the previous thought had been wrong: he was doing what he was doing because there were no rioters and no provision for riot in his inner society, and so there was no one for the job but him. His trouble, perhaps, was that his inner society was not sufficiently different from the outer one: too many of the same things were done and not done. And having no interior colleague to whom he could assign the task or delegate the responsibility, he himself had to take off his shirt and ride his bicycle in circles at a traffic light and shout. And it must have taken something out of him to do it.

Now my inner society, on the other hand, has always had that shirtless shouting cyclist in it. I know him of old as I know myself, even though I hadn't given him much thought until I actually saw him in the outer world. So it isn't likely that I shall ever have to go out into the street and do that myself; he's always there to take care of it for me. There may, of course, come a day when I shall riotously put on a bowler hat and a neat black suit, buy a tightly furled umbrella, and mingle in wild silence with the brokers in the City. One never knows what will come up.

Which brings me, by cobweb bridges perhaps invisible to the naked eye, to a book I once threw into an incinerator.

The book was *Robin Hood*. My edition, an American one, was bound in what I think was Lincoln Green. I don't remember who it was that wrote that particular version of the story, but it had large black type and was illustrated by an artist named Edwin John Prittie with line drawings and paintings in full colour. I used to read that book up in an old wild-cherry tree, and it was the cosiest reading I can remember.

But there came a time when I got to be eighteen years old, and there was a war, and I was going off to be a soldier, and it seemed to me that I had better stop being a child and be a man altogether. So I took *Robin Hood* and pitched it into the incinerator. It's a crime that I am driven to confess from time to time, as I do now.

When I came home from the war and found myself, surprisingly, alive and having to go on with the business of growing up, I looked for that same edition that I had thrown away. Years later I found a copy. I haven't it with me now; it is gone again, lost in a removal. But I remember how it was when I held it in my hands again. There were all the pictures looking just as good as ever, and that whole dappled word-world of sun and shade with nothing lost whatever—Little John and Robin fighting on the plank bridge with their quarterstaves; the hateful Sheriff of Nottingham in his arrogance and his scarlet cloak; the beautiful Maid Marian and all the merry men in Lincoln Green; Robin in the *capul hide*, standing over the corpse of Guy of Gisborne. I've always liked the sound of the words *capul hide*: the skin of a horse, with the eyes of a man looking out through the eyeholes in the head—the skin of a dead beast hiding a live man, magical and murderous.

Obviously Robin Hood is a part of my inner society and has never stopped being in my thoughts, but it's only recently that I've become fully aware of how much he is to me, of how far the theme of that child's book has gone beyond childhood. Now as I think about him Robin Hood grows deeper and darker and stronger. Constantly he takes on new shadowy identities, and in his *capul hide* he sometimes evokes the dancing *shaman* in the drawing on the cave wall at Les Trois Frères, sometimes Fraser's *Rex Nemorensis*, doomed King of the Wood, the killer waiting for his killer who will be the next king.

In the absence of my found-and-lost-again edition I bought Roger Lancelyn Green's Puffin *Robin Hood*. On the title page was a stanza from the Alfred Noyes poem, *Sherwood*, and it gave me gooseflesh when I read it:

Robin Hood is here again: all his merry thieves
Hear a ghostly bugle-note shivering through the leaves. . .
The dead are coming back again, the years are rolled away
In Sherwood, in Sherwood, about the break of day.

I wanted it to be Sherwood again, about the break of day.

I turned the pages, reading with impatience. But it wasn't the same. This book started with Robin Hood's birth, and I didn't want that, I wanted the opening that had been in the cherry-tree book of childhood, and it wasn't there and I couldn't remember it.

Then, on page 19 I found it—the incident in which the Sheriff of Nottingham and his men capture a serf who had killed a royal deer. The beginning of my book came back to me then, just like Proust's Combray—all at once and clear and vivid. 'Saxon hind' was what my book called the serf, and I could see the scene again as it first came to me through the words in the cherry tree. I could see that sunlight through the passing leaves, the prisoner trussed up on the sledge like meat, helpless, rolling his eyes in terror as the Sheriff's foresters drag him to his death. Robert Fitzooth, not yet Robin Hood the outlaw, encounters the group and questions the Sheriff's men. The Chief Forester taunts him about the power of the bow he carries, doubts that such a stripling can wield such a weapon. Fitzooth shows his strength and skill with a long shot that brings down one of the King's deer. And with that he has fallen into the forester's trap—like the prisoner, he has forfeited his life with that shot. The Sheriff's men attempt to take him, but he kills some of them and frees the 'Saxon hind'. They escape into the greenwood, and the outlaw life of Robin Hood begins.

The light and the air of that first encounter have never left my mind, and the sounds of the forest, the hissing of the sledge runners over the grass, the rattle of weapons, the shouts, the whizzing arrows. It is the metaphorical value of that action that has made it so memorable for me: the free and active wild self of the forest, armed and strong, freed the bound and helpless captive self and so became the outlaw self I recognized within me—the self indwelling always, sometimes kept faith with, sometimes betrayed.

Free and savage, the Robin Hood who has always walked the pathways of my inner society has been exemplary—a standard and a reminder to the unfree and unsavage boy that I was who lusted for that greenwood world: excellence was the price of Robin Hood's freedom, his untamedness, and his power. He was able to be what he was only because of his matchless skill; he was the archer who could shoot farther and truer than any other; he was a hero and a winner who had a thing that he could do better than anybody else.

Heroes who can do something well are still considered necessary for children. And if many of today's books for grown-ups offer us a selection of the infirm and the awkward, the losers who lap up defeat like chicken soup ladled out by a Jewish-mother kind of fate, we need those too: the composite hero of the collective, cumulative, juvenile-adult imagination has got to have some antiheroism about him in order to be complete. Certainly anything that closes the gap between the real and the ideal makes the hero more useful for everyday reference—and here I can't help thinking about the god Krishna, who disported himself with fifty or sixty cowgirls at a wonderful party out on the meadows that lasted many nights, during which he made all the cowgirls think he was making love with each of them. But despite his divine powers—or because of them—he did it all with his mind, which I think is charming. A hero no better than the reader, however, will scarcely last a lifetime. And I think that heroes who excel and win all kinds of good things are the best kind. Myself, I can't use a mythology in which there is nothing to win and consequently nothing to lose. I have to have something to try for, and the more excellence I can manage the better I feel. In that respect Robin Hood has been a great help to me all my life.

Reading the Roger Lancelyn Green version, I realize that there was a great deal more to the story and the archetypes than I had thought before. In my edition Marian was simply called Maid Marian, and nothing more was said about it. Once or twice as I grew older and more cynical I may have questioned the validity of her title. She was, after all, presumably sleeping rough like everyone else in the outlaw band, and Robin being her lover, what could have been more natural than for them to sleep together? But Green spells it out and no mistake: Marian *was* a maid; she kept her virginity the whole time that she and Robin lived together in the forest. Although she had pledged herself to him the marriage was not to be consummated until the return of Richard the Lion-Hearted, the true and lawful king.

Robin Hood has no other woman that I ever heard of in any of the stories. So I have to think of him as celibate, as putting off the assumption of a full male role, as being less than a complete, grown-up man. He is asexual and pure, mercurial, airy almost, Ariel-like—a natural innocent, murderous but sweet-natured, light and quick. And he shares with Marian that mystical virtue that chastity confers, so useful for catching unicorns. The male and the female elements, the *yang* and *yin* of this legend, are allied but not conjoined at the peak of their vigour, and when later a legitimate union is formed, they decline.

Robin Hood is more often with Little John than with Maid Marian. He and his giant companion are like a clean-cut, somewhat prim ego and id. They continually test and prove themselves, tempting fate, daring all comers, looking for trouble, never content with safety and boredom. They fight with quarterstaves at their first meeting; they quarrel from time to time; they rescue each other from capture; they compete with each other against the terrible strong beggar with the potent quarterstaff and the bag of meal that blinds the usually cunning Robin. And so they stay young and jolly until King Richard, the lawful ruler, the inevitable mature authority, returns.

And with that return Robin Hood is absorbed into grownupness and legitimacy. He is pardoned, and no more an outlaw; he is married, and no more a child-man. His best men are called into the service of King Richard. Robin Hood's power is drained off into the power of lawful authority. The outlaw self is assimilated into the lawful self; the puissant youth becomes the waning man.

I'm no scholar, and I have no idea of the origin of the legend that is Robin Hood. What is inescapable is that the stone of legend is worn into shape by the sea of human perception and need that continually washes over it. Legends, myth and fantasy both ask and tell us how life is, and there seems to be a strong need in us to think about the theme that is in *Robin Hood*: the absorption into law and order of that mysterious, chthonic, demiurgic power that we vitally need but cannot socially tolerate. We regret the loss of it and we rationalize the necessity of that loss. We say to it, 'Yes, be there. But lose yourself in us at the proper time. Grow up.' But I wonder what the proper time is, and I wonder if the loss is necessary. And I wonder what growing up is. And I wonder whether young people now are not validly reconsidering and reshaping that theme, reclassifying it as well, so that the values assigned are no longer the same as those agreed upon until now. Maybe what we've always called growing up is sometimes growing down. It bears thinking about.

Robin Hood is only one development of that theme; there must be many others. In *Great Expectations*, for instance, Magwitch, the outlaw self, is content to subsidize anonymously Pip, the lawful self. And it is Magwitch the outlaw who refines what is base and shallow in the respectable youth. Pip thinks that Miss Havisham is financing him, but the money that makes it possible for him to cut a dash as a young gentleman does not come from her decaying beauty, wealth and gentility, but from the starveling and tenacious humanity of what in us is violent, inchoate, unshapen and fit only to be put in prison.

Again, in Conrad's *Secret Sharer*, a young captain, a young lawful authority in his first command, is appealed to by a young man who closely resembles him, a fugitive fleeing trial for killing a mate on another vessel. With characteristic genius Conrad opens his story with the unfledged captain taking the anchor watch alone at night on his ship that is still unfamiliar to him. He looks over the side and sees looking up at him from the water a face like his own, the face of a desperate swimmer. The captain shelters his criminal *doppelganger* aboard his ship during a period of self doubt before putting to sea. But when the barque leaves port the fugitive must be put ashore to take his chances alone. A wide-brimmed hat, given him by the captain as protection against the sun, falls into the water and becomes a sea mark by which the young master gauges the current while negotiating a difficult offing under sail in light and baffling airs.

The fugitive's hat gets the lawful master safely out to sea, but the fugitive cannot go with the ship. Magwitch gives Pip what he can and dies. Robin Hood is killed by the establishment that has no use for him. The predatory church that he has always fought will take him in, ailing and ageing, will bleed him to death at the end by the hand of the treacherous Prioress of Kirkleys Nunnery. Robin Hood, supported by Little John, will loose his last arrow from his deathbed and be buried where it falls. Marian, first magical maid and then magicless woman, will become a nun and Prioress in her turn. Robin in the earth and she in the nunnery will both regain their innocence and power.

After the first reading of the book, the death and the last arrow were always there waiting for Robin Hood and me; he carried that death with him, carried that last arrow in his quiver always. He seems such a year-king! He seems, in his green and lightsome strength, always to hasten toward his sacrificial death that will bring forth from the winter earth another spring. And like a year-king, he must be given up, cannot be kept.

But I cannot give him up entirely. I think that we need our outlaw strength alive and brother to our lawful vigour. The one is not healthy without the other. I keep calling the elements outlaw self and lawful self, but that is unfair, really, to the essence of the thing. Society defines the terms of lawful and unlawful, because society makes the laws. And society is a retarded child with a loaded gun in its hands; I don't completely accept society's terms. Something in us makes us retell that myth; some drive there is in us to find and name the demon in us that is more real than laws and conventions that tell us what is right and what is wrong. And that demon is, I think, the radical spirit of life: it is the dark and unseen root system of our human tree whose visible branches are so carefully labelled and scientifically pruned by us. Maybe we think we don't need to know more about that nameless creative chaos, but we do, because in it we must find all real order. Polite gentlemen wearing suits and ties and with neat haircuts sit around tables with the death of the world in their briefcases, and they do not hesitate to tell us what is order. But to me it seems disorder. Other polite gentlemen some years ago sent up human smoke signals from the chimneys of crematoria, and they too defined order with great clarity. I think that fewer definitive definitions and many more tentative ones are needed now.

The fantasy of our legends, myths and stories helps with

those new definitions. It is as close as we can get to noumena through phenomena, as close as we can get to the thingness of things through the appearances of things. Fantasy isn't separate from reality; it is a vital approach to the essence of it. As to its importance, it is simply a matter of life and death. If we don't find out more about the truly essential thingness of things, then some future generation, if not this one, won't have anything left to find out about. So we must have fantasy constructed as scaffolding from which to work on actualities. And to work with fantasy is a risky business for the writer: it can change his whole world of actualities.

Which brings me back to the man on the bicycle, shirtless and shouting. I was sorry for that man. I know how he felt. I wish he had been able to do something better with the baffled demon in him. I think he might have found something better to do if he had had more workable material in his mind, more useful people in his inner society. Robin Hood would have helped him, perhaps Captain Ahab too, and Lord Jim and Raskolnikov and goodness knows who else, functioning as surrogate actors-out of extreme and exaggerated degrees of the human condition. They might have taken on for him certain time-consuming and self-defeating tasks. They might have shown him other ways to be, might have freed him to do something more effective than what he was doing, might have helped him to find an identity in that wild surge of random creation that vanished into silence on the indulgent and indifferent air.

Well, you may say, perhaps that man wasn't a reader, and whatever is in books won't help him. But books permeate both the outer and inner societies, moving through readers to non-readers with definitions and provision for societal roles, expectations and probabilities. Always more figures are needed to people our inner societies—personifications of all the subtly different modes of being, *avatars* of the sequential and often warring selves within us. Books in nameless categories are needed—books for children and adults together, books that can stand in an existential nowhere and find a centre that will hold.

From *Children's literature in education*, No. 4, March 1971

E.B. White's Unexpected Items of Enchantment

Marion Glastonbury

Marion Glastonbury taught in various schools and technical colleges after reading English at Oxford. She now works with overseas students at University College, Swansea, and has two children.

SHORTLY BEFORE Christmas 1938, E.B. White wrote an article for *Harper's Magazine* complaining that his Maine farmhouse was overrun with children's books sent to his wife to review. 'Throw open the door of our kitchen cabinet, out will fall the Story of Tea.' This contact with children's literature inspired thoughts which have themselves a random haphazard look, as if ideas fell out of cupboards onto a man who was not expecting them.

He reflects that one should keep abreast of what the children of the country are reading because it is a mirror of the age. He notes the paradox that old familiar literary paths lead to new destinations and laughs hollowly at the irony of books on domestic safety in 'this year of infinite terror when the desire of everyone is for a safe hole to hide in'. He concludes that 'it must be a lot of fun to write for children—reasonably easy work, perhaps even important work'. Particularly exciting would be the search for 'a place, a period or a thing that hasn't already been written about'.

Around this time White started his first children's book in the hope of amusing a six-year-old niece; by the time he finished it, she had grown old enough to read Hemingway. A prolific journalist and a professional meeter of deadlines, White has produced only three books for children in the course of a long life: *Stuart Little* published in 1946, *Charlotte's Web* 1952, and *The Trumpet of the Swan* 1970. I believe the reason for the long intervals between the books is that the subjects he hit upon, so far from being easy, involved the distillation of much experience and the synthesis of problems which exercised him, in theory and in practice, throughout his life.

White was born in 1899 in a suburb of New York and was educated at Cornell University where he edited the *Cornell Daily Sun*. Before he joined the staff of the *New Yorker* in 1926 he wrote automobile ads for a Madison Avenue agency, a job he hung onto longer than his friends expected because he had 'no confidence in my ability in the world of letters'. His editorials had a certain influence in the city—he got the lights on the tower of the Empire State Building changed from coloured to white, and freed the passengers in Grand Central Station from broadcast commercials. His main ambition was to be esteemed as a poet but he collaborated with James Thurber in producing cartoon captions and satirical sketches. The book they wrote together, *Is Sex Necessary?* was illustrated by the first Thurber drawings to appear in print. Both writers moved out of the city in the thirties—a colleague remarked that the *New Yorker* was run by two country bumpkins—and while White admits that the animals got into his stories, there is evidence that Talk of the Town got into the animals. The books encompass the elements of the earth and what man has made of them, politics and privacy, innocence and experience, confrontation and retreat.

Thurber's definition of humour, 'a kind of emotional chaos told about calmly and quietly in retrospect', applies in some measure to White, who described himself as celebrating 'trivial peaceable pursuits knowing all the time that the world hadn't arranged any true peace or granted anyone the privilege of indulging himself for long in trivialities'. As a youth in the First World War he had written a poem strongly advising himself to get killed in action; in the Second World War, his liberal ideals and his observation of racialism in America convinced him that the times needed heroism which a writer could preach but not practise.

The rueful comedy of *Stuart Little* emerges from these pre-occupations. Stuart is a model hero, cool in a crisis, dauntless in a quest, unflinching in the defence of principle—but he is a mouse. Endlessly resourceful, Stuart is the converse of White's Mittyesque depiction of himself 'at the mercy of inanimate objects which deliberately plot to destroy a man'. The son of Mr and Mrs Little of New York masters the intricacies and hazards of the apartment and the city by pioneering zeal and technical ingenuity, adjusting piano keys from inside and boarding trams in trouser turn-ups. His triumphs of self-help are contrasted with the unproductive brainwaves of his brother George, who litters the bathroom floor with tools. White is particularly good at rendering boisterous boys and sorely-tried parents, and this realism sets off the paragon of American family life which Stuart embodies, with his adventurous spirit, courtesy, early rising and well-exercised stomach muscles. Virtue is exposed to discomfort and indignities. When he retrieves his mother's ring from the drain he needs to be deodorized. He gets caught up in the window shade and remains there, despaired of, until George pulls down the shade to show his respect for the dead. When he is carted off with the garbage by mistake, he is the envy of his father whose business prevents him from travelling far from home.

Stuart combines many heroic traditions and the eloquence of literary pastiche enriches the comedy of his exploits. A clubland dandy with his hat and cane, he requests a 'nip of brandy' after being shut accidentally in the fridge. A crack shot with bow and arrow, he quotes speeches from the movies as he chivalrously rescues his bird friend Margalo from the cat. In the epic boat race on the pond in Central Park, he is a swashbuckling champion and, returning home, is too sophisticated to boast. 'George asked him where he had been all day. "Oh knocking around town," replied Stuart.' When danger at home puts Margalo to flight, Stuart takes to the road in a car powered by five drops of gasoline, and, a picaresque wayfarer, comes to the aid of a pensive stranger.

' "You see, I'm the Superintendent of Schools in this town." "That's not an impossible situation," said Stuart, "It's bad but it's not impossible." ' Stuart's moral courage matches his physical daring. While deputizing for an absent teacher Stuart dismisses the conventional curriculum as trivial and irrelevant— ' "Who knows what is really important?" '—and leads a discussion of universal ethics. An autocrat within a democratic procedure, he discovers that being Chairman of the World takes more running and leaping and sliding than he had imagined, and leaves the class with a benediction: ' "Never forget your summertimes, my dears." '

Significantly the only setback in Stuart's career occurs with the failure of his romantic overtures to a girl of his own size—a well-rehearsed evening on the river which turns into a muddy fiasco. It has an inauspicious start since the paddles for the birch-bark canoe are cardboard spoons for eating ice-cream, disquietingly inauthentic. ' "I would hate to meet an American Indian while I had one of these things in my hand." ' Rejecting comfort and compromise, the solace of a dance at the Country Club with wealthy Harriet, Stuart resumes the challenge of his original task, the search for Margalo in which nothing is certain or guaranteed. He journeys northward (White's own route home from the city) encouraged by a telephone repairman:

'I have sat at peace on the freight platforms of railroad junctions in the north, in the warm hours and with the warm smells. I know fresh lakes in the north, undisturbed except by fish and hawk and, of course, the Telephone Company, which has to follow its nose. I know all these places well. They are a long way from here—don't forget that. And a person who is looking for something doesn't travel very fast.'

Some readers find this conclusion inconclusive; my six-year-old son was moved to write a sequel in which Stuart and Margalo reached home 'and never went away again without coming back.' This book reads you.

I think the intensity of the tale comes from White's own predicament: his frustration as a teacher who knew 'what is really important' and was not hopeful of getting it across; as a modest writer with topics on his mind too big to express; as an idealist whose aspirations for humanity exceeded his powers and position. 'Law is extremely solemn,' Stuart tells the class.

Yet this solemnity does not detract from the entertainment of the book. For the young, Stuart provides a chance to identify simultaneously with underdog and topdog. His mastery of the world is achieved through the universal paraphernalia of miniature boats and cars with which children rehearse their own adult performances; his feats complement their fantasy. There are scatological jokes: ' "Phew Stuart, you do smell awful" '— and wordplay with a touch of *Schadenfreude*—the strangulated talk of the patient in the dentist's chair—which in my experience children find side-splitting.

Stuart's infancy is unusually short—less than a week. White's second book, *Charlotte's Web,* dwells on babies—piglets, goslings, lambs, children. Stuart is a detached self-sufficient character, soon independent of his family and pitting his wits against the domestic sub-culture of cats and dogs, a wise guy making his own way in a predominantly public world—street, park, store. The narrative is linear, a solo with a supporting cast. The farm by contrast is densely populated with intimate relationships; the characters live in and through each other; the strand of each individual destiny is enmeshed in the collective fabric. Stuart's deepest feeling, his commitment to Margalo, is unfulfilled, a goal in the distance; in *Charlotte's Web* emotions are reciprocal, realized and followed through. The dynamic of feeling within a complex community *is* the movement of the book—nurture and maturation, attachment and loss. The mock heroics of Stuart Little depend on your consciousness of incongruity; the difference between the hero's picture of the figure he is cutting and our own. In the second book, the satirical core is the interdependence and mutual influence of the public image and the true self, social valuation and its effect on personality. Within the web of the title, Charlotte the spider contrives a publicity stunt to ensure the survival of her friend the pig. By advertising his noble qualities she turns him into a celebrity and Wilbur and the farm flourish in the ensuing fame which culminates at the County Fair, the great occasion which brings to each character his heart's desire.

E.M. Forster remarked on the rarity in fiction of 'the facts of birth'. Characters usually 'come into the world more like parcels than human beings'.[1] But birth is White's special province. Nests abound—White says he spent the war years 'publishing my belief in the egg'. Wilbur, the runt of the litter, owes his life to the intervention of Fern, the farmer's eight-year-old daughter— ' "If I had been very small at birth, would you have killed *me*?" '—and is passionately cherished with bottle and doll's pram. When he is weaned and transferred to the barn, Fern's tender vigilance continues and more lives begin—the miracle of creation, the slog of parenthood. Birth has a social dimension: when seven goslings hatch out, Charlotte formally congratulates their mother on the lucky number. ' "Luck had nothing to do with this," said the goose, "it was good management and hard work." '

Waiting and working are in some forms familiar to children but the rarity of birth in their literature is related to a deeper omission which corresponds to a limitation in their lives—the dimension of time. Just because children's temporal span is so short and their experience of relationships necessarily one-sided, it is difficult to convey gradual transition; the pattern of changes which make up the full compass of a life. Since the child is conscious of so few years, so few seasons, he lacks—and needs—an imaginative grasp of the facts of growth and generation. In the absence of time as the element in which lives are lived, people in fiction are incomplete and their acts lack significance. Hence the static, eventless quality of many novels for children. Scenes tend to be 'stills' with dramatic devices sandwiched between. If the plot requires a character to grow up, the parts are played, as it were, by two actors, one small and one large.

White transcends these limitations. His solid evocation of shifting seasons, the perpetually changing landscape, the ceaseless mobility of 'here and now' is the foundation of his achieve-

[1] E.M. Forster, *Aspects of the Novel,* Arnold, 1927.

ment in making us believe in his characters and care about the events which affect them. Risk and pleasure combine in the unifying imagery of height and flight which symbolizes the launching of new life—the children swinging from the barn roof, the spider-balloonists sailing off into the unknown, Henry and Fern on the Ferris wheel. ' "They've got to grow up some time," said Mr Arable, "and a fair is a good place to start, I guess." '

The child reader's own history is charted in Wilbur's archetypal journey from private bliss with Fern to public exposure and hard-won friendships in the wider community, amid the rumours, rivalries, business meetings and formal procedures of the barn. Having been Fern's nursling and Charlotte's protégé, he becomes in his turn a protector entrusted with an egg sac containing five hundred and fourteen unborn children just before the spider dies.

'When the first light comes into the sky and the sparrows stir and the cows rattle their chains, when the rooster crows and the stars fade, when early cars whisper along the highway, you look up here and I'll show you something. I will show you my masterpiece.'

Animals mature quickly, their successive roles have a short term and can be readily perceived. Human development is slower, more obscure. In anxious phases parents seek reassurance from the longer perspective of experts; Mrs Arable consults the doctor about Fern's obsession: ' "I would say off-hand that spiders and pigs were fully as interesting as Henry Fussy. Yet I predict that the day will come when even Henry will drop some chance remark that catches Fern's attention. It's amazing how children change from year to year." ' The doctor is right; Fern turns from her pets to the love of her contemporary and is soon 'careful to avoid childish things like sitting on a milk stool near a pigpen'.

White's depiction of the natural order includes conflict as well as cooperation and mutual support, destruction as well as survival. Charlotte herself is a predator:

'I'm not entirely happy about my diet of flies and bugs, but it's the way I'm made. And furthermore, do you realize that if I didn't catch bugs and eat them, bugs would increase and multiply and get so numerous that they'd destroy the earth?'

Stuart Little's cat suffers psychologically from his repression of his hunting instincts; the collecting urge of small boys is a natural threat to the spider, a danger which the hoarding mania of the rat happens in this case to avert. White has given much thought to rats and their place in the scheme of things. They are the outcast species which Stuart insists should be granted full citizenship in the reformed world system. They exemplify the least likeable aspects of our society—acquisitiveness, alienation, self-seeking. Templeton is recognizable as one of us with his profiteering 'I handle this stuff all the time', his contempt for play and his lust for high living. Yet within the fictional world he has created, White is 'fair to rats' for Templeton's actions are better than his motives. Cynicism and callousness notwithstanding—' "Let him die. I should worry." '—he is an agent of salvation for Charlotte, Wilbur and the eggs, since self-interest lies in Wilbur's feeding trough. Destinies are chronologically linked; no animal is an island.

Walter Benjamin wrote, 'An orientation towards practical interests is characteristic of many born storytellers'. White's books are rich in skills and strategems, solid with feasts, tools, gear. You could stock your farm from his inventory and go away on holiday with the bags he packs. You could also choose your car from his traffic jam: 'Fords and Chevvies and Buick roadmasters and GMC pickups and Plymouths and Studebakers and Packards and De Sotos with gyromatic transmissions and Oldsmobiles with rocket engines and Jeep station wagons and Pontiacs.' Actuality is a brand name; even *things* have a history, a past and a future. There is a lot of twentieth-century junk around the garbage that entraps Stuart on the East River, the stormblown newspapers and candy wrappers in the Philadelphia Zoo. But the trash dump raided by Templeton is the repository of the media, food for fantasy, and speaks the twentieth-century message. ' "Bring me back a word," Charlotte called after him.' The rat tears our ads and labels—'Crunchy', 'Pre-shrunk', 'With New Radiant Action'. "Actually," said Wilbur, "I *feel* radiant." '

Commercials are satirized with affection: 'People will believe almost anything they see in print'. Everyone but the farmer's wife assumes that it is the subject of the slogan and not the creator who is remarkable and this delusion saves Wilbur from slaughter. Yet it is precisely his ordinariness that makes Wilbur lovable and his rise to fame a source of joy. Appreciation is a self-fulfilling prophecy: ' "But I'm not terrific, Charlotte. I'm just about average for a pig." "You're terrific as far as I'm concerned," replied Charlotte sweetly, "and that's what counts." ' The unreality of competition and status is exposed by the uniqueness of love.

Charlotte's Web ends with a tribute to 'a true friend and a good writer', perhaps referring to the author's wife, who was literary editor of *The New Yorker* for many years. (*The New Yorker,* like the web, is influential and renewed at regular intervals.) White's latest book celebrates music, the universal language that transcends even the power of words. The Trumpeter Swan of the title is called Louis; the book pays homage to Armstrong and the men who composed his tunes.

Once again the traditional formula of a meteoric career is parodied and the story describes the struggles of an animal hero to overcome an initial handicap within a relationship with a maturing child. This time the human hero, Sam, is adolescent, concerned with what he is going to be when he grows up, while in the life cycle of the swans, attention is focussed on courtship and marriage. The sanctuaries of the wild and the centres of society are further apart than ever; the flight of the swan is paralleled by Sam's air travel, and the ventures of each into the territory of the other have the quality of 'firstness' which John Berger has characterized as the essence of sexual experience. Sam meets the swans' brood while camping by a remote lake in Canada. One cygnet turns out to be voiceless. The cob's distress at this discovery: ' "Fatherhood is quite a burden at best. I do not want the added strain of having a defective child," ' becomes determination to provide for Louis's future since a voice is vital for courtship. Louis attends school with Sam but, though literacy enables him to communicate with humans, he can make no headway with the swan he loves. The impotence of muteness is finally mastered by art when Louis learns to play the trumpet which his father has stolen for him, earns money to pay for it and successfully woos Serena. The fulfilment of Louis's love has a more than personal importance since we learn from the game warden that Trumpeter Swans were once almost extinct, ' "But now they are making a comeback," "*I'll* say they are making a comeback!" ' says the storekeeper and donates Louis's money to the Audubon Society.

White's technique uses time-honoured literary conventions as a sort of ambush for originality. Psychological insights lurk behind clichés of the genre. Louis's rise to stardom, fame and fortune reveals the grind of making a living in show business. The standard adventure story rescue occurs when Louis saves from drowning a boy who doesn't like birds, but without the standard conversion of the rescued—' "I still don't like birds." "Really?" said Mr. Brickle. "That's quite remarkable." ' Sam hopes Serena won't marry Louis for his money (which hangs in a bag round his neck) and when at last the deus ex machina of a storm blows Serena into the Philadelphia Zoo and the conventional happy ending is in sight, she is too 'mussed' and 'pooped' to be approached. It is a measure of White's success in creating the romance that he can afford to tell this kind of unglamorous truth. The more exalted the theme, the more down-to-earth the treatment. Sentimentality is a sin of omission. White's completeness is the converse of this. He shows us priceless things and tells us honestly what they cost. When the mother is incubating her eggs, her husband asks, ' "Don't you ever feel the pangs of hunger or suffer the tortures of thirst?" ' "Yes I do," said his mate, "as a matter of fact I could use a drink right now." ' The parent swans epitomize the enduring intensity of what survives satire, what can be laughed at and still loved. (Thus humanizing the modern American reversal of the patriarchal tradition which treats fathers as buffoons.) Sources of emotional strength can also be sources of comedy just as true poetry can withstand parody. When Louis plays Brahms's Cradle Song it is interrupted by the ping of pellets from an airgun—only good tunes make jokes.

The points of the compass are a recurring symbol in White's work and this book is remarkable for its impression of space and flight, distances travelled and contrasting landscapes. The secret life of wild places—frog, chipmunk, jay, fox—is matched by the panorama of metropolitan fauna—lobby clerks, bellboys, people drinking cocktails, chambermaids in bedrooms who pause to listen to the trumpet. White's comic scenes are played on a wide screen, often with choral effects, as in the cob's invasion of the vibrating music store. Melodrama serves to illumine the reaction of bystanders to momentous events. Most observers are as unmoved as the horse in Auden's poem who 'scratches its innocent behind on a tree.' Alfred Gore, deadpan, sees a swan laden with money shot by a storekeeper and covered with blood; then, still thirsty, he continues his journey to the candy store. Others leap joyfully onto bandwagons: the boatman sees a chance to 'sextoople' his business; the teacher wants to get her picture in *Life* magazine. The wise are neither blasé nor opportunist. Miracles give them food for thought; they are left pondering the mysteries of life. And their meditations bring these old men of authority, the telephone engineer, the headman of the zoo, into relationships with the young, earnest, questing, eager for knowledge. The result is a sort of fusion of seriousness and frivolity, rather as if *The Leechgatherer* and *The Aged Aged Man A-sitting on a Gate* had both been composed by the same author.

The reader is left with an impression of charm and wisdom, two qualities which may appear somewhat antithetical. Charm involves a self-effacing responsiveness, an awareness of one's audience; wisdom responds only to truth and tells it, welcome or not. Charm is compliant; wisdom is uncompromising. Charm implies ease; wisdom urgency. I suspect that White's dissatisfaction with himself as a writer in troubled times stemmed from the fact that he knew that he was charming and yet wanted to be wise. His touch was too light to take the weight of what needed to be said. Yet in stories for children the contradiction resolves itself; there is no tension between the demands of style and content. In the witty handling of serious themes, a modest undertaking with immense potential influence, White found the exact mode of expression for his gifts; more appropriate than either advertising with its overtly seductive aim or journalism which would change the world if it could.

Thurber repeatedly used the word 'perfection' of White's work. White himself is fascinated by images of natural perfection. The artifacts of instinctive skill, the spider's web, the swan's nest—'Nobody ever taught her'—are set beside the processes of teaching and learning, the effort and frustration involved in mastering human skills, writing and making music. White has said that he finds writing 'difficult and bad for one's disposition'. Yet he seems driven to it by the need to acknowledge particular blessings and to pay particular debts of gratitude. His readers have reason to be grateful to one who wrote in 1962:

> As a writing man, I have always felt charged with the safekeeping of all unexpected items of worldly or unworldly enchantment, as though I might be held personally responsible if even a small one were lost.

From *Children's literature in education*, No. 11, May 1973

The Problem of C.S. Lewis

David Holbrook

*David Holbrook is well known for his five books on English
teaching which include the seminal* English for the Rejected. *
He has written four books resulting from the study of the
psychology of culture on Dylan Thomas, Gustav Mahler and
Sylvia Plath. The extract* here is now included in a new book,*
The Mirror and the Witch, *on symbolism in children's literature.*

AS I WORK on a study of C.S. Lewis's 'Narnia' books the Par-
ish magazine comes through the door. In it there is a review of
The Silver Chair. It seems quite clear from this Church paper
that people believe C.S. Lewis offers children a Christian message:
The Sign tells us that:

> If your children have not yet been introduced to Aslan, it
> is high time they were: he could accompany them for the rest
> of their lives. And beyond . . . a spiritual journey for anyone
> who reads . . . it is hard to believe that there are many Chris-
> tians in this country at all who need an introduction to the
> land of Narnia, to Aslan the Lion, or the children who jour-
> ney in those wonderful, if sometimes perilous, regions . . .

In the rest of the magazine there are articles on Africa, and
on Ireland. I am reading *The Last Battle* at the time. I try to
imagine an African reading this—or someone (say) in hospital
after an IRA bomb attack:

*All the chronicles of Narnia were considered in the original article. In this
extract, David Holbrook discusses the final book, *The Last Battle.*

116

Eustace stood with his heart beating terribly, hoping and hoping that he would be brave. He had never seen anything ... that made his blood run so cold as that line of dark-faced bright-eyed men. ... Then he heard twang-and-zipp on his left and one Calormene fell: then twang-and-zipp again and the Satyr was down. 'Oh, well done, daughter!' came Tirian's voice; and then the enemy were upon them. ... The Bull was down, shot through the eye by an arrow from Jill. ... 'That's a rotten shot!' she said as her first arrow sped towards the enemy and flew over their heads. But she had another on the string next moment: she knew that speed was what mattered ... one of her own arrows hit a man, and another a Narnian wolf ... . 'Oh well done. *Well* done!' shouted Jill. ... The Unicorn was tossing men as you'd toss hay on a fork. ... 'Tash made one peck and the monkey was gone!' 'Serve him right,' said Eustace. ...

I am aware, of course, of the whole tradition of 'fight the good fight' and I know this symbolizes a moral struggle. But the way in which it is done—the way in which one is involved in feeling that aggression is commendable: is that a Christian message?

Or, if one is not a Christian, but an agnostic humanist (as I suppose I am)—is this an artistic message one can respect?

One cannot, I think, escape this question by saying that there is violence in all myth and fairty tale. There is also love in many tales. In C.S. Lewis there is a particular emphasis on a *continual* aggressive stance: indeed, in a sense, nothing happens in the Narnia books except the build-up and confrontation with para-noically conceived menaces, from an aggressive posture of hate, leading towards conflict. And in this there is often an intense self-righteousness, which must surely communicate itself to children.

Lewis himself was capable of making this explicit—in terms of the reality of everyday life. In a radio talk he said:

What I cannot understand is this sort of half-pacifism you get nowadays which gives people the idea that though you have got to fight, you ought to do it with a long face as if you were ashamed of it. It is that feeling which robs lots of magnificent young Christians in the Services of something they have a right to, something which is the natural accompaniment of war—a kind of gaiety and whole-heartedness.

This, in fact, is the main message of the Narnia books: *it is no good being half-hearted about fighting*. The most valuable thing is to fight and kill the 'enemy' and one must not be ashamed of it.

*   *   *   *   *

In *The Last Battle,* C.S. Lewis turns to that ultimate battle which, in so many mythologies, has to be fought, to find one's way through to the final meaning. The book is full of hate.

At once (characteristically) the children enter into a paranoid-schizoid situation—and have to toughen themselves. They put colouring on themselves, Calormene helmets, swords and shields. They go through something like a Hell's Angel ritual:

> There was no sword light enough for Jill, but he gave her a long, straight hunting knife which might do for a sword at a pinch.

Jill is not bad at archery: she shoots a rabbit (not, of course, a talking rabbit!). It was now already skinned, cleaned and hanging up.

> He had found that both children knew all about this chilly and smelly job . . . .

They are properly 'blooded' children.

The unconscious message is that the child C.S. Lewis needed to toughen himself by imaginative flights of fancy, in which he became an assertive warrior. So, here, the incident in which Jewel is freed is very much like an incident in a James Bond novel. Eustace is told, 'If he (the sentry) moves, rive him to the heart.'

Then the two children and King Tirian meet a party of dwarfs with four Calormene guards. Eustace kills one.

Eustace, who had drawn his sword when he saw the King draw his, rushed at the other one: his face was deadly pale, but I wouldn't blame him for that. And he had the luck that beginners sometimes do have. He forgot all that Tirian had tried to teach him that afternoon, slashed wildly (indeed), I'm not sure his eyes weren't shut) and suddenly found, to his own great surprise, that the Calormene lay dead at his feet. And though that was a great relief, it was, at the moment, rather frightening. The King's fight lasted a second or two longer: then he too had killed his man and shouted to Eustace, ' 'Ware the other two'.

But the Dwarfs had settled the two remaining Calormenes. There was no enemy left.

The savagery of killing is made quite genteel—'a great relief', 'rather frightening', 'to his own great surprise', 'the Dwarfs had *settled* the two remaining Calormenes'. It is a phantasy exercise in cold-blooded destruction, in which the Calormenes (who are more like men than the Narnians) are simply regarded as 'gooks'. (We may recall, in Mark Twain, the exchange about a riverboat boiler explosion, 'Anybody hurt?' 'No, mum, killed a nigger.') Here, it is *rather* frightening, but it is only a *Calormene* who is 'settled'. 'Three cheers for Aslan'—and the dwarfs (Jill tells them) can 'have fun again'. We are almost (are we not?) involved in fun killings? Again, the parallel to the Hell's Angels' syndrome is evident.

Later, there must be another battle; the scene is satisfyingly blood-thirsty:

Two [Calormenes] lay dead, one pierced by Jewel's horn, one by Tirian's sword. The Fox lay dead at his [Eustace's] own feet, and he wondered if it was he who had killed it. The Bull was also down, shot through the eye by an arrow from Jill and gashed in his side by the Boar's tusk. But our side had its losses too. Three dogs were killed and a fourth was hobbling behind the lines on three legs and whimpering. The Bear lay on the ground, moving feebly. Then it mumbled in its throaty voice, bewildered to the last, 'I don't—understand', laid its big head down on the grass as quietly as a child going to sleep, and never moved again. . . .

The battle with the Calormenes (ill. by Pauline Baynes, from *The Last Battle* by C S Lewis. Bodley Head, 1956; Macmillan [U.S.], 1970). Reprinted by permission of Bodley Head Ltd.

The illustration shows dogs tearing at a fallen satyr, sword-play and a fallen Calormene with an arrow in his back. Now the Talking Horses came rushing up—only to be shot at by the Dwarfs.

> 'Little *swine*,' shrieked Eustace, dancing in his rage.
> 'Dirty, filthy, treacherous little brutes.'

The protagonists are 'our' side: so, we identify with such hate. What we must *not* do is be tender. Tirian says to Jill:

> 'If you must weep, sweetheart, (this was to Jill) turn your face aside and see you wet not your bowstring.'

Such a lapse would be like failing to dry your sword: like Rauschning, Lewis declares, 'we will have no weakness or tenderness in our youth'.

> Feeling terribly alone, Jill ran out about twenty feet, put her right leg back and her left leg forward, and set an arrow to her string. She wished her hands were not shaking so. . . 'Eustace seemed to Jill . . . to be fighting brilliantly. The Dogs were at the Calormenes' throats. It was going to work! It was victory at last. . . .

At this point the Calormenes are reinforced; and one grabs Eustace and hurls him into the hut containing Tash:

> Even then Jill remembered to keep her face turned aside, well away from her bow. 'Even if I can't stop blubbing, I won't get my string wet,' she said.

What does it mean—this concern not to be so humanly feeling, that one must not spoil one's weapons? And what is the 'reward of it all'?

After the last battle, the protagonists eat the golden fruit from a grove of trees. They are momentarily touched by guilt:

> Everyone raised his hand to pick the fruit he best liked the look of, and then everyone paused for a second. This fruit

was so beautiful that each felt 'It can't be meant for me . . .
surely we're not allowed to pluck it.'

'It's all right,' said Peter, 'I know what we're all thinking.
But I'm sure, quite sure, we needn't. I've a feeling we've got
to the country where everything is allowed.'

At last we have reached the Golden Age, that old Rousseauistic
dream, of total permissiveness.

> What was the fruit like? Unfortunately no one can describe
> a taste. All I can say is that, compared with those fruits, the
> freshest grapefruit you've ever eaten was dull, and the juiciest
> orange was dry, and the most melting pear was hard and
> woody, and the sweetest wild strawberry was sour. And there
> were no seeds or stones, and no wasps. If you had once eaten
> that fruit, all the nicest things in this world would taste like
> medicines after it. But I can't describe it. You can't find out
> what it is like unless you can get to that country and taste it
> for yourself. When they had eaten enough. . . .

This fruit, surely, bears a sinister resemblance to the White
Witch's Turkish Delight in *The Lion, the Witch and the Ward-
robe*? What makes the difference? There, to be greedy was to
lay oneself open to sin—the loss of one's autonomy. What is the
difference between Edmund's greed and the greed of these
Kings and Queens? Of course, we can see that they are in Heav-
en but the point surely was that one should not be self-inter-
ested, but think of others. Is the ultimate reward for this going
to be a Super-hedonism, of Absolutely Guiltless Self-interest?
Death is merely no-longer-having-the-pain-of-a-sore-knee:

> . . . There was a frightful roar and something hit me with a
> bang, but it didn't hurt. And I felt not so much scared as
> —well, excited. Oh—and this is one queer thing. I'd had a
> rather sore knee, from a hack at rugger. I noticed it had
> suddenly gone. And I felt very light. And then—here we
> were.

This surely is as inadequate as Barrie's work shows itself when
he makes Peter say 'Dying will be an awfully great adventure.'

To analyse these stories reveals the deep ambivalence in C.S. Lewis's Christianity: his fear of love is not least a fear of Christ's love—until one overcomes that schizoid fear by paranoid self-strengthening (wiping one's sword, and not wetting one's bowstring) it is not possible to accept (and enjoy) that love. But this is so personal a myth that it is barely reconcilable with Christianity at all, surely.

In the end the children are happy dead. Aslan says:

> 'There *was* a real railway accident . . . . Your father and mother and all of you—as you used to call it in the shadow-lands—dead. The term is over: the holidays have begun. The dream is ended: this is the morning.

But what kinds of joys could heaven bring? It would be interesting to have C.S. Lewis's account of them—in which 'every chapter is better than the one before'. Could there be such joys for him, without more paranoia and fighting? We are left with no feeling that Lewis could find peace in simply *Being*.

And because there is no such sense of existential security, there is no going outward to serve goals beyond the self of any relief (even in Heaven) from the confrontation with paranoiac chimeras. Nowhere in the Narnia books are there causes to be served, in terms of the mysteries of this world, the possibilities of man, or the satisfactions of interpersonal encounter between human beings: love. There is only plotting, marching, moving about the terrain, and killing—in opposition (mostly) to non-human creatures, helped by magic, in world after world in which events are already *determined*. The children never escape from magical control and determinism: they never question what they do, or their motives—and they never make existential choices. They never suffer. As we see, by the way in which even Tash is made an instrument, the world, universe, and all transcendental realms are governed and manipulated by the White Witch, Tash and Aslan. While the former two represent Lewis's hate, which he fears will devastate the world, the latter is his split-off, benign male element—which he hopes will be benign. But in his dictatorial power Aslan is often exercising a disguised predatoriness, which is a form of hate, too, since its most harmful effect is to rob human beings of their autonomy—and so of their freedom, and their quest for authenticity.

The Narnia books can thus hardly be accepted as Christian fables, while from an existentialist point of view they could be said to encourage dependence and the forfeiture of one's moral autonomy to magical control. As imaginative literature I doubt whether the hate, fear and sadism in them is relieved by humanizing benignity.

Most children probably read the stories as spooky yarns, and probably little harm is done. But under cover of his apparent religious intentions and his mask of benignity C.S. Lewis conveys to his readers a powerful unconscious message that the world is full of malignancy; that one must be continually alert; that aggression is glorious, exciting and fully justified; that tenderness, cowardice and reticence are weak; that one may easily be assured as to one's righteousness; that magic works—and these messages are sometimes conveyed with undertones of a sadistic-sexual kind, or with powerful phantasies rooted in hate. This must surely raise doubts as to the wisdom of exposing children to them, from a writer of such clarity, persuasiveness and power.

From *Children's literature in education*, No. 10, March 1973

The Flambards Trilogy: Objections to a Winner

Dominic Hibberd

Dominic Hibberd has taught English at Manchester Grammar School and at Northwestern (U.S.A.) and Exeter Universities; he is now a lecturer at the University of Keele. His doctoral research was in the literature of the First World War.

Introductory Note

In 1969, K.M. Peyton enjoyed the unusual distinction of winning both the Carnegie Medal and *The Guardian's* annual award for fiction written for children. Discussing the award of the Medal, Colin Ray, chairman of the Carnegie selection committee, wrote:

> The Carnegie Medal is awarded, necessarily and wisely, in accordance with clear and binding terms. It is inevitable, none the less, that from time to time one would wish them temporarily away. While there are years of relative dearth in which an outstanding book must almost select itself, there are others in which it becomes an almost painful task to choose one, only one book to honour in this exclusive way. It seems almost wilful, therefore, of an author to provide as eligible in one year two books as serious contenders—and then to set the committee the task of examining each of these as an individual work and as separate from the whole trilogy of which each forms a part. Both of the relevant books by K.M. Peyton, *The Edge of the Cloud* and *Flambards in Summer,* were widely supported both in nomination for the award and in the committee's discussions. In each the

author's outstanding ability in evocation of atmosphere and conveying a sense of place was admired. Her skill in delineating and developing character could be followed through the two books, as Christina grows from adolescence to young widowhood, and her insight into her heroine's acceptance of the relationship with Will—acceptance of the inescapable rivalry for his concern between herself and his other love, aeronautics—raises issues of fundamental significance to adolescent self-awareness. The third book of the trilogy suffers a little, perhaps, from the need to draw together threads from the whole sequence, and in its complexity both of plot and ideas is outshone by the winner, *The Edge of the Cloud,* which concentrates its resources to a single theme. A story which includes so much almost documentary detail of the history of aeronautical development in its early days is a surprise in this area of fiction, and it is a singular achievement that this book is read, unlike most fiction for the upper age level, by both boys and girls. And not only by them; this book, the whole trilogy, is a piece of literature for all ages. Unlike *The Guardian*, whose annual award this year was given to the Flambards trilogy, the selection committee considered each book in itself. It is unprecedented for one author to both receive the Carnegie Medal and to be acclaimed on the Honours List, and it is a measure of Mrs Peyton's quality that the committee found itself happily obliged to take such a step this year.[1]

*   *   *   *   *

THE CARNEGIE MEDAL and *The Guardian* award carry high prestige and the people who give them have an important literary responsibility. By what standards should a work for 'the younger reader' be judged? By special standards? Or by the kind that one would apply to any other sort of literature? It is my contention that the Flambards trilogy, though a lively and enjoyable story, is, if judged like any other group of novels, very definitely not of the first rank; and I shall suggest that,

[1] *Carnegie and Kate Greenaway Medals for 1969:* Library Association Record, June 1970.

even if there are special standards to be invoked, the Carnegie judges do not seem to have used them in this case.

We have K. M. Peyton's word for it that she did not plan to write two more volumes when she started *Flambards*, but if the trilogy is viewed as it stands it does look very much like something designed to be a commercial success. Suppose we were to set out to write a story for the respectable teenage market. We must aim at three parties in particular: girls, boys and teachers. Safe subjects to choose would be horses for girls, planes for boys and some fairly reliable history for teachers (then our book will be ordered by the school library). To work all three topics into one book is not easy: a trilogy would give us more scope and would look more impressive, without having the disadvantages of one fat volume. So we put horses into one book, planes into another, and tie up our plot in the third. But that means girls will not read book two nor boys book one. Solution: the horses are part of a masculine, hunting world, though seen through the eyes of a girl; and the same girl (she'll be the connecting link then) must somehow be got up in an aeroplane. A new snag arises. If she's nuts on horses, as she must be, why does she give up a whole volume to planes? Because she's in love, of course — she's got an aviator boyfriend who attracts her away from the stables to the hangars (chance for some vivid place descriptions here). And what gets her back to the horses in book three? Death of husband (she'll have to marry him, of course) naturally—aviators are easily disposed of. As for history, there's only one period in which both hunting and aviation were open to young amateurs and that's the years around 1914, before the decay of the country landowner and the introduction of strict rules about flying. There was a war then too, so that makes it even easier to dispose of aviators.

Perhaps we can bear other sorts of reader in mind while we're about it; parents, for instance, and Progressives. We've got a love motive in the book already, but parents quite like a 'frank' approach to sex these days as long as you don't actually tell the kids anything; and this suits the 1914 period, when advanced novelists like H. G. Wells were always taking a 'frank' approach to sex without giving anything away. So we can have a baby or two and perhaps even a bastard (but the characters must sometimes refer to it only as a 'b———', in deference to the headmistresses). And the Progressives, who are way behind the times as usual, will like a bit of good Proggy stuff about servants being maltreated and the groom being better than the master. Indeed, since the aviator is going to be killed, we can marry off the heroine to the groom when she goes back to the horses in book three.

It would be churlish to press this further or to suggest that Mrs Peyton thought in quite so crude a manner. Nevertheless, Teenlit for O.U.P. is big business and Mrs Peyton is a prolific writer. The Flambards trilogy does bear the marks of something written and printed in a tremendous hurry. My paperback copies were full of malapropisms and misprints — 'accede' for 'concede', 'avid' for 'fervent', 'consciousness' for 'unconsciousness', 'like' for 'as' everywhere, 'handsom' cabs and other oddities. A careful writer would not slither into clumsy repetitions like these:

> She (the aeroplane) nosedived *sickeningly into the* thorn
> *hedge* beyond. Her tail cartwheeled, one wing dug in with a
> *sickening* rend*ing of* crack*ing* timber. Bury*ing* her nose deep
> *into the hedge . . .*

or mix this remarkable image:

> This pain, compounded of frustration and loneliness, shot
> through with nerve-flicking stabs of doubt and seamed with
> chasms of confusion, had dogged her for the whole
> fortnight . . .

But if you're a critic of the Carnegie kind you don't notice the bad style here. You don't wonder how pain can be shot through with stabs and seamed with chasms, how stabs can flick and shoot (or is it shot silk that we are supposed to think of?), or how the whole weird concoction can be said to dog somebody. No, you seize upon those dear old chestnuts 'frustration and loneliness' and praise the author for 'raising issues'. Mrs Peyton's insight into Christina's relationship with Will 'raises issues of fundamental significance to adolescent self-awareness', according to the chairman of the Carnegie Medal committee. This dusty mouthful of cliches is supposed to be a compliment; but any book can raise an issue and far too many do. Indeed, if the old sorcerers had been as good at raising the dead as we are at raising issues, they would have left scarcely a corpse underground. Unless an issue can be made to do some useful work and not just stand there in its cerements, one ought not to disturb it. I imagine that what Mr Ray really means by 'raising issues' is 'asking questions in such a way as to encourage the reader—and the writer—to search for truthful answers'. As I shall suggest, I do not think Mrs Peyton goes in for this sort of questioning. If, however, Mr Ray simply means 'introduces subjects', then I insist again that any book can introduce a subject without earning special merit for itself.

The Carnegie committee gave its medal to the second volume only — a revealing choice. Mr Ray admits that they found the third volume too complex. Established critical practice requires us to consider the trilogy as a whole, and in terms of the whole the second volume is the weakest link while the third is by far the best. The complexity of *Flambards in Summer,* which frightened off the committee, is an essential part of the trilogy and is quite well handled; the various themes of the three books are interwoven and resolved. The committee seems to have valued two things in particular—depth of characterization and accuracy of historical detail. We are not concerned here with historical detail. One hopes (though sometimes the hope wavers) that nobody would try to pretend that a novel is a good one because it is well 'researched'. Mrs Peyton knows about early aeroplanes and makes them interesting; but the novelist has to know about people and society. We are concerned with social history and with characters, and we must take all three volumes together.

The central character of the trilogy, Christina Parsons, is one of those tough, active women that have abounded in English fiction ever since Emma Woodhouse. (One only has to think of Emma to perceive Christina's flatness.) We meet her first while she is still a girl of twelve, and within a few pages we have picked up enough clues to know how much depth there is to this portrait. 'Life had already dealt her some cruel surprises'; she shows 'iron self-will' and even takes 'a long, cool look'. She enters the story in—of course—a pony-trap, driven by an old retainer into the estate which will be the background of the tale, a very useful way of introducing us to her, the estate and the old retainer, and one which proved its worth often enough in the last century. However, it is startling to find her apparently capable at the age of twelve of recognizing Flambards (which she has never seen before) as a 'mid Victorian pile'. Christina's age is a sham. From the start she is a young woman, and she belongs much more to our own time than to hers. These hackneyed phrases of character description are the language of the sixties and they set a tone which Mrs Peyton never quite succeeds in changing. This opening failure to make Christina really a child seriously weakens the first volume. Indeed, it weakens all three, because she never has a chance to grow up or to learn. The young mother and widow of the third book is no more mature in her understanding of the world than the girl in the pony-trap. She's a fine young filly but Mrs Peyton always has a hand on the leading rein, as a moment of bathos in the second volume makes clear:

> She steeled herself to get out of bed, not to cry. Her warm
> feet flinched on the linoleum, like the feel of a horse
> going to refuse. 'Horses have courage,' Christina thought.
> 'They have to do whatever is asked of them, however hard.'
> She would have to be a horse. She had stopped the threat
> of tears now.

O, enviable steel (or was it iron?) self-will! The old-fashioned critic, searching the trilogy for its moral teaching, would have had to surface with this pearl: Be a horse.

Christina, like everybody else in the book, is certainly far from cowardly, but one wishes that her intelligence had functioned at a less equine level. Her inability to foresee the certain disaster into which she leads Dick, the groom, when she persuades him to rescue a favourite horse from being fed to hounds, is barely credible. As soon as the rescue is discovered, Dick is sacked. She, like us, has had frequent hints that this would happen, but she has ignored them all: as usual, she neither foresees nor learns, unless such processes are required of her by the plot. Her lack of insight into the other characters is a useful excuse for superficial portrayals of them also. Her cousin Mark, for example, is seen entirely through her eyes and remains more or less incomprehensible because Christina herself never understands him. He is thus a much more successful character than she is, because we are less tempted to question his behaviour. His eventual admission that he wanted to marry her because she rides so well is accepted as a nice joke, and we even swallow his extraordinary plunge into seriousness at the end of *Flambards,* when he suddenly delivers a speech about the approach of war.

Mark's brother, William, is the aviator. He hates hunting and his cruel, horsy father, and in the second volume he escapes with Christina to an aerodrome where he can pursue his passion for flying. Will is a victim of Mrs Peyton's plot. He has to be disposable and the story is not his tragedy, so we must be prevented from getting fond of him. He has to be left, by us as by his fellow characters, to his own devices. Eventually, he crashes. In fact, he's shot down in the war, but he might as easily have been killed in a civil accident, and his death occurs between the second and third volumes. This is, I think, the greatest single weakness of the trilogy; the worst of all the 'cruel surprises' dealt to Christina by 'life' vanishes into the formless void that lies between two outside covers. If we had been faced squarely with Will's death, we should have seen at once that it wouldn't do. The smoothness of Christina's inevitable acceptance of Dick in the last volume would have been intolerable, for one thing, and the quality of writing the crisis would have called for would have shown up Mrs Peyton's shortcomings all too clearly. The climax of the trilogy is avoided so that the plot can continue; we are swept on into the new volume so quickly that we hardly notice the trick that has been played on us. Any readers who may have lingering doubts about this treatment are expected to be content with a spurious re-enactment of Will's death when a German plane is shot down over Flambards. The sight of the dead German is supposed to show Christina what her husband's death had been like. So it does, of course, as far as physical details go; but the dead man is not Will, whose image is already fading in Christina's mind, and her emotional reactions are almost perfunctory. The reader is still not allowed to feel the strain of the suffering that Will's death ought to have caused. Our feelings are spared because we must be free to enjoy the rest of the book. Pain is an embarrassment in fiction of this kind; the trilogy is about events, not minds.

There is another reason for the plane crash in *Flambards in Summer:* the theme of aviation has to make an appearance. In the same way, Christina has to have one ride on a horse in the aerodrome volume. These are elementary pegs but they help to hold the structure together. Mark's occasional entries serve a similar purpose, and Dick, who is the least solid of all the principal characters, links the end of the trilogy to its early stages. Having used the war to get rid of both Will and Mark, Mrs Peyton can pair off Christina and Dick as ushers of the new, classless dawn. On a personal level, this match shows again how Christina is led by the plot. She has treated Dick throughout with remarkable insensitivity, first ruining his career and indirectly causing his mother's death, then taking away his beloved nephew and finally, having quite forgotten that he used to love her, finding him in Rotherhithe and asking him back to Flambards to work. However, he has golden hair, as we are frequently told, and he's only a servant.

The status of servants is a major theme in the trilogy. It is introduced on the first page when the hunting gentry are seen by a farm labourer who thinks to himself: 'They'll get no help from me. Or as much as I get from them, which is the same thing.' This is presumably what Mr Ray would call 'raising an issue'. The author reveals her own opinion and we know we're on safe Proggy ground. The master-servant relationship is a bad one; servants are ignored completely and only cooperate because they have to keep alive. This topic is tackled frequently and it leads us first to a consideration of Mrs Peyton's treatment of history.

Prewar Flambards is not made to seem an exceptional household in the world of its time, partly because no comparisons are made with other estates and partly because it is described in a firmly matter-of-fact manner. The story deals with subjects and social patterns that form part of this century's history: changes in parent-child relationships, new and old forms of transport, masters and servants, town and country, the effects of war. It is difficult not to conclude that Mrs Peyton is deliberately trying to set up a microcosm of the social history of the 1914 period. Perhaps, indeed, this is the justification for any work of historical fiction, that it should show its characters as integral parts of their time. At any rate, I believe I am not the only reader of the trilogy who felt that one is expected to take the Flambards estate as representative of its period and to suppose, perhaps rather vaguely, that most masters treated their servants heartlessly, most country estates were decaying, and so on. However, Flambards is a special case; its patterns of relationships and economics are breaking up largely because of the incompetence and sadism of its old owner. Old Russell has something like the effect on the house that the war might have done. I do not myself find him a convincing character. His dismissal of Dick, the perfect groom, is a most unlikely act from a man obsessed with horses and hunting; and Will's acceptance of violent beatings from the grotesque old cripple, whom he could escape by simply going upstairs, is unexplained. (John Rowe Townsend, who suffers a little from the same malady as Mr Ray, makes no critical comment on this violence except to observe that it is 'disturbingly powerful' – one realizes with dismay that these may be words of praise.[1]) Whether one finds Russell credible or not, however, does not affect the fact that Mrs Peyton does not let the war play its historical part. Servants ceased to exist largely as a result of social and economic forces which the war got moving, not because they were terrorized by men like Russell; and the decay of Flambards, well under way before the war, is not the typical case that it might appear to be to a young reader. Similarly, Mrs Peyton's use of the war as a means of getting rid of redundant characters is brutally misleading. We actually find ourselves *glad* when Mark goes back to the Front after discovering a suitable fiancee; we forget that he is going to almost certain death. Christina gives barely a thought, it seems, to Dick's having joined the army, and her attitudes to war, beginning with exaggerated ignorance and developing through patriotic pride in Will to her final angry feeling that she can't understand war but that it's 'mere foolishness', are little more than a vague acknowledgment of introductions

[1] John Rowe Townsend, *A Sense of Story,* Longman, 1971.

to various anthologies of war poetry in which these ideas are set out and documented. Wilfred Owen said that his *Strange Meeting* was about the 'Foolishness of War'. The comparison speaks for itself. Christina's conclusion is this: 'She wanted these things to make sense, and they didn't. Is Mrs Peyton excusing herself for failing to examine the impact of the war more closely? She and Christina abandon the whole business.

The social conditions at the aerodrome represent the society that will replace the old regime that Russell stands for. The social history here is heavily camouflaged under aeronautical details. As the acknowledgments rather brazenly admit, two of the passages about aviation are lifted whole from a history book. Borrowing of this kind can easily damage the unity of a piece of writing. Many bits of *The Edge of the Cloud* feel second-hand, the result of hard work in a reference library, perhaps, but not part of the 'organic whole' that we should expect a novel to be. Without their aeroplanes, the people at the aerodrome do not seem to me to be distinguishable from young people in respectable novels set in the present day. But my objection here again is that the aerodrome society, though such communities no doubt existed, is presented as both too ordinary and too significant. Its lack of horses, servants and parental control, and the easy, informal way of life of its inhabitants, are typical of post- rather than prewar years. These things were made common by the war, not by the brave, pioneering efforts of a few young people who broke away from their parents to enter the flying machine age in mildly socialist style.

The master-servant relationship is dealt with as superficially as the other historical themes in these books. Tories will approve, I suppose, of my claim that the behaviour of old Russell is not typical of that of his contemporaries; Marxists, perhaps, will agree that Mrs Peyton does not go nearly far enough. She does offer an alternative to servants, but it is only sketched very briefly: at the house of Mr Dermot, Will's benefactor, where cool Georgian architecture contrasts with the mid-Victorian pile of Flambards and announces the triumph of reason, everybody is on Christian name terms and equality seems to be the rule. We are not shown such a situation,

however, when Flambards passes into Christina's hands. The old
retainers are retained and new ones are added. Christina gives
orders as sharply as any Russell and only behaves better than
her relations because she happens to be sane. And her
engagement to Dick, which seems at last to remove the class
barriers, actually does nothing of the sort; it is just the good old
traditional ending when the handsome poor boy marries the
heiress—an evasion of the 'issue' worthy of any Victorian
sentimental novelist. Under Christina, Flambards will have
servants, horses and hunting as it always did; but I fear many
readers will be duped into thinking that a revolution has
occurred.

By his romantic marriage, Dick has escaped the
unemployment and privations that faced returning soldiers,
saved Christina from living as a war widow, and prolonged the
life of an estate that would have been doomed to extinction in
the postwar world.

This habit of evading the issue can be seen working again
when Christina visits Rotherhithe. Here she is faced with urban
society at its worst: romance is no use here, nor is individual
effort. And what does she do? She clears out as fast as she can.
For her, town memories are 'memories best forgotten'.

It would be absurd to attack a book about the country for
not being about the town if it had no pretensions to deal with
the social problems of the Great War years; but if the *Flambards*
trilogy is meant to be seen as a microcosm of its time, then its
refusal to face urban problems and its failure to grasp the
significance of the war itself are weaknesses of a pretty serious
kind. And Mrs Peyton really ought not to be allowed to get
away with passing off a corny Victorian ending as a
revolutionary change in the social order. It may be, however,
that these matters receive only accidental emphasis in the
trilogy; perhaps Mrs Peyton is really not concerned with topics
beyond those of the technicalities of aviation and hunting. If
that is the case, we must recognize that the trilogy is not of any
importance as an historical novel.

Some readers will by now have decided that I am going much
too far, that it is not fair to apply adult critical standards to a
work written for teenagers. It is true that some books for young

readers do set special standards for themselves— *Alice through the Looking Glass,* for example, or possibly *The Owl Service*—but this is also true of some adult novels, such as *Titus Groan* or *Wuthering Heights.* The *Flambards* books are not presented as an exceptional story, as I have said before. Their elements of fantasy and the grotesque remain in embryo; their symbolism is firmly explicit (Christina's ball dress falling off the chair, for example, 'symbolized her feelings exactly'); their scenery, though often well described, is standard fare. Places play a big part but if one compares Mrs Peyton's use of the old house with Forster's use of the house in *Howards End* or with the part played in folk tales by castles and palaces, one is left with a clear impression of the trilogy as a straightforward, 'ordinary' narrative. If it had been serialized anonymously in a woman's magazine we should not have thought of it as aimed particularly at teenagers; but Mrs Peyton is known as a 'children's writer' and the appropriate expectations start operating as soon as we see the cover. I think these expectations operate in the reader rather than in the writer—there is no reason to suppose that Mrs Peyton herself is trying to meet them. She has recorded that her 'idea of a perfect book' is Sassoon's *Memoirs of a Fox-Hunting Man,* which is not surprising to anyone who has read *Flambards;* it is an odd ideal, when one thinks of the wealth of literature she has to choose from, and it suggests that her standards are modestly simple. However, there is nothing in the *Memoirs* that makes them especially attractive to adolescent readers. Mrs Peyton just enjoys writing a lively tale, and her readers very properly enjoy reading it, but by adult standards the trilogy is not an outstanding work. By what standards, then, did the Carnegie Medal judges honour it so highly?

The judges' chairman is not very helpful: 'outstanding ability in evocation of atmosphere . . . conveying a sense of place . . . skill in delineating and developing character . . . documentary detail . . . read by both boys and girls . . . and not only by them . . . a piece of literature for all ages'. The last comment, of course, gives the game away. If the committee had thought about this admission more carefully, they might have wondered why they were not considering adult fiction too for their award, whether *any* literature can be classed as being for teenagers only, and why books merit special treatment just because they come from publishers' children's fiction departments. The chairman's only reference to adolescent interests is the remark we've met before, that Mrs Peyton's 'insight into her heroine's acceptance of the relationship with Will . . . raises issues of fundamental significance to adolescent self-awareness'. As I have said, I suspect we should substitute 'introduces subjects' for 'raises issues', but I agree that adolescents are more likely than anyone else to be interested in subjects to do with adolescent relationships. I do not, however, see this as an adequate reason for exempting the trilogy from adult critical criteria. Would we make such an exemption for *Sons and Lovers* or *Romeo and Juliet*? Indeed, I myself doubt that an exemption could be justified on any grounds. This is a problem which needs much more discussion that it has had in the past, though it is beyond our present scope. At any rate, Mr. Ray appears to be using standards which in kind are the same as adult ones, but which in degree are lower and less demanding. If they were as high and as demanding he could not, for example, have praised Mrs Peyton's skill in characterization or her evocation of atmosphere with such marked enthusiasm.

The growth of the Teenlit industry begins to be a little worrying. That there should be interesting, readable and decent stories available for younger readers is an excellent thing. My complaints about the trilogy would scarcely be worth making if it were not for Mr Ray and his colleagues. I enjoyed these books and was sorry when I'd finished them. As Christina herself realizes at several climactic moments, her life is much the same as that of any heroine in the sentimental novels to which the Flambards housekeeper is addicted:

> He held her closely, and she put her cheek against his shoulder. 'Just like Mary's novels,' she thought.

Well, we think so too and read on cheerfully. But why is a novel of this kind showered with honours when it is presented as being 'for teenage readers'? Is it for teenage critics too?

From *Children's literature in education*, No. 8, July 1972

'The Edge of the Cloud' — A Reply to Dominic Hibberd

Colin Ray

Colin Ray is chairman of the Children's Work Subsection of the International Federation of Library Associations and a former Chairman of the Youth Libraries Group of the Library Association. He is now Senior Lecturer at Birmingham Polytechnic Department of Librarianship.

THE CARNEGIE MEDAL selection committee, and its chairman, change each year. There would be no point in resurrecting that which sat in the early part of 1970, were it not for Dominic Hibberd's critical article. (I was delighted, incidentally, to find myself linked with John Rowe Townsend, and only regret that he escaped with one comment—was Mr Hibberd scared of the more eminent name?)

Mr Hibberd's complaint of my 'dusty mouthful of cliches' is unimportant, though he may agree that more can be said, more fully, in his several pages than in the brief paragraph in which I had to introduce the committee's choice. But what use does he make of his space?

He objects that Mrs Peyton doesn't discuss in any great depth the problems of war, the social history of the period, the wartime urban situation. He is, of course, right: she also fails to write a treatise on prewar economics, changes in agricultural technology and so on. One good reason for these 'failures' may be that this is a novel about a young woman growing up, and about her response to the external pressures and problems to which she is exposed. Whether Mr Hibberd finds this an interesting or a rewarding exercise, whether he believes in her responses, is a matter for him: but it seems unfair to complain that it isn't a different book. (But fairness is not important: the 'two of the passages about aviation (which) are lifted whole from a history book' amount to three sentences, quoted by Christina as if from a newspaper.)

Another complaint is that the trilogy has a lot of matter about horses and aeroplanes, which many young people find interesting. Is that a bad thing? Are we to have a list of topics which, because they may encourage reading, should be avoided? For myself, I should be hard put to it to decide which of these two topics holds less interest for me: and yet I enjoyed the books. Does this suggest a 'sales appeal' approach?

This trilogy was clearly intended *primarily* for adolescents' reading, and published as such by Oxford University Press. There is good evidence to show that these books, like many others of high quality presented to this market (*The Owl Service* is a good example) are read by adults as well. It has often been said that a mark of a good children's book is that adults enjoy reading it. Does that invalidate it for consideration as a book for young people?

The real trouble, I think, is that we are up against Mr Hibberd's 'critical standards'. These are not defined, but appear to be those of *literary* criticism. If he will refer to the terms of the Carnegie Medal, he will find that the award is for an 'outstanding' book. I would personally criticize that adjective as being vague: but one thing it does not explicitly mean is that the Medal is a literary award. Many previous choices for the Medal have been criticized precisely because of this fallacy.

What the committee seeks, in my experience, is a book, not necessarily breaking entirely new ground, but of the highest quality in its genre. And in considering quality, literary quality is only one aspect: its potential impact on the young reader, its ideas, its chances of being read, its individual aspects which make it stand out from the rest, all are relevant. The committee, of the year in question or of any other year, would not claim infallibility: it can bring to bear only its accumulated knowledge of children's literature and the experience of children's reading of its members. But dogmatic statements, unjustified by any argument, that 'the third (volume) is by far the best' will hardly shake their confidence.

Fiction for Children and Adults: Some Essential Differences

Myles McDowell

Myles McDowell has taught English in Middlesex and London and more recently at Settle High School in Yorkshire. He is now deputy head of J.H. Whitley School, Halifax, in Yorkshire. This article was written during a period of secondment at S. Martin's College, Lancaster.

> *Is there such a thing as a children's book? Is the children's book an art form, distinct from other fiction, having its own particular excellence? Or is it just the novel made easy, in which everything is the same as in an adult book, only less so?*[1]

THE ONLY DEFINITION of a children's book, John Rowe Townsend avers, in *A Sense of Story,* is that its name appears on a publisher's list of children's books.[2] The distinction between adult and children's fiction is an artificial one maintained for administrative convenience. Now there is enough of truth in this to make us stop and ask, is there really no difference at all? But it seems to me to be the sort of special pleading to expect from one who is known as a writer for children, and is hardly the assertion one would expect from a purely 'adult' novelist. Townsend's statement is more important for the questions it raises than for the truth it contains, for while clearly the line between children's and adult fiction is blurred and broad, equally clearly there are vast numbers of books that fall very

[1] Jill Paton Walsh, 'The Rainbow Surface', *Times Literary Supplement,* 3 December 1971.
[2] John Rowe Townsend, *A Sense of Story,* Longman, 1971.

definitely on one side or the other. For the sake of examples one might pick, almost at random, Joyce's *Ulysses* and Clive King's *Stig of the Dump*. Now this is not to say that there is nothing in *Stig* that an adult might read with pleasure and profit, nor indeed that there are not bits of *Ulysses* that a child might confidently approach. C.S. Lewis was undoubtedly right to claim that a book that could only be read by a child was a poor children's book, but he might have added that an exclusive diet of children's fiction can hardly be satisfying to an adult, any more than an exclusive diet of the 'available bits' from adult books is a satisfactory diet for a child. An adult reading *Stig* does not read it as a child, full of wonder and delight and discovery, but as one perhaps blandly aware (because it is a rather 'thin' book), of an evocation of childhood, and aware too of some rather naively oblique comments on the Consumer Society. Neither does the adult read *Stig* as he reads an adult book. His mental approach and his expectations would be markedly different.

Is then the distinction we think we discern between *Tom's Midnight Garden* and *The Shrimp and the Anemone,* between *The Piemakers* and *Mill on the Floss,* merely one conditioned in us by publishers anxious to serve their own conveniences? Or are there real differences; are there two distinct general categories, even if the two merge and run together freely at the point of contact? A pot of green and a pot of orange paint might be spilled on the floor. The two pools have a yellow base in common, and where they run together a murky brown is formed that doesn't happily belong to either pot, but he is a fool who cannot distinguish the green from the orange. Unless he's colour-blind. But then the difference is a fact, only he is inadequately equipped to see it.

As between the green and the orange, there are observable differences: children's books are generally shorter; they tend to favour an active rather than a passive treatment, with dialogue and incident rather than description and introspection; child protagonists are the rule; conventions are much used; the story develops within a clear-cut moral schematism which much adult fiction ignores; children's books tend to be optimistic rather than depressive; language is child-oriented; plots are of a distinctive order, probability is often disregarded; and one could go on endlessly talking of magic, and fantasy, and simplicity, and adventure. The point here is not to legislate for essential differences but simply to note observable general orders of differences between the large body of children's fiction and that of adult fiction. The question immediately to be raised is how far these observable differences are inherent rather than accidental or conventional. Must a child's book necessarily be different from an adult book, or are the reasons for the differences merely conventions introduced by publishers, or by teachers, librarians, parents or others who direct choice and influence the supply?

Wherein lies the difference between the two following extracts? The first is from Philippa Pearce's *Tom's Midnight Garden* and the second is from Angus Wilson's *Late Call*.

Only one thing went badly amiss that Thursday. Just as he was getting into bed, he remembered: 'I never wrote to Peter yesterday!'

'Never mind,' said his aunt, tucking him up.

'But I promised to.'

'It's bad to break a promise, but I'm sure you didn't mean to. Luckily, it won't matter very much to Peter. Why, he'll be seeing you the day after tomorrow.'

Tom knew that it did matter. The broken promise was bad enough; but he knew, as well, that Peter would be feeling desperate without his letter. Peter needed all that Tom could write to him, to feed his imaginings—to feed his dreams.

'Write to me more about the garden and Hatty,' he had begged Tom. 'Tell me what you did. . . . Be sure to tell me what you're going to do.'

'Sorry, Pete,' Tom murmured into his pillow, and felt wretched. He hoped that Peter had by now got over the bitterness of this betrayal. Peter went to bed earlier than Tom, so that probably he had already ended his day of disappointment with sleep.

*   *   *

Mrs Longmore put on her white silk nightgown, unloosened her long black hair and sat brushing it before the little stained dressing-table mirror. Then suddenly she thought of something. She opened one of the trunks she had so painfully packed in the afternoon, and rummaging at the side, pulled out a long lemon-coloured piece of tulle. She had worn it one evening round her head, to the little Tuffield girl's great wonder. Now, tiptoeing across the corridor, she entered the Tuffield children's bedroom. She had not somehow expected to find them all sleeping in one large bed, with the eldest girl lying on her stomach in the middle. She was moaning still, but it seemed, in her sleep. Mrs Longmore bent down and placed the chiffon scarf on the hump which she guessed to be the little girl's feet. She was glad to get out of the stuffy, ill-smelling room. It was little enough she had done, God knew, but it was something.

In both the character involved is facing regret. Tom regrets his failure to write to his brother, and the reasons why a letter would have been important are complex; so is the sense of responsibility, of accountability, that it raises. A child reading this passage may well grow in an important dimension of awareness. But though complex and potent, the experience is made available to quite a young child reader by the carefully unobtrusive way Philippa Pearce leads him through it by the hand. Angus Wilson offers very little help. The confusion of regret, culpable blindness, guilt and insensitivity, rationalization, despairing ineffectuality in the face of brutal atavistic emotions (she has been the cause of the little girl being whipped 'till the blood run') is created by Wilson in all its complexity. He has evoked the emotional condition; it is not his function to analyse it and to present the elements separately to the reader. And I think this comes close to the heart of the difference between a children's and an adult novel: a good children's book makes complex experience available to its readers; a good adult book draws attention to the inescapable complexity of experience.

These differences are essential, I think, simply because children think quantitatively differently from adults. The peculiar variety of emotional response in Mrs Longmore simply isn't conceptually accessible to children (and perhaps, in fact, to many adults), and the reason is that the average child has not reached, until the mid-teens at the earliest, a sufficiently advanced stage of conceptual maturity to understand, to grasp, let alone appreciate, such a condition.

Piaget's work on the stages of mental growth is well known. Paul H. Hirst and Richard Peters speak of the work of Kohlberg:

> Children, Kohlberg claims, start by seeing rules as dependent upon power and external compulsion; they then see them as instrumental to rewards and to the satisfaction of their needs; then as ways of obtaining social approval and esteem; then as upholding some ideal order and finally as articulations of social principles necessary for living together with others. Varying contents given to rules are fitted into invariant forms of conceiving rules. Of course, in many cultures there is no progression through to the final stages, the rate of development will be different in different cultures, and in the same culture there are great individual differences. All this can be granted and explained. But his main point is that this sequence in levels of conceiving of rules is constitutive of moral development and that it is a cultural invariant. Also, because of the conceptual relations involved, which are connected with stages of role-taking, it could not occur in any other order.[1]

There are, it seems, whole areas of moral, emotional, and psychological understanding which are beyond the child's cognitive range, exactly as there are physical skills like walking which are dependent on maturational factors. St Paul put it more simply: 'When I was a child, I spoke as a child, I understood as a child. . .' Tom, in pushing at the frontiers of understanding, is exemplary in that he is as aware as one could hope any child might be; Mrs Longmore has regressed into an emotional and rational infantility in order to escape the pain of accountability, and is therefore blameworthy.

If therefore some peculiarly adult emotions and experiences are not accessible to children this does not necessarily mean

[1] Paul H. Hirst and Richard Peters, *The Logic of Education*, Routledge, 1970.

that a writer will find himself excessively restricted in his range nor compelled to simplify experience. Restrictions there are, of course, but then every writer is restricted to some degree by the cultural expectations against which he writes. It has been argued, indeed, that present-day 'adult' writers are peculiarly restricted to themes of personal relationships or to man in society, and that to be free to write of adventure, of fantasy, of initiation and personal growth, to write of a period other than our own, to explore some of the great archetypal experiences such as the quest or the great dichotomous morality patterns, a writer must turn to children's fiction, or to the adult 'pulp' market. 'Keep off sex', it seems, is rather like 'Keep off the grass'. Not so much a restriction as a licence to walk anywhere else you choose. And it has been said that Dickens, were he writing today, would not be expected to command a large adult audience.

But what of simplicity? Is to write in terms of a child's experience to write up experience simplistically? I don't think this need necessarily be so, though of course some writers do just that—some notoriously so, such as Enid Blyton, some because their concern is not principally with individually felt experience but with, say, wider historical themes. Cynthia Harnett is a case in point here. One also thinks of Rosemary Sutcliff, whose concern is with typical, even archetypal experience in distanced, powerfully evoked, historical settings, rather than with the psychological study of one child's experience. Those children who follow Drem's adventures in *Warrior Scarlet* easily sense that this is the story of the runt of every litter that ever was, and that Drem exemplifies a recurring, universal experience. In a sense Drem's story reiterates the experience of every reader, offering comfort and encouragement rather than new knowledge. This is at a far remove from the intensely personal discovery of the complex notion of another's individual worth and sanctity, of the necessary distinction between wishful dreaming and reality, and the responsibilities of reality, the tempering of values in the fire of experience: the discoveries, as I see them, which can be made by a sensitive child reading *A Dog So Small*. There is new knowledge discoverable here; a child might grow in reading it rather than, as it were, consolidate what he already has (and this latter, of course, were no inconsequential thing).

What is one to say, moreover, of the view of life expressed in, for example, *Smith*, by Leon Garfield: is that simplistic? The word hardly seems an apt description for a kaleidoscopic view of fortune and deservings such as Garfield presents. Schematic, I suggest, is the more appropriate word. And in this word, I think, is contained one of the essential differences between an adult's and a child's view of life. By and large adults have effected a bifurcation between the moral and the physical imperatives. But this understanding is itself of fairly recent growth, having its springs in the development of scientific rationality during the last three centuries; and in popular terms perhaps is restricted to presently living generations of 'advanced' countries. A common nineteenth-century European view, in all strata of society, would have been that a moral power could, and frequently did, overrule the physical laws. A personal accident that befell one was not explicable in terms of a chain of physical cause and effect, but as a 'judgement' for some earlier moral failing. This schematic moral view of life is essentially childlike; and what is more, it is inconceivable that one should reach the more sophisticated state of discriminatory thinking about the varieties of cause and effect without going through the more primitive stage of belief that an omnipotent, omnipresent, omniactive power controlled all manifestations. From a child's point of view not only is such a view safe and reassuring, it is also optimistic. Good *will* triumph, and not because it has public support and sympathy (that being almost one of the characteristics of what we call good), but because it *must*. Evil *will* be punished, again not because a prudent society has taken pains to protect itself, but because a benign power reigns.

Part of Leon Garfield's, William Mayne's and others' optimism rests in their acceptance of this schematic view, not, I suggest, as an article of personal belief, but as an appropriate matrix against which to present details of experience for children. In *A Parcel of Trees* Susan wins from the Railways the right of possession of the orchard because on the whole she deserves to. She has proved herself worthy of the heritage.

It isn't merely a conventionally happy ending; no other ending for the child reader would have made sense.

A schematic view of life is then not merely an observable difference between adult and children's literature—it is an essential difference. What of the other observable differences, are they essential too?

Children's books are shorter than adult books. It depends on the age of the child, but it is common sense that the younger the child the less he will be able to grasp and retain, the shorter will be his period of concentration. Indeed, we wouldn't want a child to concentrate on reading all day, believing that varied experience and activity is beneficial. Not much need be made of this. It is obvious that a four or five hundred page novel is something of an acquired taste, something one graduates towards.

More important is the bias towards an active rather than a passive presentation of the material. By active I mean that the text concentrates on dialogue and incident rather than on the more passive mood which characterizes description and reflection. Again it is more obvious: good children's books do follow the rule; those which ignore it risk rejection by the child reader. Children, in their readings as in their lives, are more active than ruminant: it is just happily so. And a skillful writer such as Leon Garfield accepts this, as the following extract from *Smith* shows.

His favourite spot was Ludgate Hill, where the world's coaches, chairs and curricles were met and locked, from morning to night, in a horrible, blasphemous confusion. And here, in one or other of the ancient doorways, he leaned and grinned while the shouting and cursing and scraping and raging went endlessly, hopelessly on—till, sooner or later, something prosperous would come his way. At about half past ten of a cold December morning an old gentleman got furiously out of his carriage. . . .

This is description, but *active* description, loud and colourful: 'met. . .locked. . .confusion. . .leaned and grinned. . .shouting. . .cursing. . .scraping. . .raging. . .' It is achieved in short

bold strokes and quickly moves on again to action: 'an old
gentleman got furiously out of his carriage. . .' Furiously?
Not surprisingly, and in gleeful anticipation the fun begins.
The reader wishes to move in for a closer view, and, being with
Garfield, gets more than he bargained for.

In *A Parcel of Trees* Mayne evokes a languid, summery world
of long and lazy days and slow quest. He unfolds his story
unhurriedly, drowsing and droning, so it seems. But the
impression is deceptive—a retrospective impression. In fact,
the story seldom stands still, and then only for the shortest
passages.

> Susan felt melancholy rise in her like joy. Here she was
> alone, but there was a way back. Here she was not in the
> year that surrounded the rest of the world, but in the first
> year and the last year of time. This vision was perfect. It
> began in the mist, like a dream, and then the sky began to
> be blue overhead, and the mist sank, until the treetops were
> out of it and the sun shone on the apples. Then it was warm
> on her face and warm on the wall, and then was slanting
> across the grass and mottling it with the indistinct profiles
> of the branches above. The sunshine showed in the still
> heavy air, and the shadows were hollow, so that the air
> was veined. The day began to be hot. Susan thought she must
> have been out all morning, and went back in again, hoping
> not to be late for dinner.

Back to action again! Though the sun has been active and
changing throughout this relatively still passage, Mayne's art
is to give the impression of languidness without lulling the
reader to sleep. He does this, among other means, by the
obliquity of his dialogue.

> Mr. Ferriman looked into the shop on his way home at
> midday.
> 'Burwen rock,' he said, and went at once.
> 'Caerphilly Castle,' said Rosemary.
> 'Don't stock it,' said Mum, shaking her head, 'I don't

believe it's made. Weston-Super-Mare is what he's thinking
of.'

'Tom Royal,' said Susan. 'That's the name of something.
He doesn't mean seaside rock.'

'Are you sure?' said Mum. 'We'll go and look at Burwen
Hill and be certain.'

She went outside. Susan went with her. Burwen Hill, with
its rocky top, stood out clear against the paler edge of the
sky. 'That's it,' said Mum. 'It looks no different, so he
must mean what you think.'

'He does,' said Susan.

There is with Mayne a sense of a slow, deep, steady current
of understanding underlying the lighter surface show. The
surface carries the reader buoyantly; the undercurrent it is
which is remembered. And this, of course, is Mayne's strength,
this hiding of the introspective, reflective quality in dialogue
and incident.

'It must be water,' said David. 'It's water rocking a stone
about, or a boulder or something, and then it's going to
break out here and be another spring. At least, it won't be
another spring, because there isn't one in this field, even
though it's called High Keld. This must be the High Keld
itself, and it dried up and went. Now it's coming back.'

'Oh well,' said Keith. 'I'd rather have badgers.'

'Of course,' said David. 'Of course.'

What a wealth of private understanding, of a history of
reflection, of a scale of values, of a way of life shared is conveyed in those short strokes, 'Of course. . .Of course.'

Another major difference between the children's and the
adult novel is the almost invariable use in children's fiction of
the child central character, which rarely appears in adult fiction,
and then most frequently from the adult point of view as a
recollection of childhood (L. P. Hartley is the great exception
here, and perhaps Joyce Cary). Wallace Hildick says that:

Assuming. . .that identification is the key to one's enjoyment of a story and to the refreshment and sustenance to be had from it, it is possible to see why so many children's books deal with child characters. A child *can* identify with adult characters—but only if they are sympathetically drawn and simple enough. By this I am not suggesting that the only adult characters a child can get under the skin of are simple-*minded* ones. Quite complex adults—adults who can be presumed to have complex personalities by virtue of their positions in life, like kings, prime ministers, witches, wizards and wise old nurses—abound in fairy tales of high quality. But in such a context only single aspects of their personalities are presented at a time: the predominantly greedy become greed itself, the generally envious become envy, the honest honesty, the brave bravery—and so on.[1]

The central character of the novel must be created in the illusion of fullness, roundness—must be made to 'live', and that almost necessarily means must be shown as a complex being. There are complexities of adult being that are beyond the comprehension of a child, and an author is left with little choice; either he writes of simple, child-like, adult characters (for example George and Lennie in Steinbeck's *Of Mice and Men*—one of those awkward books that defies the classifications I am dealing with here), or if he wants to draw a complex character he must draw a child. This, I think, accounts for the recurring similarities between many of William Mayne's adult characters. They have their individual traits, of course, but they are, many of them, remarkably similar too. And for children adults *are* alike. They have the common quality of being adult, which perhaps looms larger than all their differences in a child's eye.

Adults are, however, often conveniently absent from the world of the children's story. Either they are ill, or they are too busy to notice, or they are misty background figures lost in their own tea and conversation. George Layton dismisses the mother in *The Balaclava Story* with the economical line, 'Well, it's my bingo night, so make yourself some cocoa before you go to bed.'

Whatever the design, the convention is that they don't in-

[1] E.W. Hildick, *Children and Fiction*, Evans, 1970.

trude for a large part of the story, and *conventions*, of one sort or another, are an essential ingredient of children's fiction. There is, I think, a certain assurance to be found, and also a certain necessary, aesthetically pleasing sense of the predictability (as in music) in meeting a story that runs on predictable lines.

The old conventions, therefore, are much used. The quest is a favourite. But this is really, in the hands of a clever writer, the general form of the story rather than its substance. Within the 'form' of the quest the experience can be unique. Compare *Ravensgill*, where the object of the quest is unknown until it is found, with *A Parcel of Trees*, where the ostensible object is always in sight, and what is really discovered is a sense of place, and continuing time and change and adjustment, a sense of community.

Travel in time is another recurring convention. This varies from the use of the idea of time travel to produce simply another exotic locale, to the use of time to explore a philosophical concept (*Earthfasts*) or an emotional one (*Tom's Midnight Garden*). In many respects, the use of the time travel convention is similar to the convention of historical setting. Again it can be a mere exotic locale (C. S. Forester's *Hornblower* stories), or the deliberate distancing of a story to a relatively simpler and less cluttered time, where the issues can be presumed to be clearer and bolder. Again, one thinks of Rosemary Sutcliff and Cynthia Harnett. A geographical distancing, as in *Walkabout* or *Lord of the Flies*, can be used for a similar purpose. Initiation into manhood, or womanhood, is another much-used convention or theme, but this can vary from the relatively simple task and achievement outline of *Warrior Scarlet*, to the complexities of self-discovery forced upon the protagonists of *Walkabout* or *To the Wild Sky*. The initiation can be into reality-based self-confidence, as in the case of the plain girl, Maggie, in Zindel's *My Darling, My Hamburger*, or into the responsibilities and self-abnegating role-playing of young womanhood as in *Marianne Dreams*, or into self-knowledge, as in *A Dog So Small*.

The rise and fall of fortune is another favourite theme (*Black Hearts in Battersea*) which on occasions can be neatly inverted as in *Devil-in-the-Fog*, with its happy 'riches to rags' theme. But, of course, children's fiction has no monopoly of conventions, though it might be thought richer in available conventions than much adult fiction which retreads the 'boy meets girl' theme, or the 'eternal triangle' theme, endlessly.

There are other aspects of plot which characterize children's stories. Not many threads run through the story. There will be twists and turns and reversals as much and as often as you like, but the main thread, or threads if it is a two-in-hand, must be kept going and not be held up by sub-plots rising and dying across the path of the action. *Devil-in-the-Fog* is, I think, a good example of a plot running smoothly two-in-hand. The story of George Tweet-Dexter and the story of Captain Richard trot along comfortably together to a final resolution which draws them together satisfactorily.

There are possibilities of growth in the plot. If the hero emerges substantially the same as he began the book, then the story has very little but romance to offer. Nicholas Tucker refers to the value of building something of the unknown into the known areas of the plot: stretching the child's knowledge, especially his self-knowledge, or extending the story beyond the reader's expectations. He instances *The Intruder* of John Rowe Townsend which, he says, starts off very black and white, but the colours merge and dimensions of uncertainty enter and force Arnold Haithwaite to adjust and grow.[1] *Smith* would be another fine example of colours continually changing and merging and forcing independent reappraisal onto the young hero. Tucker is right, I think, and Joan Robinson hopelessly confused when she says,

> Before. . .making judgments we must start with some basic assumptions. And we can't arrive at those by just thinking about them. They are emotionally based, which is why I am only interested in books which, apart from helping myself, may help children in their growing up.[2]

Judgments that are emotionally based, far from helping growth, will just precisely retard it. The system is closed. Emo-

[1] *Cle 9*, November 1972. (See p. 177, this collection.)
[2] *Cle 6*, November 1971.

tions and judgments both must be based, if they are to be capable of development, on increasing knowledge, on growing understanding, on confrontations with the details and truth of experience, and not just emotional reaction to it. That would be to have Tom emerge from his midnight garden with no more than a feeling of regret for a passing dream, instead of a growth in understanding of the meaning of time and change and loss.

Such growth is usually linked with the optimism of children's literature, upon which I have already touched. I think however that it is as well to recognize that this optimism is perhaps as much a part of the cultural traditions of Christendom as it is an essential ingredient of children's fiction. Adult literature today tends often to be depressive simply because ours is an optimistic culture, and optimism is so often betrayed. In other cultures which are perhaps more melancholy, or fatalistic, other sorts of children's literature might be written, but optimism is ingrained in our habits and traditions of thought. This is why I think that the newer sub-Salinger writers, such as Zindel, despite their virtues of freshness and an authentic teenage voice are on the whole unsuitable for children. There is such a cynical, depressive quality throughout Zindel's books, which seems to me to be destructive of values before values have properly had time to form. It is the depression I would want to protect emergent minds from, rather than the promiscuity. For even the sexual adventures of his young heroes and heroines are presented in a depressive light, and this presentation of sexuality arguably is as potentially harmful as direct licentiousness. So though Zindel obviously understands the confusion and amorality of teenagers and their frequent failure to associate consequences with actions, rather better than does K.M. Peyton, I feel the work of the latter is preferable because of its underlying optimism, even if it is sometimes clumsily handled (the professor, deus ex machina, of *Pennington's Seventeenth Summer*, for example), although Peyton's language does not have the same adolescent ring as Zindel's.

For at its best, Zindel's language does provide an illustration of the peculiar qualities of writing that distinguish good children's fiction. In this passage from *I Never Loved Your Mind*, he manages that awkward mixture of irony, strained posing, uncertainty of touch, throw-away affectation and hollow pretentiousness and ingenuous charm, that gaucherie that *is* adolescence:

> I remember regaining consciousness (I only passed out once before in my life, and that was last summer when I was bombed at Lake George and went water-skiing at midnight with a lantern in my teeth) and still thinking I was unconscious because when I opened my eyes, I couldn't see anything. It took me a minute of blinking before I realized I was staring at a white ceiling. Anybody else would have been relieved they hadn't croaked, but I let out a scream. It was a little, manly scream, like the kind an actor lets out when he's playing the movie role of an archaeologist who pooh-poohs the mummy's curse but the mummy gets him anyway. I knew I was looking at a white ceiling, but I was scared because the thought crossed my mind that maybe that's what death was—one big white glossy ceiling.

Eleanor Cameron, in *The Green and Burning Tree*, talks about 'an elusive quality (of language) . . . it may be its flavour, tone, atmosphere, or its force of association, all of which have deeply to do with meaning.'[1] One can see immediately how 'right' is the text of Sendak's *Where the Wild Things Are*, for example. Again, consider this extract from *Black Hearts in Battersea*, by Joan Aiken:

> 'Mr. Cobb,' said Simon that evening as he mended the springs of a lady's perch-phaeton. 'What would you do if you thought you had discovered a Hanoverian plot?'
> Mr. Cobb lowered the wash leather with which he was polishing the panels and regarded Simon with a very shrewd expression. 'Me boy,' he said, 'it's all Lombard Street to a China orange that I'd turn a blind eye and do nothing about it. Yes, yes, I know—' raising a quelling hand— 'I know the Hanoverians are a crew of fire-breathing traitors who want to turn good King James, bless him, off the throne and bring in some flighty German boy. But, I ask you, what do they

[1] Eleanor Cameron, *The Green and Burning Tree*, Little, 1969.

actually do? Nothing. It's all a lot of talk and moonshine, harmless as a kettle on a guinea-pig's tail. Why trouble about them when they trouble nobody?'

Simon wondered whether Mr. Cobb would think them so harmless if he were to see the contents of the Twites' cellar. But just as he was opening his mouth to speak the Chelsea church clock boomed out the hour of nine and he had to hurry off to Battersea Castle.

and the appropriateness is obvious. In this example there is raciness, there is fun, there is inventiveness and a mad kind of logic— 'harmless as a kettle on a guinea-pig's tail' —and the plot is effortlessly forwarded, time moves on. It is as easy to pick good as bad examples. But why are some uses not appropriate? Vocabulary might be too remote (though a few long words will often add to the fun of language), the concepts it handles too abstract. A child's most telling condemnation often is, 'It's boring!', and perhaps there it is. The language must have an attractive or interesting personality of its own. It might be a benign adult voice (*Tom's Midnight Garden*), or the authentic voice of childhood (*There Is a Happy Land*). There will perhaps be musical qualities, rhythms, unexpected moments of delight, variations in texture. Eleanor Cameron quotes Kipling:

It was indeed a Superior Comestible (that's magic) and he put it on the stove because *he* was allowed to cook on that stove, and he baked it and he baked it till it was all done brown and smelt most sentimental.

Impossible to lay down rules. Perhaps it springs from a writer's caring for his tale and caring to set it down well. What one misses in the following extract from a story in the magazine *Fab 208* is precisely this sense of caring; one regrets also the missed opportunities:

It was a hot sunny afternoon and the end of another failure day. I didn't think much about the failure, I was used to all that. It was one of the conditions of my life and

I had to live with it. But it was a long climb up the hill to the common. The brown paper carrier bag was heavy and the string was biting into my fingers, so I changed hands and took a look inside it. It wasn't groceries I was carrying. Nothing so sensible. Being me and my daffy sort of universe it had to be a cat inside the carrier bag.

I want finally to say something about probability, the last of the 'observable differences' mentioned at the outset of this article. To say that probability is not terribly important for a child is really only another way of saying that it looms large for an adult. The adult's habit of rational enquiry and explanation gets in the way of enjoyment of the book with improbabilities written into it. But it seldom occurs to children to seek rational explanation of some parts of the plot, probable or improbable. The world of the story is there, it is given, and is accepted as a schematically coherent whole. To listen to a group of adults frantically searching for a rational explanation of time in *Tom's Midnight Garden*— 'Is it happening *now* in Mrs . Bartholomew's dream?' 'Then how can Abel see Tom?' 'Are they real skates or imaginary ones—which are the imaginary pair?' —is to realize that they, like Uncle Allen, have quite simply failed to understand. The explanation is conveyed in a metaphor, not a logical system of relationships:

> He had longed for someone to play with and for somewhere to play; and that great longing, beating about unhappily in the big house, must have made its entry into Mrs Bartholomew's dreaming mind and had brought back to her the little Hatty of long ago.

The child reader who accepts the 'thirteenth hour' as being as unnecessary of explanation as any of the everyday phenomena described in the book is operating more totally in the world of the novel than the unfortunate adult hindered from full response to the experience by his shackling habit of rational enquiry. Adults, indeed, may make intrusive interpreters for the child reader, for it would seem that a child's book (and I hope I have established that there is such a thing) is one a child can enter and need no other guide than the author.

From *Children's literature in education*, No. 10, March 1973

Reading Children's Novels:
Notes on the Politics of Literature

Fred Inglis

Fred Inglis was a school teacher for some years, and is a lecturer in the advanced studies division of the Bristol University School of Education. He contributed to the Schools Council's research project on Children's Reading Interests and has written several books, including The Englishness of English Teaching *and* Ideology and the Imagination.

READING FICTION, like watching television, is not something which you do by yourself. It is a transaction. It involves at least the story-teller and you listening to him: but further, since a man is both himself and his history (and himself *because of* his history), it is the conversation between two histories and between the two odd beings who give those histories shape and meaning. Reading fiction has a total context, like any other human action, and while it is always impossible to recover that total context, at least we should remember that it is always there. One way of reminding ourselves is to change our modes of understanding; when we understand things differently, we value them differently. There is a cue for any understanding of human experience to be taken from children's novels.

In this paper, I want to think hard about the relation of the adults who write and choose novels for children to the experience and the art which renders it; I want, that is, to look at what we as adults—as parents, teachers, librarians *and* as novelists—decide we want to tell our children. And children's novels,

157

after more than a century of such writing, and at a time when
more and better children's fiction is available than ever before,
provide a developed and distinctive subject for inquiry. To
read them closely and intelligently is to launch a sustained
and collaborative inquiry into the institutionalized fantasy
which fiction is. It is a social, sociable, heavily conventional
means of exploring and defining our fantasies and their relation
to our realities. Even though we tend to read novels in a rather
isolated, absorbed way, we are immitigably engaged in a social
and cultural transaction—with the author and with the sense
we have of our social identity. Consequently to study fiction
(and, being teachers, to study children's fiction) is to stand at
the intersection of various perspectives, and to stand there in
an attempt to sort out some bearings, bearings which will help
chart the main question of humane and conscious teaching—
where does the essential life of a society flow? Where is full
life in the present maintained? Whereabouts does our culture
renew and transmit itself?

There is no knowing of course whether the area of life which
we choose will reward inquiry, but even if we return with a
bleak and desolate report—'no life there'—we know, to that
extent, better where we are. We are then able to take bearings
as to value and significance from a more precisely drawn map
of our culture. Clearly we don't expect children's fiction at
the present time to justify such a negative report. Clearly, too,
there appear to be many familiar routes into the territory. We
know, now, how to handle and weigh out fiction. Well, that is
right. We must begin where we can. But this familiarity of
material may be itself deceptive, for there are accents, procedures and sightlines that I propose to take up which modify
our literary-critical appraisals in radical ways. The special nature
of children's novels makes them relevant.

At a time when there is widespread recognition that we
must redraw the boundaries of our intellectual properties
(curriculum reform), English studies provide us with a grammar
and a vocabulary which will permit such redistribution. The
language of English studies allows us to raise matters of life
and death with dignity and conviction. It has permitted its

students to draw connections between a work of literature and its genesis in a society. But its own historical genesis equipped it with a number of reach-me-down stereotypes about reading fiction and ways in which fiction gets written, which are cramped and ungenerous. If we come to children's fiction without at first being in too much of a hurry to read as critics, we may see what familiar critical remarks are dismissive but inappropriate. Now I am absolutely clear that, responsible as we are to the life of our society in its fiction and in its children, we must at some stage get our value judgments right about children's fiction, as about adult fiction. But to report accurately from this segment of our culture requires a novel series of procedures. In a muddled way we recognize this. We come to read children's fiction with an eye on our literary notions of a classic tradition. At the same time we keep at the back of our minds vaguely pedagogic notions of psychological and linguistic development. And even more vaguely, sociological echoes of stratification theory and class bias in literature drift somewhere across our imaginations. Each of these preoccupations rises at times to the top of our consciousness. Half of our feelings, tangled in psychology—conscientiously anxious cliches about class differences and subcultures, and that rather half-baked, soft-middled, low-keyed humanitarianism which passes for a value system amongst English teachers—pushes us towards saying 'let the child find and choose his own books in his own good time; my books aren't necessarily his books'. The other half, under the impulse of the great tradition and the moralism which as index of the strength of English studies so widely penetrates school, university and college teaching, pushes us on to say, 'Here are fine books; read them; they'll do you good'. The tension between a vivid sense of social justice and individual values and a no less keen response to a continuing tradition and a common destiny is the source of our moral (and teaching) energy, as it is of many contradictions and confusions. To see this is to abandon the arid dichotomy between 'child- and subject-centred teaching' which in turn gives rise (on the Left, as it were) to a lot of rather canting rhetoric about the privacy of the child, and on the other side (the Right) to the stiff-lipped defence of set readers, *explications de texte* and salutary hard work on the notes.

These complex forces come into subtle and irresistible play when we, as teachers and students, decide to read children's fiction. We shall be reporting from a segment of our culture—children's experience—to which we give a quite unprecedented attention. We are now at a high point of enthusiasm in the study of children's experience, a point which would have looked to its earliest instigators, Blake, say, or Rousseau, manic in its intensity. To understand and to judge this state of affairs is to say something of final importance about ourselves and the meanings we give our lives. It is to face a question of which the political resonance is as deep-seated as it is inescapable: what is the life of an individual child worth? Or to put the same question in another way: what is the life of an individual children's novel worth?

We are going back to the total context within which a fiction has its genesis and is read. We try to recover that context. Or rather, since that can't be done, we change the set of highly selective frameworks with which we have learned to understand and value literature for another set. And then we find, inevitably, that different contours are thrown into relief by our new procedure. We value the novel differently for seeing and interpreting it differently. The emphasis for our purposes is changed if we put the novel down into a process: a process of exchange and transaction. That is to say, we want in what will be an inevitably patchy way to understand the interplay between the elements of our study: between reader and author, reader and his social experience, author and his social experience. We try to see how they know (or read) what they know (and read). In trying to perceive these contexts we must draw on vocabularies and stand in positions which have been unfamiliar.

The second stage of adequate cultural inquiry is to relate what we study to our ideas of social and moral change. If the first stage concentrates (in reading fiction) on the expectations of authors and readers towards each other, the second stage may roughly be said to apply itself to the experience shared and what each contributor makes of it. It is here that we raise explicitly political questions about the relation of the shared experience to its society, and questions too about the discrepancy between what the author makes of his experience and what the readers make of it, in their various ways. A further effort at detachment is needed in order to throw into relief the fact that we are adults appraising the significance of these forms of cultural life—these children's novels—partly on our own terms but partly on children's. That is to say, we must know in as inclusive and searching a way as possible what it means to us to invite children (as children or as incipient adults?) to read these books and not others. And as we become conscious of the need for this knowledge, our intention must then be as Leavis says 'to make fully conscious and articulate the sense of value which "places" the book', to bring to an unusually developed intensity the specific gravity of the work, its moral weight. This is the final stage of a continuous process and of course it penetrates the whole enterprise. Not that the value judgment is itself anything to settle for finally; like any judgment worth having it is subject to 'testing and retesting and wider experience'. Nor is it, as by this stage of my argument should be clear, a matter of simply deciding whether the book is any good. What we hope to have done instead is to provide as rich an account as possible of the context within which the work occurs and within which our act of valuing must also take place. We cannot, at this time of day, ascribe a timeless value to a work or see it with the eyes of God. The work and our judgment of it exist within coordinates of time and space. This is absolutely not to say that acts of valuation lose themselves in a meaningless jumble of relativist signals, any more than it is to say we can make arbitrary contemporary meanings out of past works But we find in literature what we need. We take from literature what we are looking for. The integrity rests in being sure that what we are looking for is there.

The study of children's novels catches us at an exceptionally important moment. It is the moment at which we decide what we as teachers and as novelists want to tell our children. The novels which we recommend to our children represent the organization of history as we want children to see it. And 'history', it is worth pointing out, 'may be servitude', or 'history may be freedom', but in either case it is not simply something which happened once upon a time, but is the action, the living, inexorable principle, of the past in the present. To speak like this constitutes a strenuous effort to resist the evils of specialization, themselves the products of an accelerating technology, and this means in turn carrying our efforts to understand into many areas of cultural life, and carrying them there in liaison with other specialists. 'Down these mean streets a man must go.' Well, the streets I propose to go down aren't very mean: amongst the houses of fiction I intend to visit only Rosemary Sutcliff's. At the same time I would like to maintain liaison with a student of literature who keeps up his politics, and beforehand it is timely to summarize what a social psychologist tells us about the transaction between readers and their authors.

Denys Harding starts out from the main premise that reading a novel is an inescapably *social* action. Our response (and children's) to situations in a novel is instantly evaluative, though the value judgment may change with time. For the novel (*les nouvelles*), perhaps more than any other artistic form, makes nonsense of the distinction between literature and life. Novels cannot ever be said, as it were, to lie along a scale at one end of which is raw, day-to-day living and at the other heavily stylized and diagrammatic novels like Ivy Compton-Burnett's, or semantic jokes like *Tristram Shandy* or over-elaborate, occasional verse like the eighteenth-century pastoralists. If we are faithful to our experience, we surely recognize that novels occur to us much in the same way as gossip, anecdotes, large areas of conversation, even larger areas of experience in which we take part as onlookers. Think how readily we watch a couple of people, or a group, in some kind of conflict. As we watch them we come to a complex evaluation of what has happened, guessing at what some people feel while others make their feelings explicit in words or gesture. Similarly, when a colleague or friend tells us some piece of school or college gossip, we instantly range ourselves sympathetically with various sides in (say) a dispute, not only feeling with our friends but also against other factions, yet able at the same time to imagine one's opponents' feelings and in our sympathy feeling *for* our friends as well as with them, feeling protective, irritated, surprised. Thus we are socially involved in such events, even in gossip across a cup of coffee.

The nature of this involvement is not just analogous to the involvement we feel with the characters in a novel; it is at many points coincident. In either situation we are never 'mere' or passive listeners or spectators; our range of interest may extend or modify itself as a result of what we watch. We never see only a reflection of that range thrown back at us. Our psychology is endlessly busy, moving swiftly from reality to memory to fantasy and back to supposition. We constantly imagine, evaluate and discard possibilities other than those in front of us, and we perform this astonishingly rapid filtering and sorting operation during a dialogue with our interlocutor and the rest of his audience. If he is really there in front of us relating what the pupil said to the principal, the dialogue is spoken aloud, and our reactions to the story, our appeals to the other listeners and our interjections into the story become part of the total experience which we recollect and weigh up.

A similar dialogue is going on when we listen to an author, even a dead one. We hold a silently evaluative conversation with him and make it clear by our appeals to other readers in discussion that we are looking for endorsement of our responses. ('This is so, isn't it?' 'Yes, but. . . .') Even if we never attend a formal discussion we still make the appeals to a shared and social context of experience, as we read. At the same time therefore as we respond to, sympathize with, like or dislike characters in a narration, we see them alongside the author, as his voice selects and distorts and renders. Even very small children are sometimes aware of this refracted relationship with the people in the story. They ask 'Was it really true or are you having me on?' or 'Why does it say that?' Quite often, for example, Beatrix Potter or A. A. Milne break the storytelling convention, or give it a double focus within the tale itself. Even a four or five-year-old can be quite clear that fiction is 'a convention for enlarging the scope of the discussions we have with each other about what may befall' (Harding's words). So a four-year-old knows that Peter Rabbit is naughty in ways that he may be naughty, but is in danger of much more drastic reprisals—becoming a rabbit pie for Mrs MacGregor. The four-year-old, like the adult, discusses with the author his imaginary and offered judgments, and may well reject them, either out of an intense sympathy or by being bored. The discussion with the author, and the subsequent discrimination, will be according to the limits of more or less advanced criteria.

These processes are immediately recognizable. It is important to remember that they are not truistic. English students and teachers at all levels have for so long made such confident play with very different models of the psychology of reading that there needs to be an explicit challenge made. Conventional teaching accounts of reading behaviour deploy as their essential concepts 'vicarious experience', 'identification', 'escape', 'light entertainment', 'wish-fulfillment', 'fantasy'.

But a novel is not vicarious experience; it is reported and (perhaps) imaginary experience. We do not 'identify' with the characters; we respond in complex ways with, to, and for them out of the framework of all our prior experience, literary or not. No reader imagines that his alleged desires are gaining actual satisfaction. Rather, what is happening is that his desire for affection or romantic love, for adventure, prestige or cheerfulness, defines itself in a new context. The reader discusses with the novelist the possibilities of giving his desires statement in a social setting. This is not to say that the level of such discussion may not be embarrassingly low, nor that the desires themselves may not be horrifying. But this is not at all the same as saying that the reader identifies with a character and lives through vicarious experience. We are not satisfying our desires in any fiction (obviously including TV); we are defining them. And it is worth remarking that to relinquish one's desires, fantasies and aspirations is to give up hopes for oneself as a free man and in a profound sense to release one's grasp upon life.

As a function of our humanity, then, we constantly imagine entry into other people's lives and derive from these excursions an extension of what we imagine to be possible in life. We do this with snippets of overheard conversation or glimpses through half-curtained windows, with three-line paragraphs in

Titbits, or the evening paper, with fragments of news on TV or radio. These scraps alert us to human possibilities, trivial or important, which have occurred to other people but knowledge of which develops, refines or coarsens our personal maps of humanity and our own significance upon them. To an expanding degree as we experiment with more adult and intelligent literature we live through the same process. Our study of the cultural life which flows through a novel must therefore include our imaginative estimate of what the novel means to the life of its various readers. If the novel is institutionalized fantasy, what do we learn of that society which at the first hand generates the fantasy in an individual writer, and at the second takes the new work back to itself and makes it part of continuing social experience? Perhaps I can go over this social psychology again before laying another scanning grid across the inquiry.

1. Reading a novel is a social transaction.
2. Novels or any fiction are a continuous part of social experience.
3. Reading a novel is very similar to being an onlooker of human actions.
4. We do not 'identify' with characters in a novel nor live through wish-fulfilment; we respond to a total situation which may clarify or confuse our wishes.
5. Reading novels, like any other experience, is evaluative.
6. In our rapid and elaborate processes of evaluation, we understand ourselves to be considering new human potentialities in the company of the author.

Last, a further note on the idea of 'escape'. I cannot now discuss the multifoliate purposes to which we put our reading— quite literally, the uses of literacy. But I suggest that the idea of escape is often too happily used in the condemnation of what are obviously poor works of literature. We may 'escape' from our immediate world into a much darker and more horrifying one; 'escape' may be narcotic or reassuring. When we escape with the most intense relief into a novel, it may be that the novel is a relief because it is much more intelligent and rewarding than the tedious staff meeting from which we have 'escaped'. We regularly need respite when repairs (or repression and evasion) can go on. 'Repair time' is a valuable concept in any developmental graph worth having. We cannot say any work is necessarily a form of 'escape', though we can say a good deal about its quality. We can speak censoriously of escape as regression only when the activity is self-deceiving, a deliberate manipulation of our humanity in order to alter feelings without altering conditions, a pursuit of a fraudulent solace in which we purposely retreat from our usual level of cultural interest and stamina.

These last remarks may too often be fired point-blank at teachers and parents reading children's literature. For it is necessarily true that the present flowering of children's litera- ture is, in its genesis and sociology, an adult product: the conditions of production, distribution and consumption are created by adults. It seems to me further true that the enthus- iasm amongst many adult readers for Alan Garner, Henry Treece, William Mayne, Philippa Pearce, John Christopher, Cynthia Harnett, Rosemary Sutcliff and the rest is often a disguised taste for *Kitsch*, for the thoroughgoing, rank, tasty meat and gravy of an old-fashioned bestseller. For reasons which are surely part of our study, a number of intelligent adults may be said in their wholesale enthusiasm for some children's novelists to be reading well below their proper· standards. This is best exemplified in the extraordinary pop- ularity of J.R.R. Tolkien (most of all when he writes allegedly for adults), but I am taking the altogether more distinguished Rosemary Sutcliff for my example. One opens any of her novels at random, and finds at once these late Gothic reson- ances, the misty accents and landscapes of an iambic rhetoric which wrings the solar plexus of all those of us brought up on Rider Haggard, Kipling, Stevenson, Scott and Sir Henry Newbolt:

> They looked back when they had gone a few paces, and saw him standing as they had left him, already dimmed with mist, and outlined against the drifting mist beyond. A half- naked, wild-haired tribesman, with a savage dog against his knee; but the wide, well-drilled movement of his arm as he

raised it in greeting and farewell was all Rome. It was the parade-ground and the clipped voice of trumpets, the iron discipline and the pride. In that instant Marcus seemed to see, not the barbarian hunter, but the young centurion, proud in his first command, before ever the shadow of the doomed legion fell on him. It was to that centurion that he saluted in reply.

Then the drifting mist came between them.

Listen to her fatal mastery of plangent cadences:

> The murmur of prayers in the Latin tongue reached him in the quiet. It was the first time that he had known a Christian place of worship since the summer when his world had fallen to ruins. He remembered all at once the grey stone preaching cross in the hills, and behind all the silence of the service the deep contented drone of bees in the bell heather; he remembered, as he had not remembered them for years, Priscus and Priscilla, who would have shared their cloak with him. . . . slowly the sore hot place of his heart grew quiet within him.

Think of her boldly drawn villains, men born straight into the dynasties of Sapper's Carl Peterson, Buchan's Dominic Medina, Baroness Orczy's silkily impassive French inquisitor:

> 'Ah yes, I had forgotten that you both contrived to come alive, together, out of that fight.' Vadir's light eyes flicked him, like the careless flick of a whiplash, and came to rest on the long white spear-scar that ran out of his torn sleeve. His pale brows rose a little, and the mobile mouth lifted into a half smile. 'I have never seen you stripped. How many scars the like to that one are there on your back?' he asked softly. 'Or can you perhaps fly faster than a spear?'

The doglike subordinates, taciturn, resourceful Men Friday, Chingachgook to the hero's Natty Bumpo (a part of Rosemary Sutcliff's development is the story of the subordinate-become-hero in *The Lantern Bearers*):

> Esca tossed the slender papyrus roll on to the cot, and
> set his own hands over Marcus's. 'I have not served the
> Centurion because I was his slave,' he said, dropping un-
> consciously into the speech of his own people. 'I have served
> Marcus, and it was not slave-service . . . . My stomach will
> be glad when we start on this hunting trail.'

Remember the commanding simplicity of the dramatic climaxes
in the novels: Aquila's lighting the symbolic beacon on Rich-
borough tower in *The Lantern Bearers*; the death of the villain
Vadir on the god's horse in *Dawn Wind*; the return of the Eagle
in the middle of the initiation rites in *The Eagle of the Ninth*.
Behind these moments stand Kipling's memorable tableaux
(the late Imperial subalterns of the Wall in *Rewards and Fairies*,
the powerful evocation of Sussex in July right through *Puck
of Pook's Hill*); and before him the great nineteenth-century
melodramatists—Walter Scott, Marie Edgeworth, Charlotte
Brontë, the early George Eliot—the scaffold scene in *Adam
Bede*, the flood in *The Mill on the Floss*; supremely, the master
of such moments, Dickens; the death of Bill Sykes; the house
split down the middle in *Little Dorrit*; Lady Deadlock in
Tom All Alone; Sidney Carton's execution; Magwitch recap-
tured; on and on, an incomparable roll-call.

In a much smaller way, of course, Rosemary Sutcliff stands
in this line. Now there is no doubt that a great novelist com-
mands as part of his qualifying equipment a popular rhetoric—
Lawrence is the great example of this century. But Rosemary
Sutcliff's muted trumpets do not have the orchestration of an
authentic popular voice; one can hear in most of the examples
the prose ring with a certain wistfulness; a faded, regretful
glimmer plays over its surfaces and rhythms, and her popularity
amongst school teachers seems marked more by a need to hear
these antique harmonies again rather than by a fully mature
response to a great gust of elemental feeling—the kind we
respond to in Mrs Dombey's death, that astonishing combina-
tion of horror, prurience, pathos and magnificence.

> 'Mamma!' said the child.
> The little voice, familiar and dearly loved, awakened some
> show of consciousness, even at the ebb. For a moment, the

closed eyelids trembled, and the nostrils quivered, and the faintest shadow of a smile was seen.

'Mamma!' the child cried, sobbing aloud, 'Oh dear Mamma! Oh dear Mamma!' The doctor gently brushed the scattered ringlets of the child aside from the face and mouth of the mother. Alas how calm they lay there; how little breath there was to stir them! Thus, clinging fast to that slight spar within her arms, the mother drifted out upon the dark and unknown sea that rolls round all the world.

The collusion of writer and audience which we need to study in the case of a children's novelist is perhaps explicable by comparison with Dickens, but only in a very much more local way. Yet this is where we might start: by comparing Rosemary Sutcliff to bestsellers of the past, and by defining her relationship with a certain social group, a group which contains but goes beyond her audience. For the explanatory relationships between society and culture are not only a matter of content. We shall of course learn a great deal by drawing up a system of the typical features of bestselling or popular literature or of the characteristics of a social system. But we shall learn more about the life of a society (and its unnoticed deaths) by trying to see the nonconscious structures which shape a writer's work and are the inescapable product of his having written within the framework of a particular social group.

When I say nonconscious this does not mean subconscious. The English mode of criticism tends to overestimate the individual in understanding the significance of a work of literature. Thus we undertake the fruitless business of charting the influences of one writer upon another. Such studies see meaning as linked only to biography and psychology. In addition we must scrutinize the contexts of a novel for its significant structure, the shape of which fixes the arc of a writer's gesture, much as it determines the inflections of everyday speech. To understand the situation of a present-day, liberal-spirited teacher with a training in the humanities and a struggling sense of history is to understand the genesis of Rosemary Sutcliff's novels. It is also to draw in the heavily political overtones of any literary study.

We learned once at our critic's knee that we must never

look for simple social messages in a novel, and that if a novel were set upon by its ideology, so much the worse for the novel. Trusting the tale and not the teller was a way of putting it, not very satisfactorily. Times have changed, and as they have done so, it has become clear that such a way of talking about literature was itself time-serving: for to study a novel as *immanence* —as rendering all its meaning from within (set up in front of a painted 'background')—amputated many of the strong political and social veins which gave it blood and life. A novel without ideology is like experience without knowledge. Or an action without belief. It could not mean anything. So when we shied off the politics, what we jibbed at were *those* particular politics, as in conjugating the well-known verb: 'I am moderate; you are staunch; he is rabid.' The liberal teacher may not think of herself as looking for politics in these children's novels but I think that that is what she finds, caught in that grander music which seems to have been extinguished in the universe of adult novels—to have been absent indeed in modern literature since the death of Yeats. There is a need to hear those notes struck which have gone mute in the rest of literature, to find a prose which moves with ceremony and amplitude, with a portly courtesy and a forgotten grace.

I cannot help it if this analysis comes near the complaints of letters to *The Daily Telegraph*—'The age of chivalry is dead'; Rosemary Sutcliff is the best of a mixed group of writers who register objection to a gaunt and toneless language, inept as to rhetoric, graceless as to manner. These writers have no academy to sustain them, and their only set of beliefs is that pale, anxious and rinsed-out liberalism which is the best most of us can do by way of a contemporary world picture. What therefore comes through as the strongest impulse to feelings is often an intensity of loss and regret, not bitter but intensely nostalgic, for the sweetness of a youth and a landscape intolerably vanished. Rosemary Sutcliff invokes time and again the great images of an organic literature—pure water, oak, ash, may, blackthorn, a cleansed and abundant landscape; sorrel, heart's ease, eglantine, laurel; wren, nightingale, lark; honey bees, fresh milk, woodsmoke. At moments her over-descriptive prose begins to sound like a catalogue of Habitat living—the scrubbed tables, the sheepskin rugs, the scoured flags. But this country lore is another symptom of a disinherited present. She appeals to a symbolism which is largely destroyed and she does so because she needs to disbelieve in the reality of that destruction. The appeal is one detail of the significant structure of her novels. It signals that relation in which she stands as the most telling representative of children's novelists to a certain body of ideas—the ideas of an amorphous and lumpen-intelligentsia with a strained notion of social function, a confused but tenacious responsibility towards a theory of social justice and towards national high culture, whose only fixed points of reference are certain principles of personal relations and individual privacy best expressed in the way they treat their children. Rosemary Sutcliff's novels define the response of such a group to the loss of the English landscape both in itself and as a symbol of one version of Englishness; they further define a powerful and unfulfilled longing for a richer moral vocabulary and an ampler, more graceful and courteous style of living such as at the present time can only be embodied in a stylized past. The novels go on to sort and clarify an absent centre in the lives of so many of the social group whose structure of beliefs, economics, aspirations, moral rhythms and intellectual effort she embodies. The novels reconstruct a moral authority carried by the idea of the metropolis (Rome) and become a ritual in the archaic and beautiful system of allegiance, fealty, gesture and rite which characterizes the tales. To uphold the authority gives meaning to men's lives, and this meaning is conveniently discoverable in epic battle. It is a tautology to say that the tribal ceremonies and ritual battles appeal to adolescent readers. That is my whole point. She writes of these experiences because they express for her (and her social group) in the only available language an adequate response to the times.

For the group of Roman-British novels is an adequate response. The attitudes I have summarized add up to a powerfully conservative and elegiac view of history. But there is much more to be said for the courage and moral stamina of liberal ideology. The history of the twentieth century has not left it unmarked. Rosemary Sutcliff's novels are also stained deeply by a profound sense of the possibilities of change, of an unknown future, neither finite nor apocalyptic, but with a subtle, palpitating play of alternatives deriving from its past. Even though in the early *Eagle of the Ninth* and *The Silver Branch* the young heroes take it for granted that loyalty is unquestioning and any usurper morally outrageous, the heroes themselves suffer and change. In *The Lantern Bearers* the presence of violent change is the theme of the book, and the bitter suffering of the hero is the rendering of a writer who knows the refugees' experience of post-1933 Europe. This novel makes Rosemary Sutcliff's gradual search explicit in its title. Aquila is much less confident, much more morally adrift than the earlier heroes. He registers a strong sense of historical dialectic: of forces in shifting conflict and collision, the new direction of which is the necessary result of social contradiction.

> 'I sometimes think that we stand at sunset,' Eugenus said after a pause. 'It may be that the night will close over us in the end, but I believe that morning will come again. Morning always grows again out of the darkness, though maybe not for the people who saw the sun go down. We are the Lantern Bearers, my friend; for us to keep something burning, to carry what light we can forward into the darkness and the wind.' Aquila was silent a moment, and then he said an odd thing. 'I wonder if they will remember us at all, those people on the other side of the darkness.'

This note is the prelude to *Dawn Wind* in which we see the politics of change clear their lines a little. For the second time the hero is forced into slavery, and the subjugation and cruelty of the twentieth century gets onto the page. This hero does not escape brutality in order to fight against it from the other side; he lives through it to win a new sort of identity, a balance of uneasy forces meeting yet another new interruption from an unknown ideology. What he emerges with, in its slight, stoical, bruised way, is a positive response to the new dawn, the determination to make a life, of sorts, more or less where he is.

I have tried to indicate the political nature of literature by brief reference to a single writer. In this argument I have suggested that to account for a politics of literature we have to go further than inward study of the work. By politics I have meant not just the obvious clash of generals and rulers, the sanctions and punishments, the conflict of freedom and slavery, the wars and parleys which we are already familiar with in folktale. The political structure of these novels (or of any novels) is provided by the system of responses to a given historical situation at the time they are written. Rosemary Sutcliff is an honorable representative of her tradition struggling with the idea of change in our time. The decency and limited range of her politics mean that in some ways she speaks up for a largish and not unimportant group of people. The fact that she writes for children and is widely read by teachers further means that her politics are those most likely to go into circulation at any level above that of wage bargains and productivity settlements. She cannot, as Leavis unforgettably tells us Dickens does, 'see how the diverse inter-playing currents of life flow strongly and gather force here, dwindle there from importance to relative unimportance, settle there into something oppressively stagnant, reassert themselves elsewhere as strong new promise.' She is writing too simply to maintain tension between multiplicity and organisation. She doesn't allow sufficient life to the characters she condemns, and there is therefore no radical criticism within her own work of what she affirms. There is little occasion therefore to study the meanings—moral and political—of antagonisms within her novels, which is what gives range and tragedy to a larger work. But her position as a children's writer makes her a figure peculiarly worth our attention if we would read our own cultural bearings with any accuracy. She is a writer of undoubted grace and strength. She rewards the searching treatment I have attempted. And having read her, we find that she has spoken up in the present-day accents of that unkillable member of our society since 1800, the Liberal intellectual woman.

From *Children's literature in education*, No. 5, July 1971

Part Three
CHILDREN

How Children Respond to Fiction

Nicholas Tucker

Nicholas Tucker is a former educational psychologist, now lecturer in developmental psychology at the University of Sussex. He has written widely about children's reading and edited Suitable for Children? *(Sussex University Press, 1975). He has also written four books for children themselves.*
In this article, which was originally delivered as a conference paper, he considers children's preferences for books according to their stage of development.

TO GIVE an account of how children respond to fiction is a near impossible task but it is perhaps less impossible than we sometimes think. At first sight it would seem that whatever book the teacher likes, the children like. So often if the teacher likes a book she will say 'All my seven-year-olds adored it'; and if she did not like the book she will say 'For some reason it did not go down too well.' Reports from libraries about the popularity of books show striking variations, with one library saying that William Mayne and Alan Garner are the most unread authors on the shelves, while another library down the road will say that they are the most popular authors. The question that arises is whether the picture is totally anarchic, with children's responses determined by the particular enthusiasm of the teacher or parent, or whether there are a few guidelines. I hope to show that there are a few guidelines.

In the few surveys of children's reading that exist one nearly always finds folk stories and legends top of the popularity list

177

for younger children up to about eleven, and of course there is
the ubiquitous Enid Blyton, who has sold more copies than the
Bible. There must be a reason why she is so popular. It cannot
be parents' or teachers' enthusiasm. Equally one could say with
confidence that Henry James's *The Awkward Age* would not be
very popular with most children, however enthusiastic the
teacher. So what in fact is the difference between Enid Blyton
and Henry James? If we could arrive at that, we might be a little
closer to finding out what is the difference between books that
children on the whole seem to like and that on the whole they
do not seem to like. One should say at this point that it is a
well-known fact that any psychological generalization which
attempts to cover all children is bound to be wrong, so of
course there are going to be children who do like *The Awkward
Age* and are bored stiff by Enid Blyton. But we are concerned
here with mass trends, not absolute laws.

The question of what books children like has been made
baffling for us by our building up on past experience. Before
the turn of the century there were very few books actually
written for children at all, and that is why we find some
puzzling choices. Charles Lamb wrote beautifully about the
books he read as a child, and one particular book that caused
him endless nightmares was an illustrated Bible with a graphic
picture of the raising of the Witch of Endor. I thought, poor
boy, seeing a book like that, and then I turned over the page to
find that his favourite book was Foxe's *Book of Martyrs,*
particularly the illustrations.

Then of course there are the English classics—*Robinson
Crusoe, Gulliver's Travels, Pilgrim's Progress*—which children in
the past have always claimed to have liked and which many an
English undergraduate sweats and struggles under now. Of
course no child would have read those lengthy puritan bits of
Defoe or Bunyan, but they would have extracted from these
stories the bare bones of a child's adventure which is in fact
there. *Pilgrim's Progress* is written very strongly in the shadow
of the fairy story as well as in the shadow of the Bible, and
Robinson Crusoe was one of many books written about people
on an island fending for themselves—very much the child's

mode of life when he tries to build up some sort of autonomy and independence around him.

We cannot say from all this what books children like and produce a formula—heaven help us—but we can discuss some purely cognitive, intellectual limitations that most children have at some ages that do apply to books just as much as they apply to how we teach them maths at seven or Nuffield Science and so on. This psychological approach has obliged us to abandon the belief that a child is simply a cut-down adult, somebody who knows things rather like an adult but fewer of them. Psychologists like Piaget have persuaded us that young children think in ways not quantitatively but qualitatively different from adults, and if we allow for this we shall be closer to understanding young children's choices. The psychological approach is not widely found because on the whole whenever people talk about psychology in children's books it nearly always turns out to be a psychoanalytic approach. Freud as well as many others speculated widely on why certain stories were popular with children, and we could produce many interpretations of *Jack and the Beanstalk,* probably all coming back to some sort of phallic symbolism, depending upon which bit you interpret in what way. But perhaps a more interesting way of looking at this is in terms of intellectual limitations—the conceptual boundaries that a child has at some age or another.

The first of these is a very simple and obvious one, namely length. One of the clues to the popularity of Enid Blyton, fairy stories and the like is simply their shortness. Short sentences and a short repetitive plot are very important in stories for the young. Enid Blyton used to write a book a week, and the plots and even the dialogue go along extremely well-worn conventions, in the same way that fairy tales are full of conventions: the rule of three, three tasks to be done, the younger son being better than the older, the exchange of riddles at some point, the sudden overturning of fortunes at the end, and so on. For a child who has not much experience of stories there is a certain amount of safety and reassurance about plots that run along the same clearly demarcated lines. A child does not always know that a thing heard once will be the same next time, and there are children who have sat through a frightening story and who when it has been suggested they might hear it again some time have said no in case it ends a different way. Children have to learn conventions and some stories with very clear conventions are helping children who are trying to build up some ways of predicting the immediate future.

The second psychological limitation relates to the concrete and the abstract. In books we sometimes distinguish between action and dialogue, between things that actually happen and passages of description and introspection which are more to do with things that are happening inside a person, things you cannot touch or look at. Piaget suggests that children up to the age of seven do tend to think in much more concrete terms than they do later on. So one can understand a preference for tangible results, clear cut rewards and punishments, plots that work out, clues that all come together in the end and present some overall picture that can be clearly understood. The popularity of detective stories and mystery stories among children as well as adults can be understood in this light.

More important than this perhaps is the child's moral view of life. We know from Piaget that for a child up to a certain age the idea of chance or coincidence has very little importance, because for him to admit of chance or coincidence is for him to admit that the universe is in fact an unordered, amoral place. But if he sees the universe as a place where everything falls into place, where A follows B not by strict causation but because morally it should follow, then this will be reflected in the books he enjoys. Piaget has a good illustration of this from when he was testing children's moral perception. He told a story about a thief who stole some money, ran over a bridge and then the bridge broke. Piaget would then ask the child why he thought the bridge broke. Older children would go for things like the rottenness of the timbers or the box girders or whatever we have nowadays. Younger children would say that the bridge broke because the thief stole the money. The bridge had its part in a whole universe which had a moral meaning where on the whole good had to win in the end because if it did not, the world would be a fairly meaningless place. It is very important to remember that children begin looking at the world in this very egocentric way, by trying to make meaning out of it, and for a long time they see it in terms of this type of meaning rather than in terms of physical causation or something that we would recognize. Tolkien once said that when children listen to a story they are much less likely to ask whether or not it is true than who is the goodie and who is the baddie, to get people into their proper moral stations and then sit back and wait for things to work out as they have got to. The more clearly people are demarcated as goodies and baddies the easier it is for the child to know what is going on. I remember my bewilderment on reading *Candide* at quite a young age to find the hero depicted in reverse, that things did not work out correctly, that the good did not win and the bad sometimes prospered. Growing up is learning to accommodate the fact that the universe does not always make good moral sense unless you are very lucky. For a small child this would be incomprehensible.

There is a beautiful book written about post-revolutionary Russia by Kornei Chukovsky called *From Two to Five* that tells how the Russians after the revolution tried to banish all fantasy from their literature and had stories about how rubber galoshes were made and about tractors and so on. A Russian professor of pedagogics kept a diary and found over and over again that all her rational explanations were turned by her own children into fantasy stories. Ernest Jones and others have said that the idea that filling children's heads with fantasy does them a disfavour is wrong. When in fact you do not provide a child with some fantasy, when you have a Leigh Hunt who brought up his child as a rationalist, that child may often have worse fears than others, sometimes still along very traditional lines of witches, ogres and other immemorial figures. These may be part of us anyhow, reflected in fairy stories, rather than just put there. If you choose to work outside this framework too soon for a child you may leave him behind.

The child needs somebody in a book with whom he can identify as a child. This accounts for the presence of many animals or children themselves in children's books and the comparative paucity of adults, especially parents — it is striking how parents are always got rid of so quickly. Although a child has parents he doesn't necessarily want to read about them, perhaps because he is experimenting with fantasy, with learning about himself, projecting himself into a book where he is not tied down to the fact that he has to go to bed at half past eight and clean his teeth. A widespread mistake about children which is made very often by people who talk about social realism in children's books is to imagine that familiarity breeds content. It is not a question of having details which children can recognize but much more a question of having details which they want to recognize. If we have a picture of a school, children will certainly recognize it but they won't necessarily like it.

A popular book should have some sort of connection with the tasks of childhood. Animals and children will use play as a way of learning to be an adult. Thus a kitten practises jumping at the mice and the child will practise changing nappies and being daddy going off to work and all that sort of thing. There is perhaps no great difference between the function of play for children and what you do when you read as a child. Reading is a type of internalized play and the interesting thing about fantasy and escape is that it can have two quite contradictory functions. The function of fantasy for a young child is very often to enable him to travel in years in his imagination and practise at being a grown-up—usually in the most romantic sense. In the seclusion of your own bed you can open the batting for England or score the winning goal. You are testing yourself out at being an adult. If things go well, gradually this fantasy will get less important as you start finding out what growing up is really about. If things go wrong, then the child will stay in this fantasy world, and the fantasy will cease to be a preparation for adult life and become an escape from it. One of the most poignant statistics is about love-comics for adolescent girls which have two peak readerships: one is about age twelve to fourteen when all the little girls who are not terribly attractive at that age are practising and imagining that they are attractive and falling in love. The other peak is between forty and fifty where women who feel they have missed something will now travel back in fantasy to make up for what they haven't had rather than go on hoping. Fantasy has both these aspects.

If you accept this preparatory role of fiction for the child it is easy to understand why there is, for example, the perpetual theme of a journey in children's books. The picaresque is pervasive from Ulysses to Tolkien. The journey gives the child a chance of escaping from being a dependent child to being independent. But the picaresque form imposes certain limitations on a life. It means that the author can be less concerned with psychological relationships, with relationships between people, but more concerned with events and things people do. At a recent seminar on Tolkien with students at Sussex University some people objected very much to the fact that there are no women in Tolkien, and little psychological explanation. Tolkien himself answered this by saying that he is concerned with crisis and men testing themselves out against evil and so on, and for this you do need events. This exactly fits a child's main interest. He is testing himself out in the book, in language and in events which are easy enough to understand, and not so much seeing events in a reflective light which we hope may come later. The journey from childhood to adulthood involves becoming sexually mature and becoming independent. This you see in fairy stories, where the little boy leaves home and ends by killing the monster and marrying the princess.

In his book called *Reading Together*, Kenyon Calthrop has an interesting description of how a teacher tackled *Lord of the Flies* with his class. He gave the book to them to read, which they all did, and for the lesson in which they were going to discuss the book the teacher cunningly stayed behind in the staffroom for about twenty minutes. He finally opened the door of the classroom to find absolute chaos. That was the first point he made about *Lord of the Flies*. Then he set them for homework 'What would you do if you were on the island with all those boys — Piggy and Jack and so on — but you had actually read the book first? Is there anything you could do to stop what happened in the book?' This is just one of the functions of literature: of testing ourselves out in an imaginary situation which in some ways is quite real and may in fact be something we may have to do at some time.

Some experience of fear is essential in reading. Any teacher knows that one way to keep a naughty class quiet for the last lesson on Friday afternoon is to read them a book which rattles them in some way or another. Children will always look in their games and their literature for some ways of testing themselves out against some of the contemporary things in their own world. This is exactly what wartime children did: they played at dive bombers, the concentration camp children played at gas chambers. They can also test themselves out against their own internal destructive elements, the devouring witches of their nightmares. The peak age for nightmares is between five and nine, just the time when frightening books can be quite popular with children, and obviously you are that much more fortified if you wrestle with this in consciousness rather than always leave it for a sleeping experience. You can also test yourself out against external things—war, your parents dying etc. Sometimes we find that both these things coincide, where the demons within us become very much the same as the demons outside us. If you read Grimm as an inter-war German child you would be testing yourself out against something not purely internal. The ogres and ovens of these tales had very close correlates in the history to come.

Another element is that books should be about desirable experience rather than realistic experience. It is asking too much of a child to expect him to see life in the raw as it actually is. Children have a tremendous capacity to see things inaccurately in a heroic, sometimes rather romantic way. In child guidance clinics it is often quite striking how some of the children from the most deprived homes are fiercely loyal and defensive about them and see their parents in a much more pleasing and endearing light than anyone else sees them. This is part of being a child, this seeing things in a light that is more acceptable than perhaps realistic. Frank Richards, who wrote *Billy Bunter*, when he was attacked by George Orwell in his famous essay about boys' comics, said:

> Let youth be happy, or as happy as possible. Happiness is the best preparation for misery if misery must come . . . . It will help to give the boy confidence and hope. I tell him that there are some splendid fellows in the world, that it is after all a decent sort of place. He likes to think himself like one of these fellows and is happy in his daydreams. Mr Orwell

would have told him that he was a shabby little blighter, his father an ill-used serf, his world a dirty muddled sort of place. I don't think it's fair play to take his tuppence for telling him that.

There are of course some things that are wrong about this, the idea that one should pump out a lot of lies to children, but I respect the basic feeling. It is not fair to children to get rid onto them adult depression and cynicism. Depression is an experience which tends to happen to children only in adolescence. Before that they are perhaps discontented and unhappy, bored and troubled sometimes, but one does not come upon this meaningless view of the world because in a sense a child is not ready for it. The trash-can school of writing, as it is called in America, is all right as long as you don't make your details the main point of the story. Even in a shabby setting, there is still always the possibility of heroic action, perhaps only in the minor sense of a boy winning a trolley race or something. Children up to a certain point see themselves in a naturally heroic way, and they go to literature in a sense looking for that. You could say that growing up is one long process of cutting down this heroic view and gradually coming to terms with what really is. *Cinderella* is one of the most popular archetypes in the world. Someone tried to count up the number of Cinderella variations in cultures all over the world and stopped when she got as far as 385. This illustrates how children would like to see themselves, as the person who may be a drudge but somehow comes out of it in the end. It is someone the child can identify with. If the hero is too big for the child to be able to do this, then often there is a kind of Horatio figure, someone who is not quite so heroic but is second in command. He is for the more retiring children. Perhaps we never lose this desire for heroics. In our relaxed moments when we go to our James Bonds and so on this is exactly what we are looking for.

One of the ways in which children learn is through cognitive dissonance, by the introduction of something a little different from the set and expected situation or outlook. For example, children in the first stage of moral development are often very harsh. Any parent who has tried to be reasonably pleasant and democratic with his children, uncaning and Spock-minded, will still have found that his children play at parents beating up the children, while the kindest primary school will still have pupils playing at teachers giving the cane. Parents will often be distressed at the way children react favourably to the harshness in Grimm and agree with this expiatory kind of justice. This is not because children are naturally hard but because this is the easiest way in which to see morality—if you do something bad you get punished hard. The second stage of moral development that children naturally seem to go on to includes the idea of reciprocal justice—an eye for an eye. If someone in the fairy story has said something bad, then it follows that she should be attacked in her mouth, she should be made dumb or have her tongue cut out. For a child this is reasonable justice. A further stage of moral development, though, is when the idea of punishment is one of restitution and reform rather than one of simple punishment, reflected again in generally more complex literature.

Moral judgments in Enid Blyton are consistently at a facile level and one which corresponds with the child's way of thinking rather than with one above it. Thus one important question is whether a writer stays entirely at the level of the child's thinking or whether, as more gifted writers have done, he takes the children on from their habitual ways of thinking by prodding them onwards, suggesting new avenues, new attitudes. It is futile for the writer to ignore all aspects of children's thinking and put adult values all the way through because he will simply not communicate with the child. But if he is good enough to recognize the child's condition and yet try to make the book concerned with growth in some sort of way, then this is a measure of literary value. This is what is meant by cognitive dissonance. If there is a difference between an Enid Blyton where you find treasure in the end and everyone goes home happy and, say, *Treasure Island* or *The Pardoner's Tale* where the real problems only begin when you find the treasure, it is in the fact that one presents a static view while the other presents a view of life involving the idea of growth in relationships and experience. This happens too in Leon Garfield's books and in John Rowe Townsend's *The Intruder* which begins at a fairly black and white level and then the colours get confused. *Treasure Island* is perhaps the best example of all. Is Long John Silver a baddie or a goodie? When a child begins to ask questions like that it is the start to learning that perhaps life is more about shades of grey than about black and white.

We speak of children going to books to extend their range of experience and at one level this can be a shift of focus as when landlubbers who see the sea once a year can nevertheless know all about mizzentops and splicing the mainbrace from their reading at home. This kind of shifting from suburban street to Spanish Main is fairly superficial, but the kind that involves a shift of focus from one person to another is not superficial. One might ask of a children's book whether it offers a child simply one viewpoint, which is perhaps rather like the child's own, or whether it offers two viewpoints, which is the beginning of wisdom. A child reading a book which has a hero and a villain may sometimes find himself looking from the villain's viewpoint, which raises the question, what is truth? Is it something easily revealed or something which has to be puzzled over and about which you are not too sure?

A children's book then is one that observes certain limitations of structure and experience. C.S. Lewis said about children's books:

> You must write for children out of those elements in our own imagination which we share with children, differing from our child readers not by any less serious interest in the things we handle, but by the fact that we have other interests which children would not share with us. We must meet children as equals in that area of our nature where we are their equals. Our superiority consists partly in commanding other areas, and partly, (which is more relevant) in the fact that we are better at telling stories than they are.

If children did write books they would probably turn out very much like Enid Blyton's.

But there is a greater case now for reading children's books than perhaps I have suggested. There is a certain crisis in adult writing which reveals itself in the lack of large themes which in fact the children's writers are now taking up. Historical novels, books with a vision of the heroic, the picaresque, books concerned with time, death and evil, have recently begun to slip over into the children's section. Many children's books now have a great deal to teach us, as have children themselves. Their response to books is not just one of curiosity. Children have a way of asking us questions which are very difficult to answer because they are the right questions—what is the right thing to do? what would you do? Adult books often do not ask these questions. Some of the best children's books have the spirit to ask them.

From *Children's literature in education*, No. 9, November 1972

Quarries in the Primary School

John Cheetham

John Cheetham is a senior advisor, with special responsibility for the teaching of English, for Lancashire Education Authority. He has taught in secondary schools, was head of a secondary modern school, and has worked extensively with primary teachers in In-Service Courses.

WHEN THE Tutankhamen Exhibition was held in London almost every primary school in Lancashire—and perhaps the British Isles—was engaged on a project on Ancient Egypt. Huge photographs of the king's death-mask dominated classroom walls; there were models of pyramids and reed boats; hieroglyphics told stories on corridor walls, and long, illustrated accounts of Ancient Egypt were pasted into scrap-books. Since then we have had Pollution, Space Travel, Wildlife and the World Cup Project with its attendant world maps, flags and what it is like to live in Haiti or Zaire. The immediacy of important events is seized upon to supply the motivation, the energy of the project, in the conviction that last night's television news holds a strong fascination for children. In the primary school the Project has become sanctified—here there are no subjects, all is integration. Children are busily engaged on a wide variety of activities which are designed to develop skills, interests and talents. Many of the projects in schools occupy timetable space which would, on a subject division, be devoted to Geography, History, Social Studies and Nature Study.

A nagging question often arises—what part do novels and poetry play in all this busy-ness? There was no evidence that literature played any part in the projects I have described.

189

Putting my fears before a group of primary teachers at an In-Service Course, I asked them these questions:

1. When we have taught children to read, how do we develop their reading ability?
2. How do we teach literature in a primary school?
3. How much time do we devote to literature?
4. Having read a book to a class, what do we *do* with it?

In the silence, I felt like a heretic or like the man who shouted 'Everybody out' at the Stock Exchange.

Then one experienced headmaster rose to his feet and slowly, carefully explained the heresy, the insensitivity implicit in my questions.

'In the primary school we read for enjoyment. To do anything with a story would mean the destruction of that story. Children would soon cease to be interested in books. We do not teach Literature (as you call it)—such work we leave to the secondary school. Story reading during the last twenty minutes of every day is a regular and accepted diet in our schools.'

This statement opened the flood gates of criticism.

During a lull I asked, 'Why don't you have set-books in the upper junior school—at least one copy between two?'

A derisive laughter swept my audience.

'We have a marvellous selection of books in the Library . . . . children are encouraged to read books. They can take books home . . . . I think any discussion of a book destroys its imaginative power—I know it did for me in the fifth form . . . . We cannot spend long on Literature because we have too many other things to do. . . .'

'But you are asking us to become secondary teachers . . . . We can't afford such luxuries . . . . Children should have a wide variety of books.'

When the furore had died down I was asked why I had put my original questions.

During my visits to schools over the past four years I had never seen a project based on a novel. I wondered why this was so because a well-chosen novel could stimulate many varied and interesting activities; it could be the mainspring of creative

work in writing, art, drama and music. Such work could surely
help the children to enjoy the book on many levels, increase
their understanding and develop their imagination. Some weeks
later, during a school visit, a Head said he had something to
show me. On our way to the classroom we walked down a
corridor where the walls were covered with coats-of-arms and
a large display of the technical language of Heraldry. In the Hall
were two large models of an attack on a castle and a jousting
tournament. Along another corridor were models of a banquet
and a medieval market, and on the end wall a lovely collage of
a procession of knights and their ladies, soldiers, acrobats and
peasants. In the classroom itself the walls were covered with
the children's paintings, poems, stories. In pride of place was
a large home-made book entitled 'Our Book of Ivanhoe'.
The children were eight to nine years old.

When I realized that the inspiration of all this work had been
a classic novel (when the teacher could have chosen a book
from the many modern novels written for children) I naturally
had many questions to ask. I summarize the information the
teacher gave me:

1. She had been on the Course and thought that she would
   try out the idea.
2. She had chosen *Ivanhoe* because she had always liked
   the book. There was a similar story being serialized
   on television. She thought 'it would be something completely outside the children's experience.' (The school
   was in the heart of a Lancashire mill town. What price
   Leila Berg?) Also, the story was full of action.
3. She had used a simplified version in the Kennet Series
   of abridged classics. She had only one copy.
4. She read the book to the children every day: she read
   the first chapter four times 'so that the children would
   really understand it.'
5. They had discussed the various episodes as a whole class,
   and she had helped their understanding by direct explanation and teaching.
6. She read the book through 'for enjoyment'.
7. The work which had come from the book was instigated

partly by the enthusiasms of the children and partly by the teacher. The language work, the teacher said, was designed to foster vocabulary, to develop story-writing, and poetry. Comprehension was mainly oral. There were also spelling lists of newly discovered words.

8. The children worked in groups or as individuals. All had to do some writing, but apart from that, free choice was given to pursue any interest. One boy, who was not very able, had tried to make a long-bow from an elderberry bush, others had made models and some had painted or created collages. One little girl said that she would much rather write about her new puppy.

9. The work was done in the time allotted to 'activities', i.e. every afternoon.

There was no doubt, as I discovered during my conversations with them, that the children had enjoyed the book; several had re-read it at home, and many had asked, 'Has this man written any more like it?'. They knew the book and talked to me at great length about the characters whom they liked and why. Some of their own stories had obviously borrowed many ideas from *Ivanhoe*, and these stories had been bound in 'Our Book of Ivanhoe'.

Since then these children have 'done' *Call of the Wild*, *A Christmas Carol* and *Carbonel*. The last time I visited the school they were trying to write their own class novel.

Many articles in *Children's literature in education* seem to be aimed at secondary schools, but there is a real need to look at the place and function of literature in primary schools. The questions to the teachers on the Course were deliberately provocative because it seems to me that primary schools are obsessed with the teaching of reading but have made few attempts to explore the possibilities of using literature as a vital part of the children's experience. The approach to literature is altogether too casual; children are not exposed to literature often enough and for long enough. There is no doubt that the junior school which produces lively, interesting, sensitive writing has a firm basis of poetry and fiction, introduced and used by the teachers. Connie and Harold Rosen in their book *The Language of Primary School Children* (Penguin Education) found similar evidence to my own.

During the past decade an attitude seems to have been encouraged and developed in junior schools that to do other than read poetry and novels to children would sound the death knell of enjoyment; that children are so vulnerable and literature such a delicate thread in their lives that it cannot be used with the same rigour as other aspects of the curriculum. Perhaps this attitude sprang from the way poems and novels were analyzed and dissected in schools a quarter of a century ago, and this form of teaching may be responsible for the present-day attitude which forbids close examination of poems and novels. A side effect of this is that children are no longer encouraged to learn poetry by heart.

Geoff Fox's editorial comment to the article 'Travelling in Time' in *Children's literature in education 13* intrigued me.

> The project-approach is increasingly popular in schools determined to work across the divisions of conventional subjects. Not all teachers of literature are convinced of the value of such work. They fear fiction may become a quarry-face hacked about by well-meaning social studies teachers . . .

His comment may apply to secondary schools, but in junior schools many teachers do not even seem to be aware that there is a 'quarry-face'. The end-of-the-day reading, as propounded by the headmaster, is not good enough. I am convinced that the 'quarry-face of literature' should be excavated by junior children.

May I suggest two ways of careful excavation (as opposed to indiscriminate 'hacking'):

1. Whatever may be the purists' fears, an injection, deliberate and planned from the beginning, of a liberal element of literature into every project or topic.
2. The use of a novel as the centre of a project.

The first is fairly obvious and open to all the criticism implicit in Geoff Fox's comment, but the second may need more elaboration.

It is illuminating to sit with teachers who are planning the next school project. Perhaps the subject chosen is 'Flight'. Within ten minutes we have ranged over the Wright brothers, balloons, the science of flight, the mathematics of world airways, holidays abroad to seagulls and gliders. Everything comes within the compass of the project. This might be called the 'Umbrella Approach'.

A subtler, and I think better development, is from one interesting fact or even casual mention in the classroom which captures the imagination of children. Such incidents can come in any lesson. From this small beginning the children, directed by the teacher, explore the various leads. This might be called the 'Evolutionary Approach', and illustrates my proposal that a novel or series of poems become the starting point of a project.

To return to the article 'Travelling in Time'. The project undertaken by the students is not what I have in mind. This is a typical Geography/History project, and one wonders whether the work done by the students enhanced their understanding and appreciation of the novel. The research undertaken by them was really the research done by the author before he wrote the novel. I do not decry research which a novel may inspire, but I think we should explore elements in a novel which will help children towards a greater understanding of the novel and a greater understanding of themselves. As Geoff Fox suggests, to treat a novel as an excuse for Social Studies is misguided. 'We must remember that *Treasure Island* is not a handbook on Piracy nor is Hickory Dickory Dock about the nocturnal habits of mice.'

The elements of a novel which need to be explored are:

1. The story—the incidents and episodes which capture the children's imagination.
2. The various characters and their relationships.
3. The relationship between people and incidents in the book and the children's own lives and experiences.
4. The physical settings and changing moods of the novel.

The work prompted by the novel should come from these elements which become the touchstones of the project; however far one may go in the creative work there must be constant return to the novel. The aim of the project is the better understanding and enjoyment of the novel, and the criterion for all work done by the children is that it furthers this end.

I should like to illustrate my points by using the novel *The Wheel on the School* by Meindert de Jong. The book tells the story of how the children in a small seaside village in Holland realize that storks never nest on the roofs of their houses. They discover that if they put a wagon wheel on the roof of the school this would make an excellent platform for the storks' nest. The story tells of the adventures of the children when they search for a wagon wheel, and how they involve the whole village in their plan.

I should use this book with fourth-year junior children. I choose this novel because it has all the elements of excitement, danger, humour and the possible experiences which, in different settings, children in the class may have had. It is about children in a community and their relationships with adults; the story of a realistic problem which children could solve; it is well-written and the details are sharply observed.

There are two main phases of work with the book:

A   Basic: The book is read by the teacher for the enjoyment of the class. During the reading there will be discussion about various aspects either in groups or as a class. There will certainly be 'positive' teaching periods by the teacher, e.g. the elucidation of matters such as the migration of birds, or the function of dikes. Much of the 'comprehension' will be oral, and some episodes may be used to stimulate writing of various kinds. New words would be collected.

Having read the book I would *not* put up a list of project topics for the children's exploration such as: the Migration of Birds; Fishing in Holland; Storks; Dikes in Holland; Why

Holland Is Flat; Life in a Dutch village; the School System of Holland etc.

Neither would I assemble a resources bank of material on Holland, because the book is not about Holland. It sets problems; how to put a cart wheel on the school and how to enlist the help of adults in the village. It is a book about relationships and how the children discover things about themselves and the older people.

B   The Project: The emphasis will be on creative work inspired by the story; the novel becomes the real reference book and will be referred to constantly.

The various aspects of creative work I would suggest are:

1 *Themes related to the children's own lives*
   a Relationships with a teacher
   b Enlisting the aid of adults
   c Understanding old people (grandparents)
   d Meeting difficult, awkward people
   e Joint solving of a problem
   f Understanding our parents
   g Why do adults help children?

2 *Art Work*
   a A class collage of Shora, the village
   b Paintings of the school house
   c Paintings of the children and characters in the book
   d Pictures of exciting episodes
   e The dike and the sea
   f A collage of storks, roofs, wheels, chimneys

3 *Drama*
   a Life in a village; an imaginary village or Shora
   b Improvisation based on certain episodes: the search for wagon wheels; the storm; helping people in dangerous situations
   c Improvisation of a problem perhaps suggested by the children, e.g. making an adventure playground

4 *Writing*
   a Writing about people we know
   b Trespassing in forbidden areas
   c People in dangerous situations
   d Exploring new areas—new woods or paths
   e Observation work on common everyday things, e.g. light on a tree

5 *Music*
   perhaps not as easy to define as other aspects of creative work but:
   a Music background to their own writing, e.g. the sea
   b Making storm music
   c Describing tension in musical terms

The suggestions outlined above show, I hope, that the creative work partly directed by the teacher (because he knows what the aim of the project is) and partly by the children's enthusiasms or interests would constantly take the children in and out of the book, referring to the text to clarify details of episodes, people and settings which help them in their own creative work. Of paramount importance in all this are the searching questions carefully devised by the teacher; for example: How would you have solved the problem? Did the finding of the wheel change anyone in the village? These questions could be put to the children either formally, in a class situation, or informally with groups of children whilst engaged on various tasks. When doing such creative work the teacher must be sensitive to suggestions by the children and encourage the 'off-beat' idea which may arise. If a boy, for example, really gets 'hooked' on the migration of birds one would use this motivating interest and, for a time, give it free rein.

When the project is finished what have the children gained? My hope would be that they have experienced the enjoyment of really knowing a book, a development of skills, a greater understanding of relationships between individuals, a desire to read other books with greater insights and the development of imagination. Perhaps this is asking too much, but this is what literature is all about, and I should like the children to have this opportunity of a shared experience.

From *Children's literature in education*, No. 16, March 1975

A Reading Policy for a Comprehensive Secondary School

John L. Foster

John Foster is Head of English at Redefield School, which draws its pupils largely from the Cowley district of Oxford. He has edited and written several successful books for reluctant readers. He also holds a part-time appointment in the Oxford University Department of Education, working with student teachers.

IN THE CURRENT hue and cry about reading standards there is a real danger that teachers may be led into adopting approaches to reading that will only partially solve the problem. A concern to increase pupils' reading ability may lead to the widespread introduction of graded reading schemes such as the SRA reading laboratories. My purpose here is not to analyse the merits and demerits of such schemes. There is considerable evidence from teachers who have used them that they are often successful in improving a child's reading ability. However, and herein lies the danger, while they may improve a child's reading skill and hence his reading age such schemes do not themselves develop the reading-habit. They are only stepping stones towards the world of books. If we are to introduce children to that world and to help them to become familiar with books as true readers then we must adopt other strategies. The purpose of this article is to outline the reading policy of Redefield School, and to suggest some of the approaches that we can adopt to achieve the aim of enabling as many of our students as possible to develop the reading-habit before they leave school.

The underlying principle upon which the policy is founded is that the development of the reading-habit is as important to the education of the child as is the learning of the basic skill of decoding. There are those who might question this, arguing that the new media make reading less important and that, while it is desirable that everyone should acquire the skill of reading, it is misguided to expect everyone to want to read books. As a publisher wrote recently: 'A high percentage of adults never open a book. Many people would rather kick a football around on a Sunday afternoon than read a book'. This is obviously true and it would be presumptuous to expect those who get pleasure from playing football to have to get pleasure from books instead. But books—the reading-habit—offer more than just enjoyment, they also offer language and knowledge. Hence, they are more important than football and, unlike football, important to everyone. Like Robert Leeson I want to create readers because 'the key to education is reading. I want 100% of children to become readers for their own good as well as pleasure. Football is for afters. Reading is the main course as well'.[1] The policy is designed to foster the reading-habit in every child in the school. That is a tall order, but it ought to be our aim.

Obviously the most direct method of doing this is by encouraging personal private reading. But a reading policy for a school should also aim to develop skills of comprehension, of reading with insight. This can only be done properly by considering the book as whole. Consequently I feel that the much maligned class reader still has an important part to play. The approach which I favour is therefore two-fold: the individual reading and, if appropriate, study of books chosen by the child himself, although in many cases recommended by the teacher; and the whole class reading and study of books carefully selected, but prescribed, by the teacher.

It is easy to talk of 'encouraging personal private reading', but how can we set about doing so? With children who come from homes where books abound, where the child has been

[1] Robert Leeson in *Signal, 14,* May, 1974.

read to throughout his childhood and where the parents are themselves readers, there is often little problem. All that needs to be done is to give such children an environment where they meet a sufficient choice of books and where adult guidance is available if they want it. In such circumstances many of them will develop naturally into readers.

With children from other backgrounds, from homes where there are few, if any, books—and statistics reveal that there are plenty of such homes—and where there has been little bedtime reading and sharing of stories in early childhood, the problem is entirely different. It is especially so in the case of children who find it difficult to master the skill of learning to read. The experiences that they undergo while doing so can leave them feeling that books are not for them. Such children often come to secondary school with their attitude towards books already well-formed: 'I don't read books'. If we are not careful all that we do to such children during the next five years is to treat them in such a way that their attitude hardens. They leave school confirmed non-readers and never open a book again. How can we help these children to become readers? We must start from where they are rather than from where we would like them to be. We must offer them what they want to read, rather than what we think they ought to be reading. We must accept the fact that any reading is better than no reading and that if a child enjoys a book that we might dismiss as 'rubbish', our literary judgements are of secondary importance to his needs.

What matters is that the child should read a book and hence take a further step towards developing the reading-habit. If the habit is developed, then discrimination will follow. As Aidan Chambers says, 'Wide, voracious, indiscriminate reading is the base soil from which discrimination and taste eventually grow. Indeed, if those of us who are avid and committed readers examine our reading history during our childhood and look also at what we have read over the past few months, few if any of us will be able to say honestly that we have always lived only on the high peaks of literature. Nor would we have it any different. The sum total of the pleasure we have had from books owes something to the ephemeral, transitory material we have frequently read. There is no reason why we should think that what is true for ourselves will be any less true in this respect for other people—children or adults."[1]

The teacher has to start from his knowledge of the child and try to find a book, irrespective of 'literary merit', that will appeal to that particular child at that particular moment. His skill lies in giving the right book to the right child at the right time.

For example, *Silas Marner* may be the right book to give to a few eleven-year-olds, but the majority of them would find it far too difficult. Similarly, the books of Mayne, Garner, Garfield, Treece and Sutcliff are the right ones to recommend to certain eleven-year-olds, but many others find them totally inaccessible. For a pupil of eleven with a reading age below his chronological age then the appropriate book might be one from Macmillan's *Club 75* series or Heinemann's *Instant Reading* series.

Finding the right book for the right child is not always easy. Unfortunately the majority of books published for children continue to be biased towards the few—those who are attracted to the world of books anyway—rather than to the many— those who are not. Consequently, there is a shortage of the books we need most—books which will capture the interest of those children who are most in danger of giving up reading for ever. Series like *Topliners* and *Pyramids* have shown that it is possible to fill the gap, but we need ten times the number of titles that they provide.

The skill in recommending books to children lies not only in knowing the child and his interests, but in knowing the books as well. This does not mean merely acknowledging that series like *Topliners* exist and making such books available, it also means reading as many of the books in such series as possible. We need to be able to show the children that we value the books that they read and this means that we need to be in a position to be able to discuss the contents of the books with them. It is important for us to be able to talk about books like Pamela Sykes's *East, West*, Christopher Leach's *A Temporary*

---

[1] Aidan Chambers, *Introducing Books to Children,* Heinemann Educational Books, 1973.

Open-Air Life and Molly Cone's *The Real Dream* with the children who read them, as it is for us to be able to talk to other children about Richard Adams' *Watership Down* and Penelope Lively's *The House in Norham Gardens*. Many English teachers find it difficult to come to terms with the books that I am advocating, because they cannot value them as literature. Until such time, however, as we can find books that both interest the less willing reader and meet all the requirements of our literary standards, then I feel we must be prepared to set aside our literary scruples.

Can we not accept and value such books for what they are—a means towards helping children to develop a lifelong habit of reading? To use them properly we must be prepared to read them and to talk about them to our pupils, whatever we might feel about them as Literature.

In the first three years the approach at Redefield is to concentrate on developing individual reading for enjoyment. There is no organized study of the books that are read, nor do we ask pupils to keep such things as reading records. There is some use of the class reader, but no detailed depth study of a class book along the lines that are used in the fourth and fifth years. This is because the aim is to develop an interest in and a liking for books before any attempt is made at detailed criticism. There is a danger that if book-study, which should in itself be enjoyable, is introduced too early then it may affect enjoyment. If the reading-habit is to be developed permanently then enjoyment is of fundamental importance.

In order to give children the opportunity to choose books for individual reading, one forty-minute English period per week throughout the first, second and third years is time-tabled as a library period. Ideally this period would also be timetabled in the fourth and fifth years, but examination pressures make it impossible at present. This lesson takes place in the library rather than in a classroom. This in itself is important, because if we are to think in terms of everyone developing the reading-habit then it is necessary for us to take all our pupils to the library regularly. It is not sufficient to send to the library only those who elect to go when given a choice. The very pupils who need to go the most are those who will not volunteer to go—unless they see the library as a place to which they can escape, free from the supervision of the teacher. It is ironic how many of our more reluctant pupils sometimes view the library as a place of refuge, not because they want to escape into an environment of books but because it is a place where they can hide away from the classroom world of books and writing.

Nor is it enough just to accompany the pupils to the library. The teacher's role in the library is a vital one, if the right attitude towards the library and towards book-borrowing is to be developed. The teacher must not allow the pressures of work to lead him to think of the library period as a time to catch up on his marking. While the pupils are browsing freely, the teacher needs to be circulating amongst them, discussing the books that they have just finished reading and recommending the ones that they might go on to enjoy next. The library period should be an exhausting one for the teacher. It is not easy to talk individually to thirty pupils and to find books suitable for all of them within a forty-minute period. One of the problems is that when a pupil says that he would like a story-book of a particular type, all too often the mind seems to go blank. For this reason we have found it useful to arrange some of our fiction stock so that it is grouped according to subject-matter rather than stacked alphabetically according to author's name. Thus we have arranged sections under broad headings such as Animal Stories, Ghost Stories, Sea Stories, Adventure Stories, Love Stories, War Stories, Science Fiction and Sport. Many stories often defy so rigid a classification, but we have found that such a system provides a useful shortcut to the time-consuming task of guiding a young science fiction addict, for example, round the shelves from Blish to Christopher and from Fisk to Walters.

If it is not possible for administrative reasons to regroup the stock then another useful method whereby the teacher can quickly recommend books of a particular type is by using Fiction Topic Cards. These are book lists, either typed or handwritten on cards, giving details of books on a particular theme suitable for a particular age group. The simplest ones, containing details merely of author and title can be made very quickly, for I think it is important not to confuse children by recommending too many books at once and would suggest that no card should list more than about 15 books.

Others, giving brief details of each book as well as the title and author's name, take rather longer to make. However, extremely attractive cards can also be produced in a relatively short time by cutting up some of the publishers' catalogues and pasting the pages onto cards. Even though the catalogues that I have used have been designed for teachers, I have found that it is possible to use them effectively in this way. In particular I have found that the Heinemann *New Windmill* catalogue, the *Puffin* catalogue and the Macmillan *Topliner* and *Club 75* catalogue can all be cut up and made into attractive cards.

These cards can be used either in the library or in the classroom, for the weekly library period needs to be backed up by making a further supply of books available either in class libraries or in book boxes. When we are dealing with large numbers, as we are in many comprehensive schools, then the provision of single copies of books in the library is obviously inadequate. We need multiple copies of the most popular books such as S.E. Hinton's *The Outsiders* and Joan Tate's *Sam and Me*. We need to have shelves of books or boxes of books available in every English lesson, so that the potential reader can dip into and rummage through the collection whenever he wants. I favour the use of boxes, because they are transportable and because they are also interchangeable. When a class starts complaining that there doesn't seem to be anything decent in a particular box, you just do a swop with a colleague and immediately you can provide the class with a different selection.

One problem of class libraries and book boxes is the number of books that are borrowed and not returned. Whatever system you devise for checking books in and out of class libraries, you always seem to lose far too many books. But we must realize that it is more important for pupils to borrow books and become readers, than for us to operate a system that might help us to lose fewer books. I regard the money that I spend annually on topping up our book boxes as money well spent.

In the economies that have been forced upon me recently by the cut in my allowance I have not included any reduction on the amount I spend on readers for the book boxes. I would rather lose 50 books and create five readers than save the £15 it would cost me to replace those books.

Another method of promoting the reading-habit is by encouraging pupils to buy books. Obviously the most effective way of doing this is to run a school bookshop and it is encouraging to hear how many schools are now running bookshops. Where it is not possible to run a shop then clubs like the Puffin Book Club and the Scoop Club can partially fill the gap. Alternatively, a Book Fair can be organized. Local shops will often co-operate, but it is perhaps easier to work through a firm like Scholastic Publications who have considerable experience in running book fairs and who have worked out a system that is easy for the teacher to follow. The hitch here is that one is limited to the books that Scholastic offer in their catalogue, whereas a local bookseller may be willing to supply a wider range of books. Whatever method is chosen to sell books is relatively unimportant. What matters is that the children should be given the opportunity to buy books, for it is another means of getting them to value books and consequently another step towards the development of the reading-habit.

In the fourth year the approach alters in that while every effort continues to be made to promote individual reading the class study of a number of selected texts is introduced. This is not done as an expedient means of preparing candidates for either the CSE or O level examinations, though of course it is a part of that process; but rather because of a belief that the whole class study of carefully selected books has a particular value at this age.

The aim of our policy, as I have already stated, should be to produce not only avid, but also perceptive, readers. The whole class study of a text offers an opportunity for developing the skills of reading with insight. The shared experience which it affords can, if cleverly exploited by the teacher, be used to help the young reader to develop skills of comprehension, criticism and discrimination. Much depends upon the type of follow-up activity that is organized. Creative activities that stem from and lead back into the book, and which involve the pupils in re-creating scenes and incidents and viewing them from different standpoints have especial value as do any activities that involve discussion. Tape-recorded interviews with characters, the re-creation of episodes as if they were scenes from a radio play, improvisations of situations which parallel those in the story and the making of sound and picture collages can often throw as much light on the themes of a book as more formal written exercises.

One of the criticisms levelled at the class reader and the organization of follow-up activities is that they lessen enjoyment. This is not my experience, nor that of many of the teachers whose work Kenyon Calthrop describes in *Reading Together*.[1] Indeed, if a follow-up activity deepens understanding, then it can increase rather than lessen enjoyment.

However, it is necessary to be very careful about the choice of books to use as class readers, especially with mixed ability classes. Too often the criteria that are used in the choice of class readers are questionable. Many class readers are chosen not for their content and suitability, but because they are available— the school has a set (and someone else has already taken the set of the text that you would like to have used)—or because the book is a set text. Others are chosen simply because they work, i.e. hold the class's attention. Obviously it is necessary to have a book that holds the reader's attention. In choosing a book to recommend to an individual this may be the sole criterion, but it should not be the only criterion when selecting books for use with whole classes. Books should be chosen for class study because their content will extend the pupils' experience and knowledge of life. Care should also be taken to ensure that any given class has a balanced diet of class readers. It would be wrong if a class during the fourth and fifth years were to study, for example, only science fiction books or only the realistic novels of Waterhouse, Sillitoe and Barstow. Similarly we should try to see that humour is included in their fare. Too often, I fear, we offer our fourth and fifth years a diet of nothing but gloom.

If we are catering for mixed ability classes there are other

[1] Kenyon Calthrop, *Reading Together*, Heinemann Educational Books, 1973.

considerations to be borne in mind. Books must not be so long as to be daunting for the less able, nor so slow-moving as to fail to hold the attention of the easily distracted. On the other hand, they must not be so slight as to fail to stretch the more able. Finding books that work with mixed ability classes and that fulfil these criteria is not easy. Nor is it possible for a school to provide as wide a range of books for class use as one would like. Among the books that we have used successfully as class readers are: *Kes* by Barry Hines, *To Sir With Love* by E.R. Braithwaite, *Joby* by Stan Barstow, *Shane* by Jack Schaefer, *I am David* by Anne Holm, *The Pearl, The Red Pony* and *Of Mice and Men* by John Steinbeck, *The Childhood Story of Christy Brown, Animal Farm* by George Orwell, *Walkabout* by James Vance Marshall and *This Time Next Week* by Leslie Thomas.

The approach to the class reader varies according to the book, the class and the teacher. However, the use of the class reader does not mean, as some critics seem to think, reading around the class. Getting the book read with enjoyment by as many of the class as possible is, of course, the most difficult problem. Depending upon the length of the book a mixture of teacher reading aloud and individual reading either in class or at home seems the most satisfactory method.

My personal bias is towards a considerable amount of teacher reading. Indeed, if the book is short as in the case of *The Pearl, Animal Farm, Old Mali and the Boy* or *The Cay*, I am inclined to read the whole book aloud over a concentrated period of time. The books I have mentioned can be read to a class within the space of a fortnight's English periods. This makes demands upon the teacher's ability to sustain interest by skilful reading, but if it can be done there are several advantages. The skilled reader can sometimes give the book an extra dimension which the child reader can not. The less able pupils can thus be helped to read books which they would otherwise find too difficult to read themselves, since the books that a child reads himself must be within his own cognitive range. Those which we read to the child can stretch him beyond it.

Critics of the method of reading whole books aloud immediately argue, 'But what about the pupil who takes the book home after the first lesson and finishes it that evening?' Most classes contain pupils who do this and allowance needs to be made for them. They can be given the choice to opt out of the other reading lessons and either to begin the follow-up work on the book or to do their own individual reading. Many of them opt to listen to the story along with the rest of the class. To allow them to do this is not necessarily to hold them back. Most pupils will gain insights from their second reading of a book that they missed during their first reading.

The aim of this class study of books in the fourth and fifth years is to help the young reader to develop the ability to probe more deeply into the books that he reads than he may hitherto have been doing. The fourth year seems to be a good age at which to do this, because the increasing maturity of the children means that it is possible to select books that raise more adult issues and that are, therefore, more demanding than the books that could be used at an earlier age. Alongside this class study, every effort is made throughout the fourth year to continue to encourage the reading-habit.

The class study of books is continued into the fifth year, but the aim is to phase it out and to replace it with individual book study once the pupils have begun to realize that there can be more to a book than just a storyline and that to read closely will often reveal meanings that they might otherwise have failed to recognize. The advantage of moving over to individual study is that it enables the individual to read books of his own choice and to work at his own pace.

The able reader can move on and study, say, Solzhenitsyn's *One Day in the Life of Ivan Denisovitch* or D.H. Lawrence's *Sons and Lovers,* while his less fluent colleague can read Christina Dickenson or W.C.C. Chalk. At the end of one fifth-form lesson in the term immediately before the CSE examinations I once asked the members of the class, who had spent the period working on literature, to note down the books that they had been studying. This list included the following books: H.G. Wells, *The Time Machine,* Helen Keller, *The Story of My Life,* E.R. Braithwaite, *To Sir, With Love,* Charlotte Brontë, *Jane Eyre,* Carson McCullers, *The Member of the Wedding,* Maureen Duffy, *That's How it Was,* Keith Waterhouse, *There Is a Happy Land,* D.R. Sherman, *Old Mali and the Boy,* Richard Wright, *Black Boy,* Dianne Doubtfire, *Escape on Monday* and Michael Baldwin, *Grandad with Snails.*

The aim is for book study and personal reading for enjoyment to become linked. For this to be possible it is necessary to follow an examination syllabus that enables choice to be made from a wide range of books. In our case this is done by following a mode 3 CSE syllabus, which demands study of a number of books from a prescribed list, while otherwise leaving the candidate free to select books according to his own tastes and ability. O level literature can be fitted into this scheme by making the set books available in the school, so that anyone wishing to take O level literature opts to read and study those books.

The advantages of such a scheme are that it enables the teacher to go on developing the reading-habit, while at the same time preparing pupils for their external examinations. The difficulty lies in planning the study of whatever books the pupils may choose, in order to ensure that they produce the course work that the examination requires. This problem can, however, be overcome by organizing a bank of worksheets. Over the years the teachers in our team have devised workschemes on over 70 different titles, ranging from some on Martin Calman's *Go Readers* (Blond), through Reginald Maddock's *Sell Out* and Ann Marie Falk's *A Place of Her Own*, to Graham Greene's *Our Man In Havana* and H.G. Wells's *The History of Mr Polly*.

The worksheets vary widely according to the book and the teacher who designed them. Some contain detailed work on sections of the book, while others consist only of general questions on the book as a whole. Each worksheet usually ends with a list of books for further reading. The worksheets are typed, stencilled onto A4 paper and stored in a filing cabinet in the English and Integrated Studies resources area, indexed according to authors. There is no compulsion for a pupil to do work on any book if he would prefer not to do so. The teacher's role is to advise the pupil about his choice of books and of work, so that each pupil can be guided to read books suitable to his needs and ability as well as to his taste and so that he will produce course work for the examination that is both sufficient and varied enough.

The organization of book study, either by individuals or by classes, to enable everyone to learn how to read books with understanding should be one aim of the reading policy of a comprehensive school. The other aim should be to develop the reading-habit amongst all pupils. The most difficult task of the teacher is to find books that will attract the interest of the least motivated of our pupils. There are still not enough books published that are aimed directly at this vast potential readership.

From *Children's literature in education*, No. 17, June 1975

Notes on Teaching
A Wizard of Earthsea
Geoff Fox

Geoff Fox has taught in secondary schools in England and the U.S.A., and at Harvard University. At present he is a lecturer at Exeter University School of Education. He has collaborated in three books for use in English classrooms, and is a member of the editorial committee of Children's literature in education.

'BUT HOW do I *teach* this book?' You could read it round the class, a paragraph at a time, checking for comprehension. Well yes, you could. You could use it as a tool in an integrated studies project and smother the book beneath a collection of maps, surveys, questionnaires, work-cards, flints and pressed flowers. You could, some might argue, expose the child to the words on the printed page and allow the alchemy to work its mystic way, bringing the child into the presence of the book, as it were.

To the teacher, such solutions are worthless. They leave the child feeling bored, conned or uncomprehending; and the book, nowhere. The 'teaching' of a book ought to allow a reader greater understanding, keener enjoyment of the book itself: perhaps greater understanding, even keener enjoyment, of his own experience.

The following contributions describe approaches to *A Wizard of Earthsea*[1] by Ursula Le Guin; through talk, choral work, drama, paint, game-making and the writing of prose and verse. The teaching contexts were very different. Readers, whether adults or children, worked with the book at their own levels.

[1] Ursula Le Guin, A Wizard of Earthsea, Parnassus, 1968; Gollancz, 1971; Penguin, 1971; Ace Books, 1973, HEB New Windmill Series, 1975.

Inset between the descriptions are some comments, transcribed from tape, of a group of three twelve-year-old boys talking about the book.

*   *   *

Actually when you read to us about the Kargs, I thought, Oh no! I don't want to read that book!

I thought it was fantastic, kind of psychedelic, when he chased after this boy's spirit and he had to leap over this kind of canyon to get at it. And then he turned round when he saw this boy going too far, he climbed up a rockface and he saw the canyon again but right by it was the Shadow and he had to get past this Shadow and he's a real hero to me at that moment because he raised his staff and he ran at that Shadow and he jumped over the canyon, no matter what and thanks to the Otak. . . .

*   *   *

At the National Association for the Teaching of English conference at York in 1972, a group of delegates discussed teaching strategies for a particular class taught by one of its members, Pamela Barnard, who teaches in Northampton. The following notes are taken from letters reporting on Mrs Barnard's work in the classroom.

. . . so, a few weeks ago, I started the book with the children: 25 mixed ability first years (with memedials removed), general ability tending to lower middle. Background—seedy working-class area, some council estate, a smattering of middle-class homes.

General problems: creative writing, whatever the stimulus, situation, experience taken, rarely brought surprises. From the 'good' children it was competent technically, from the West Indians it seemed an alien activity, from the least able the awkwardness of expression had an impact and, sometimes, a struggle emerged to say something that mattered; the middle group seemed to aim for 'what Mrs Barnard seemed to ask us to do'. Excuses, excuses, but they seemed to have little background in writing freely—where are all these lively primary schools? Also absent was any contact with 'imaginative' literature, if you'll tolerate the term.

I used the introduction to the book suggested at York and the class developed an improvisation based upon the lives and dwellings of the villagers of Ten Alders. There was some real tension when the busy village life was interrupted by a child running in and telling, without previous priming of the group, about the impending Karg attack.

Some children have already finished the book, having taken copies home, and several are opting out of class reading to write about their views—'I've written seven pages already!' Meanwhile I read extracts to them of the parts I thought exciting, interesting and/or important.

We had an interesting session the other day when I tried to get them to notice the strange language elements by letting each child choose several island names and chant them. You see, I find many of our children lacking in any experience of playing with words. We chanted in turn, loudly, and then played it back on tape. Suddenly there was a tremendous lot of talk around (e.g. 'The words sound good'). Unfortunately I couldn't pick much up and thought it would kill their response if I probed.

One of the children has made a beautifully enlarged map of Earthsea and another two are listing and looking up herbs and plants mentioned—this stemmed from my asking the biologist at school if plants such as 'moly' existed—she found a marvellous book which is all about 'useful plants' and their regional names, and, better still, their traditional healing and magical qualities. I guided three children into doing these odd things because I felt that they would enjoy it and they seem to—probably because they came from a project-minded junior school.

We have done some writing on 'Being Attacked'—their output was surprising in quantity and some of it was very good—they're a willing writing group anyway, but this seemed to have caught them particularly.

We have also written spells in 'language' and, interestingly, several of them invented their own symbols—so we got the 'English translation', the phonetic pattern and the visual 'new language'.

... Apart from 'Being Attacked', they wrote on 'The Illusion'—a piece of writing based on the Dragon sequence, spells, individual pieces (e.g. on herbs, the otak—a sort of study, the School on Roke and magic); and I also asked them to write their opinions of the book (*not* as baldly as that).

Games—this occurred to me with too little time to develop it and, on reflection, I think it was a good idea. What had fascinated me was the patterning of experience (patterning in the book's sense of the word): an inevitability and the feeling of trials leading to a fulfilment—a strangely tolerant predestination thing. This grand feeling (perhaps bathos on my part) led to games.

The children liked this—one group with little guidance (i.e. 'How about making a game based on the book?') produced a board game called 'The Wizard Game'. E.g. Start (Map of Gont) —1—2—3—Goat Drawing—'Duny learns Goat spell from aunt, advance 4 paces'. They certainly knew the book and the significance of events ('Duny keeps mist, throw a 6 before moving on'). Ogion has a positive influence; they used a part unsympathetic to them (which amused me) 'Ged picking herbs, miss two turns!'; and the Shadow, interestingly, is used to move Ged *on,* whilst human or wizard enemies delay him.

They also began to invent a card game, from which I found this scribbled list:

Good Cards: Ogion, Otak, Fog (!), Staff, Spells

Bad Cards: Dragon, Jasper, Shadow, Dead Otak, Dead Boy, Skiorh

Then a game which is like 'Scissors, Paper, Stone':

Giant Shadow—arms stretched out

Karg—hands on head

Sun—stretched hand

Embryonic, but the freer activity which this group needed.

In Art work, they produced a series of backgrounds with figures to group in front. When we mounted these, I stopped things blowing away and the Art man was the photographer. They produced an episodic sequence—I was hoping the work would be freer, but . . . .

I think the slides are rather good (the children were given little direction and little time); but they are naive and gentle, just parts of the story. We showed them one lunchtime as the

Collage work by
the pupils of
Pamela Barnard,
resulting from
reading *A Wizard
of Earthsea*.
Right: The Kargs
attack.
Below: The Mas-
ter unconscious.

group is split up now and the children remembered much more
than I did of what was what. Two slides seem to be missing,
(' 'Ere, where's my goats?'). Perhaps they'll turn up.

*   *   *

On Star Trek once I saw that Captain Kirk, who's in charge
of the ship itself, he went into this world, and his evil depart-
ed from his good and they both fought. You know, evil was
fighting good and they all parted from his body. You know,
you're like that—you've got evil in you and good. . . .
He walked up to the Shadow, when he started the battle

and when the real Ged, our Ged said that was his name, I was taken aback and the Shadow said to him, 'Ged', I didn't know what to do, and they they started to fight and they both had a hold over each other because they had the name. . . .

*   *   *

In January 1973 Lancashire Education Authority ran a one week residential course for young primary teachers. *A Wizard of Earthsea* was used as the only stimulus and some of the resulting work is described by John Cheetham, one of the general advisers responsible for the course:

The course was designed to give young teachers, who were not necessarily English specialists, the opportunity to develop their own skills in language, music, art and drama, and to explore the possibilities of interrelating these four arts. (We avoided the use of the word 'integration' because we are not sure what this means.) There were 36 teachers and four general advisers, each adviser having a specialist interest in an art.

Each member received a copy of the book to read before coming on the course, but no directions or suggestions how the book could be used. The work of the course was based on 'skill getting and skill using'. In the past we have felt that, apart from stimuli points, lectures have very little effect in in-service work, and we have found that a workshop approach is far more involving and rewarding.

During the first two days, we aimed at enjoyment. The teachers discussed the book, made music and explored sound, wrote, painted and became involved in drama work. Some examples of this work were:

In language and music, we combined words and instruments to show the joy and relief of these words; 'Estarriol,' he said, 'look, it is done. It is over.' He laughed, 'I am whole, I am free.'

And we also set 'It is over . . . It is done' to a Gregorian chant.

In drama we went on a journey (a strong element in child drama) and explored, within the journey, a series of conflicts, each group creating its own conflict, e.g., dragon, quicksand, mist, man-eating trees etc. The escape had to be made by words or a chant.

We played with place-names to show rhythm and pulse of music, e.g. Archipelago, Pendor, Gont, into a 3-part song.

We explored sounds on musical instruments to capture the moods of various incidents in the book (e.g. How do you make a *shadow* in sound? Or create an atmosphere of fear, or relief, or tension?)

We did some 'comprehension work' through Art:

(a) A language description of the ship *Shadow* gives enough details to draw the ship with some accuracy;

(b) The Dragon of Pendor, similarly;

but

(c) The Shadow, released by Ged, calls for some visual imagination.

The last three days were devoted to the development of the teachers' own ideas, following two suggestions:

(a) To take an incident or theme and explore these in two or more of the four skills they had experienced.

(b) To create their own incidents and themes derived from the book (e.g. What would have happened if Ged had spoken to the Stone of Terrenon?)

Each group had tape recorders, record player, access to a small record library and a wide variety of musical instruments currently in use in primary schools. The presentation of work done by each group was to be evaluated by the rest. All the five groups elected to present their work on tapes, with these titles: The Kargs' Invasion, Ged and the Dying Child, The Hawk's Flight, Ged Releases the Shadow, and The Last Journey of Ged. Two detailed illustrations of the work:

The Kargs' Invasion: On the tape was the linking narrative and accompanying music (Holst's *Planets* Suite and music created by the group). The group left blanks in the tape when dramatic work was going on. In this dramatic work, speech was used a great deal, whilst the death of the Kargs was mimed stylistically.

Ged and the death of Pechvarry's child. The creation of a spell to help the dying child, using place names of Earthsea or

Drawing by Peter
Sharpe on *A Wizard of
Earthsea*

the Hardad language. Guitar music as background to the
Land of Darkness when Ged goes too far. And as an epilogue,
this poem, spoken to the first track of Erik Satie's *The Velvet
Gentleman:*

I came through darkness,
Following a dying child
No stars died, nor swung with the world's turn.
The child was lost,
And I fought to reach the light.
A strong, known power—
My inner self behind the stone—
Barred my way;
But in the mage-light fled
And I awoke to sorrow.

*   *   *

Must have been terrible for him because he'd have to think
—it was me who let this Shadow loose and this Shadow's
taken over bodies, it's killing people as soon as it comes out
of this body and it was because of him the Master Mage died.

One slip-up that the woman makes, she says only black or
only dark evil may fight dark evil and then he comes out with
the suggestion that only light can defeat dark.

Last night, I thought, crikey! what's the time? 6 o'clock
and I looked through it—quite good this. Maybe I'll do the
fourth, maybe I'll do the fifth, sixth, seventh, eighth, ninth,
I finished the book that night.

*   *   *

A Wizard of Earthsèa was used as the basis for work by fifty
teachers at a workshop organized by Southampton University
Department of Education. One group discussed possible teaching strategies. Another group attempted 'a response to the novel
through movement', and worked especially on three themes:
the opening of a door and the exploration of a strange, powerful region beyond the door; the releasing of a spirit of unfore-
seen power; and the idea of hunting and being hunted. Michael
Benton, who led a third group, describes its activities:

Preliminary discussion took about 35 minutes. We were
unified by our delight in the book... 'Yes, loved it... beautifully conceived... splendid...' Enthusiasm plummets into
taut silence. We are tentative and hesitant about each other
.... Rescued by the scarcely muffled music from the drama
group next door, relaxing like mad, exuding all over the place.
But it's enough. We grin stupidly at each other and begin to talk
and I pluck up courage to hand round my outline paper, with-
drawing from its firm structure as I speak, conscious of them
gazing at that definite framework neatly tabulated. It's positive-
ly dripping with insecurity. (They've stopped relaxing next
door.) My eye catches '(4) Naming and Recognition' near the
foot of my paper; each of us names himself and we decide to
'see how the discussion goes' before we commit ourselves to the
workshop. We talk about the stress on learning a craft, achieving
self-knowledge, the morality of the book, the importance of
fantasy in the development of the child. Someone talks about

the book as a personal challenge and argues the need for *individual* reading and response rather than communal class reading and discussion. I grab this to introduce the workshop.

Hiatus. The barriers appear again temporarily. One woman says she wants to write a poem and the precedent is enough.

Everyone worked individually; there was an illustration of Ged fusing with the Shadow (felt-tips and sugar-paper); an inventive physicist who had come along drew a diagram to demonstrate the evolution of the dragon; someone took the idea of naming and made a large, stylized label of SPARROWHAWK out of sugar-paper; six or seven people wrote poems—about evil, about the four elements, about the idea of 'knowing' in their own upbringing; someone wrote the opening of his first novel; one lady sat and thought.

Thankfully people were ready to display and talk about their pictures and to read their poems. We heard from most of the group and then the lady who had not taken part in the workshop described why. The book had touched on areas of her own experience and qualities of her own character in a powerful way. She said she was an introverted person and her relatedness to others—particularly to a mentally handicapped person with whom she was living—was something she found illuminated by *A Wizard of Earthsea*, especially in the episodes to do with naming and entering the school at Roke. She felt that for her the book was about knowing oneself and knowing how to relate to others in order to trust and be trusted by them. I felt that, fortuitously, we had stumbled onto the main theme of the book. So we shut up and went for coffee.

*   *   *

I read all of Narnia—fantastic books; if you compare them with this you say, 'Oh, looks like a book for people of about fifteen' you know, you look in there and the first word you see is probably one you've never heard of before. Every other line is a word there's never been heard of—like in Narnia you've got 'lion' and you compare that with 'otak' which I've never heard of before in my life, and you say cor! this is even more mysterious!

*   *   *

Drawing by Peter Sharpe

Drawing by Peter Sharpe

M.Ed. Students at Exeter University School of Education discussed the book in a seminar. An American student commented that the School on Roke was very like the High School in California he had attended as a boy. Someone suggested that the book would make a good 'reader' for teachers in training at any stage. Various aspects of teaching and learning were particularly discussed:

As you enter a new place of learning, or a relationship in learning, you must commit yourself to the new situation: thus Ged entrusts his most valued possession, his name, his self, to the Master Doorkeeper.

Your first days in a new school or group frequently produce a strong sense of alienation: the adults appear to be talking in their own idiom, even in riddles; the initiated (Jasper) exclude the newcomer.

The ultimate lesson Ged learns on Roke, as he seeks a way out of the School, is that he must *receive* the Doorkeeper by asking his name: perhaps it is easier to give trust than it is to receive trust; for this is to share a responsibility.

The relationship between Ged and Ogion suggests the discipline needed to allow the place of silence in learning; and the distinction between apparently listening and actually hearing. Linked with this is the learner's responsibility in identifying what it is he must learn.

The need in learning and growth to embrace the negative parts of yourself, to hunt rather than be hunted.

*   *   *

When the battle came, I kept thinking Ogion was there. I thought he was watching it all—every move Ged made. If they ever write a sort of 'behind the scenes' to this, if you see what I mean, you'd probably find that he was watching it.

It was Ogion who gave him good advice—to hunt, not to be hunted. The Shadow was always hunting him.

From *Children's literature in education*, No. 11, May 1973

Feeling Like an Onion

Robert Barton and David Booth

Robert Barton is a Curriculum Services Officer, Ministry of Education, Ontario. David Booth is Chairman of Drama, Faculty of Education, University of Toronto. They are co-authors of Nobody in the Cast, *a student drama text,* Film, *a student handbook on the cinema; and* Colours, *a series about literature and language for children 8-12.*

In their original article, the authors wrote about drama work based on picture-books with older students. In this extract, they describe work which stemmed from Joseph Jacobs' collection of English Fairy Tales.

> 'According to Stanislavsky, you have to feel like an onion.
> 'Do you feel like an onion?'
> 'Not in the least,' said Harriet.
> 'Oh, come on. What are they teaching you in school these days?'
> (from: *Harriet the Spy*, Louise Fitzhugh)

DRAMA MAY BE described as struggling, doing and discovering about ourselves and our world. Learning through drama rather than learning about drama is the point of the activity. We feel that the picture-book provides an excellent source for engaging the imagination of the participants. At the same time appreciation of the literature is heightened as pictures and sounds are elaborated through movement and speaking activities. The playing out of thoughts, feelings and emotions adds much to the child's understanding of the material. The point is demonstrated in work which grew from *The Buried Moon*, a splendid tale from Joseph Jacobs' collection of *English Fairy Tales*, now available in picture-book form, hauntingly illustrated by New York artist Susan Jeffers.

In Canada, there is a growing awareness of the work of Murray Schaffer who has excitingly explored the realm of sound. Here, Schaffer's methods are employed to investigate some intense moments of the Lady Moon's adventure. Scarcely has the Lady Moon set foot upon the squishy mools and gurgling waters of the bog than she finds herself snagged in a life and death struggle with the Quicks, Bogles and other evil-doers who dwell in the darkness of the Carland. Commencing with Soundscape, a collection of sounds heard in a given place, the children move to Sound Chronicle, the telling of the story without words. At the same time as these children explore sound, they are deeply engaged in concentration and sensory awareness, both necessary if progress in drama is to be made. Although most of the work described involves individual exploration, eventually an exercise is attempted which requires the concentration of the whole class.

The room is filled with the sound of humming. It is as if a great pipe organ was slowly being activated. The children sit with eyes closed, scattered about the room each concentrating on the sound of his own voice. Moments before, the children were asked to take a deep breath, find a comfortable pitch and sustain a soft humming sound. Now the teacher is encouraging the class to increase the volume, change the pitch, experiment with the tone and vary the rate.

From the suggestions the children continue their experiments with sound, this time working with letters such as 'z', words which are onomatopoeic (pop), and colourful words like 'fuchsia'. The cacophony continues. Each child works with his sound—there are some self-conscious giggles, occasionally an eye opens, peers about and closes quickly. A routine check has been made; everyone else has his eyes closed. By and large, most faces reflect deep concentration as the sound rises and falls about the room.

The room is hushed and still, the goal now is to be aware of silence. A sigh, a sneeze, a rattle of coins all get in the way. It's hard to find silence. Yet silence is as important as sound.

The Lady Moon (ill. by Susan Jeffers, from *The Buried Moon* by Joseph Jacobs. Scarsdale: Bradbury Press, 1969). Reprinted by permission of Susan Jeffers.

The children have been asked to think about the marshes in the story. Each child is making a mental inventory of the sounds he thinks might burst forth from Quicks, Bogles and other Evil Things. And once again the air is rent with high-pitched squeaks, elongated 'oohs' and raspy 'thrafkas'. The teacher says:

Think about the Lady Moon bright and shining and how she decided to step down into the swamp and see for herself the horrors mankind spoke about. Begin with silence. . . and as the Lady Moon approaches get ready to make the sound of one of the creatures you want to be. All is well until she slips, loses the struggle with the Snag and is eventually dragged underwater and buried. Keep your eyes closed and concentrate on all the sounds around you as well as your own. If you listen hard you will know how the story is proceeding.

The children are concentrating very hard. All is quiet. . . and then a faint whispering is heard. Other baleful sounds accumulate. The volume increases, the diversity of sounds is exciting and now the thrashing death struggle of the moon is underway —for a moment the air is ripped by vocal thunder and then, as if by some unheard signal, the sound gradually dies away until only a clicking echo is heard, soft sighing, and then. . .

The children are excited and talk all at once about the composition. Little wonder, for the concentration was superb, the group sensitivity electric!

The discussion continues—only part of the story has been told—could the entire story be done this way? Might words be included? Could rhythm instruments add to the effect?

The planning continues enthusiastically. Little groups huddle in nooks and crannies, under tables and in doorways. Each group explores the sound possibilities of tambourines, shakers, drums, bells and triangles. Another clusters about a large sheet of paper printing out all the words they can think of that might be used as synonyms for moonlight. And yet another group is composing a poem to be chanted chorally about the moon's adventure.

There is talk of adding movement: someone else suggests that the room be darkened and flashlights used to add a visual 'story in light' to accompany the sound. The possibilities are endless.

The Gates: Writing Within The Community

Ken Worpole

Ken Worpole left school at sixteen and went to work in the civil engineering industry. He went to Brighton College of Education as a mature student and then spent four years teaching English at an East London comprehensive school. He now works for Centerprise in Hackney, running a community publishing project.

> Most people ignore most poetry
> Because
> Most poetry ignores most people

IT WAS with the above epigram that Adrian Mitchell prefaced his most recent collection of poems, and one could quite easily substitute 'books' for 'poetry' and the slightly altered epigram would worry us even more. For there is a truth in the proposition which for most of the time we repress, quickly moving on to secondary questions of fantasy versus realism, cash flow in the publishing trade, the 'adolescent novel', and so on. The important debate, surely, concerns the relationship between people and books, with the emphasis here on children as a section of these people. Even the order in which we put the two nouns, people and books, represents a set of priorities, for there are many people in the world of children's books who somehow find that, perhaps only inadvertently, they are always talking about the relationship between books and people, or 'getting more people interested in books' when they should be getting more books interested in people.

I remember at the 1973 Exeter conference on children's
fiction feeling very uneasy as time and time again participants
would place all the emphasis on the books, and dismiss as
irrelevant any concern for the people who actually might be—
or might not be—interested in reading them. In support of this
quite blatant commodity—fetishism—we had the following three
remarks given to us in the opening session: 'In the end what is
in libraries is more important than what is in people's minds';
'The children are irrelevant in reviewing children's books'; 'The
children are not the future, the living truth is the future', this
last being a quotation from Lawrence, a dangerous authority to
quote really, as he also said that the working class should never
have been taught to read. Apart from the philosophical illogicality that an artifact can have more value than the originating
mind, we must reassert that people—including children—are
more important than libraries, that their needs and aspirations
are relevant to the way in which we receive specific
books, and that children most certainly do represent many
aspects of the future.

Getting back to the relationship between people and books,
it is as well to remember that mass publishing and mass literacy
aren't very long established traditions, and it is probably worth
having a look at the quite significant ways in which both have
developed, *and are developing still.* Yes, it is important to
realize that we haven't quite reached the end of history yet;
there still could be quite different possibilities and options for
the future.

The idea of the social consequences of mass literacy only
became a political issue in Great Britain in the first decades of
the nineteenth century. (Although at the time of the English
Revolution, the level of literacy had been high, it subsequently
declined until the nineteenth-century revival.) There were
strong interests represented against the spread of literacy, as
can be seen in the following speech from a House of Commons
debate in 1807: 'However specious in theory the project might
be of giving education to the labouring classes of the poor, it
would, in effect, be found to be prejudicial to their morals and
happiness; it would teach them to despise their lot in life, instead of making them good servants in agriculture, and other

laborious employments to which their rank in society had destined them; instead of teaching them subordination, it would render them factious and refractory, as was evident in the manufacturing counties; it would enable them to read seditious pamphlets, vicious books, and publications against Christianity; it would render them insolent to their superiors; and, in a few years, the result would be that the legislature would find it necessary to direct the strong arm of power towards them.' Already this attitude was out of date, as the great Wesleyan Revival just prior to these debates had already taught many thousands to read, and other religious organizations were carrying on the work. What is interesting is that even once reading had become acceptable for the poor, the idea of teaching them to write was frowned on even by many of the reading teachers: 'They learn, on weekdays, such coarse works as may fit them for servants, I allow of no writing for the poor,' (Hannah More). 'It is not proposed that the children of the poor be educated in an expensive manner, or even taught to write and to cypher... It may suffice to teach the generality, on an economical plan, to read their bible and understand the doctrines of our holy religion.' (Alexander Lancaster).

Eventually, writing was allowed, although it is as well to remember that mass literacy was achieved without a statutory education system and by the efforts of the working class itself through its own religious and political organizations, often in spite of highly repressive measures against reading and writing at various times.

Today, of course, everybody supports the teaching of reading and writing, seeing them as two aspects of the same literacy process. However, if we look rather more closely at the assumptions which underpin our contemporary approaches to reading and writing, we may see that they represent nothing more than a refinement of nineteenth-century attitudes which, even at their most progressive, are in essence utilitarian. It is still a heresy to suggest that children might learn to read other than by entering the treadmill of a primary reading scheme, working inexorably through books 1 to 24, with many being called failures having not reached the end of book 6 by the end of the term. There are still thousands of children in primary schools stuck at any particular moment on book 4, *not allowed to read anything else*, until they have precisely memorized the appropriate words, and can yield them up, like poor Sissy Jupes acquiring the right definition of a horse, to the modern Gradgrinds. The structure of the majority of reading schemes is the mathematical one of compound interest—actually a metaphor which in more ways than one represents our education system—whereby the pupil starts with a little capital of basic vocabulary and compounds it day by day in strict progression. Consequently, reading for meaning, for enjoyment, is not permissible within the reading scheme (the search for meaning might delay the process). Many early writing procedures adopt the same pattern, so that the child is not helped to write what he or she wants to write, but instead is offered a series of inconsequential exercises from which to work.

Eventually, even if it is a matter of years, the children we teach are reading and writing; they have broken through, technically. We begin to get concerned with what they read and what they write. Often we are worried that they like—or have been conditioned to like—books filled with inert sentences containing plenty of action and facts, but which omit the appropriate extensions of motive, consequence, self-awareness. Their writing follows the same pattern. We bemoan their lack of imagination and in order to stimulate them we light fires under their noses and ask them to imagine they are sixteenth-century martyrs, or modern firemen, and to write imaginatively about their feelings, or take them on a visit to the local slaughterhouse and ask them to ponder on the inevitability of death. We forget that their lack of response, in reading and writing, is a direct consequence of the stilted and unimaginative materials with which we taught them earlier: their inconsequential and superficial stories are only the basic reading scheme structures writ large.

In recent years, though, quite a lot of attention has been paid to the quality of reading available to children, and this is naturally to be welcomed. There are now several comprehensive historical reviews of the best children's books; newspapers and magazines devote a fair amount of reviewing space just to children's books, often providing regular supplements; there are conferences held on the subject which has now also found itself a place on the syllabus of many colleges of education, and not least there is this journal, and one or two other special-ist journals. Our concern for their reading, therefore has taken on quite a formidable apparatus, and as a consequence raised the status of the children's book. Why is it, though, that little has developed in connection with the equally critical question of *how we respond to what children write*? There are no con-ferences on this subject, no learned articles, no specialist journ-als, not even a national association trying to struggle into existence somewhere. The only gesture towards this subject is the *Children's Literary Competition* organized, rather inter-estingly, by the much abused *Daily Mirror,* and the important work undertaken by the London University Institute of Educa-tion in its *Writing Across the Curriculum* project. I happen to find this absence of discussion on the question of why we ask children to write and what we do with their writing very signi-ficant, almost to the point of wanting to elaborate a conspiracy theory on the subject. In short, then, although there is now a recognition that children should be able to read as widely as possible, there is little seriousness or attention attributed to their writing, *which in practice fundamentally qualifies what they can potentially read.*

In the nineteenth century the ruling class's great fear of working class writing was that it would mean that a shared, and non-legitimized literary culture would be allowed to grow, and that this would have to be prevented. Two methods were used to combat this possibility of a class-specific writing community: repression of printers and publishers, and the flooding of the lower-class reading market by cheap, diversionary reading material in the form of useful knowledge magazines, blood and thunder broadsheets, comics, many of the direct descendants of these still holding sway today. It was from this that the idea developed, historically, that working class reading material, in particular, should be provided from outside that class, and not developed within it. The position is the one which still exists today and which is emphasized by the way in which we still cannot conceive of children's writing and that of their parents as having anything more than an ephemeral charm.

Therefore the position we thought we had arrived at — universal access to reading and writing, *and the integration of the two in the educational process—* is a fiction. Reading and writing in schools are two separate processes, and only mirror the wider alienation of production and consumption that characterizes the wider society. The abolition of this alienation, implying that what children write should be considered as something others can read, is a major task for all concerned with the relationship between children and the literacy process.

The above section is an attempt to set a context for a book that I have helped in publishing, and which I think in some ways makes a breakthrough in fiction for young people. It is called *The Gates*, written by two boys from Stepney, East London, and is jointly published by the Basement Writers and the Centerprise Publishing Project. The Basement Writers are a group of working class writers who meet once a week to read and discuss their work amongst themselves. It was originally encouraged to form itself by Chris Searle, who had known many of the original group either as students at the school where he was teaching, or as local people working and living in the neighbourhood. It is as well to mention, for those who may have missed the controversy, that Chris Searle was sacked from his teaching job in Stepney in 1972 after publishing a collection of poems by the children he taught, *Stepney Words*. The group has now been meeting for a year and has widened considerably in numbers and is an active presence in the cultural and political struggles of that particular part of London. In its first year it has published four individual collections of poetry: two by school-students, one by a retired docker and ex-boxer, and one by a young nurse. It has also published a political comic drawn by one of the local writers. Their frequent public readings are significant events in the area with many local people coming to listen and participate, and there is no doubt the quality of the work being written is greatly enhanced by the regular self-educational process involved in the group meetings.

The Centerprise Publishing Project is housed in a bookshop and community centre in an adjacent borough, and is a non-profit-making attempt to provide free publishing facilities for

The Gates is available from Centerprise, 136, Kingsland High Street, London E8.

local working class writers. In the past two years it has published four local children's books, two of them written by
children, six individual collections of poetry, three local working class autobiographies, and various local working class history
publications. The majority of these publications, about 30,000
copies all taken together, have been sold in the immediate area,
with one individual collection of poems, by a young West Indian boy (considered by some teachers in his school to have
been near-illiterate), selling 4,500 copies alone. As the one full-
time worker on this project, my job is to encourage and assist
local people to write, although so far there has hardly been any
need for encouragement, since it has become obvious that in
any community, an enormous amount of writing goes on that
is never allowed to become public because of the cultural inhibi-
tions that surround the idea of 'working class poetry', and other
forms of writing.

The Gates was written by two working-class boys shortly
after leaving a maladjusted school in the area, one to go to work
as a messenger boy in the City and the other to receive home
tuition in order to sit for some 'O' level exams. It is an autobiographical novel about two boys who have a pathological hatred
of school, and whose consequent truancy involved them in all
kinds of specialized educational and welfare 'solutions' until
they end up in the maladjusted school. In the introduction one
of them writes about how they came to write the book:

> When I was ill I remember thinking I was the only person
> in the world with a problem like mine. So we wrote this book
> to show school-phobics that they are not alone and that there
> is hope. And above all to show parents that when their child
> will not go to school no matter the consequences, then he or
> she may not just be having 'that Monday morning feeling' or
> 'lazyitis' . . .

It seems that one of the things about *The Gates* that
intrigues people the most is the fact that two people wrote it
without arguing so much that they couldn't carry on. Well we
did argue, and there were times when we just wanted to forget about the whole thing. But we persevered and succeeded.
A lot of people have asked us how did we go about starting
the book. Well I must confess, I didn't start it, Bill did . . .

For about six months before the start of the book he had been saying that we should write one about our experiences at our many schools. But I didn't take him seriously (much like the people who didn't believe we would write this book) then one day he turned up with the first part of *The Gates*, and I'll be truthful, I thought it was terrible, and that was how we started. Being big-headed, I thought I could do much better, and I wrote my idea of the first chapter. And for the next six months that's how it went: Bill would write his idea of a chapter then I would re-write it putting my ideas in. Sometimes a chapter would have to be written four or five times until we had it right. . . .

When Leslie and Bill had finished they took it along to the Basement Writers group, who decided that it should be published, and that this would best be done by Centerprise.

The most important aspect of the writing contained in the book is its complete honesty to the experiences involved, uncompromised by the appeal to stereotyped situations that occur so frequently in the commercially published 'concerned' adolescent fiction. The authoritarianism of many of the school situations in *The Gates* does not, in the end, turn out to be the result of a series of misunderstandings by the pupil—it is real and quite terrifying:

David followed the history teacher downstairs and into the headmaster's office.

The headmaster's secretary nodded when the history teacher asked if he could go straight in. David followed and stood looking down at his shoes.

'I was sitting upstairs in my class teaching this lad's form, and all of a sudden the wanderer returned.'

'Oh yes,' said the headmaster looking at David. 'This one does make a habit of touring London when he should be in school.'

He got up and walked round his desk and stood in front of David with his hands in his pockets.

'What's his excuse this time?' he asked the history teacher without taking his eyes off David.

'He says he had to go home to get his door key. He also

said that he told his cousin to come and tell me that he might be late. He said that he had permission from you.'

'Oh yes,' said the headmaster, 'when did he tell you all this?'

'Just now, coming down the stairs.'

'Well,' said the headmaster to David, 'that's a right load of rubbish, isn't it?'

'Yes,' said David, in a low voice.

The headmaster walked over to a high glass-fronted cabinet. He opened it, took out one of the seven or eight canes that hung on little hooks, and walked back to David. He hit the cane on the table with a loud 'whack' to test it. He turned to David.

'You are Paul Cook's brother, aren't you?' he asked.

'Yes.'

The headmaster looked at the history teacher. 'Paul Cook, he was a bit funny as well you know.'

'Don't say it runs in the family,' said the teacher.

'Unfortunately it does,' said the headmaster.

He turned to David. 'I have just about had enough of you,' he said loudly. 'You've been running away ever since you've been at this school. Your mother has even brought you, but you still insist on playing truant. Well, let's see if you still play truant after a good whacking. Now bend over and touch your toes.'

David bent over. The cane gave a loud thud as it hit him. He would always remember that caning. The feeling of injustice had never left and he doubted if it ever would.

The sympathy between individuals, when it flows, is fully human:

The Monday after, Geoff was sitting in front of a plump but friendly lady in the tutorial class.

'Well did you get here all right?' asked Mrs Cox, the teacher of the tutorial. She was a short woman, about five foot three inches tall. She had short black hair, pale blue eyes and a round face with very small features.

'I nearly didn't get here at all,' answered Geoff.

'What happened?'

'I jumped on to a bus. I had second thoughts about coming.'

'Oh I see. Would you like a cup of tea? Or maybe you would like a cup of coffee?'

'No thanks,' said Geoff.

Whenever he was nervous he could never eat or drink.

'You were saying, you jumped on a bus,' said Mrs Cox looking up from making her coffee.

'Well,' said Geoff, 'I got on the bus and I was having second thoughts about coming here,' he repeated. 'I walked down the street and stopped outside the gates and I was trying to pull myself into the class. But I couldn't. It was like there were two people inside me. One was saying, "Don't go in. Stay at home, you'll be safe there." And the other was saying, "Take no notice of that idiot. You go in the class. After all it's the best thing to do." I stopped and thought about it and I decided to give it a try and come in. And well, here I am.'

Mrs Cox looked at Geoff. 'Well Geoff,' she said, 'if your little friends ever come back, bring them in here with you and we'll give them a cup of tea.'

They both laughed. Mrs Cox poured some fresh ground coffee from the percolator.

'You sure you won't have some?' she asked.

Geoff hesitated. 'Oh well, O.K. then,' he said.

After they finished their coffee and biscuits, Mrs Cox showed him around.

'It's only a small place,' she said, 'but it's big enough for the amount of children that come here in the mornings.'

'What about the afternoons?'

'They're much the same as the mornings, only there are more children. Six to be exact,' said Mrs Cox, showing Geoff into the next room.

Geoff liked this place. It had a friendly atmosphere unlike the previous school he had been to.

'Have you ever worked in English work books?' Mrs Cox asked.

Geoff shook his head.

'Well they're books with the questions already in them and they leave little spaces for you to fill in the answers. It's quite fun. I sometimes have a go myself. Anyway, for an hour every day you'll work on this work book.'

She picked one up from the table.

'The rest of the day you've got free to paint, cook, or do some woodwork. And we've also got a record player. And if you like, you can play Scrabble.'

'What's Scrabble?' asked Geoff.

'You don't know what Scrabble is!' exclaimed Mrs Cox. 'You haven't lived! I tell you what, I'll give you a game later on.'

Later on Geoff was sitting opposite Mrs Cox for the second time that day. This time, instead of tea cups there was a Scrabble board on top of the desk. Geoff was sitting fiddling about with the small square plastic markers which the letters were written on.

'Vertigo!' shouted Mrs Cox as she placed the letters V.E.R. T.I. down on the board next to G.O.'

Geoff had found out that the object of the game was to try and make up as many words as he could. Some letters had numbers on them. Geoff found out that the player with the highest number wins. Geoff had never been so bored with any game in his life as he was with Scrabble.

The next day Geoff managed to force himself into the class. In fact, he went regularly for two months. In that time he had painted fifteen pictures (one of them being a four foot by four foot mural of Trevor Brooking, scoring a goal for West Ham from the penalty spot), baked forty cakes, (burnt twelve), made a ship out of balsa wood, and made thirty-five cups of tea and fifty cups of coffee. But the most important achievement of all was that he had only one dizzy spell in the whole of the two-month period. Things were definitely looking up for Geoff.

It was coming to the end of another coffee-making, picture-painting, model-constructing day. The smaller children (three of them) were in the painting room painting some pictures. Geoff was in the main room where Mrs Cox was talking to a lady about her son. From what Geoff could

gather, the lady's son had much the same trouble as himself.
'Poor sod,' thought Geoff, 'I know how he feels.'

Similarly, we see the complicated world of school and the
battery of supporting agencies associated with it, through the
eyes of the pupils themselves unmediated by an adult sense of
balance and artistic resolution. *The Gates* is an artistic whole,
but it achieves its completeness with a device that no adult
writer could use: that having gone through the many experiences in the book the two boys decided to transform their
knowledge:

> David went over to one of the windows and looked out
> of it. He was pleased. The show hadn't been perfect, but
> everyone had enjoyed themselves. Geoff came over to him.
> He said,
> 'The play was funny wasn't it!'
> David nodded and turned around.
> 'You know,' said Geoff, 'we've done some funny things
> these past few years, haven't we?'
> 'Yes,' replied David looking round the hall. 'We should
> write a book about it some day.'
> *The End.*

The writing of *The Gates* is of a completely different order
from what we signify as 'writing' in schools. Leslie and Bill said
that they had never written anything longer than two pages before they left school. Their first chapter, at their first attempt,
amounted to one and a half pages of writing. It was at this point
that they realised that, in a sense, they had not been taught to
write, and in the ensuing six months, in which they completed
50,000 words, they became writers. As they put it themselves,
'We learned to write by writing the book.'

By advocating the right of young people to write for each
other, and that teachers and others should assist them in publishing their work, I am not suggesting that these new sources of
literature should become exclusive. I doubt whether any six-
teen-year-old will produce a *Tom's Midnight Garden*, a *Carrie's
War*, or any of the best books written by adults for children,

and these should always be part of the reading of young people. On the other hand, I am suggesting that many young people would write better books than many of the commercial offerings which at present dominate school reading.

I conclude with one example, taken from a very popular series of commissioned novels for teenage readers, all very attractively produced—Macmillan *Topliners:*

> The sudden loud yelp of a car horn behind them made the two boys leap hurriedly for the mossy verges only seconds before a sleek dark blue Rover 2000 bumped past with a violent lurching of springs. Danny instantly recognized the grinning face behind the wheel as one he had seen many times in magazines, newspapers and on T.V. Those swarthy features, the tight black curls and the strong white toothpaste smile could only belong to 'Mad Mike' Domingues, 'The Welsh Toreador', the man who for the past two seasons had headed the list of Football League scorers and the man all Englishmen wished had been born another fifty miles east, on the Birmingham side of the Border. Beside him sat the heavy figure of Tommy McNaught, the best, and toughest, uncapped wing-half in the country and Tommy Dale's own particular hero. At this moment it came home to Danny what a tremendous thrill it was for him to be mixing with such great national figures as these. A great rush of pride swept through him only to disappear as he recognized the leering features and derisory gestures of the car's third occupant as those of 'The Ferret'.
>
> *First Season*—Roy Wilson

As an English teacher, I would feel that I had failed if a child I had taught for some time presented me with this kind of writing, full of false sentiments, comic book stereotypes, and literary opportunism. Yet no doubt thousands of these books have been presented to children in the classroom as part of their reading diet, sanctioned by all the authority of the school. Teachers all over the country are presented with writing far superior to this every day of the year, yet this gets published and their work eventually ends up in a waste-paper bin.

I said at the beginning of this essay that the historical development of mass literacy is still continuing, that the options for creating a quite different kind of literary culture are not closed, given the political will to work towards a different kind of cultural situation. The technical means of producing books outside the commercial publishing world are easily available now. Already many schools possess their own printing presses. Nothing will happen, though, unless we acknowledge that the children we teach have significant inner lives and ought to be allowed to share their experiences through the mediation of writing, just as Leslie Mildiner and Bill House have given us their lives in the form of a marvellously written book.

From *Children's literature in education*, No. 17, June 1975

That's All!*

Edward Blishen

*Edward Blishen has worked as a broadcaster, editor and review-
er and is now a freelance writer and lecturer. He has taught in
preparatory and secondary schools, and at York University. He
has written and edited several books, including* The God Beneath the Sea *(with Leon Garfield).*

A TEACHER WHO profoundly affected the relations of children and books in the school where I was taught myself was an
Irishman appointed to teach mathematics on the grounds that
he was an international lawn tennis player. He was actually a
mathematical defective. He taught us in the first form and is
certainly one of the reasons (along with some natural causes)
why I am a mathematical defective myself. He taught us by an
extraordinary method; he used to ask us what he called 'batches
of five', and these 'batches of five' were intended to be mental
arithmetic questions; but they degenerated very quickly
throughout a lesson, becoming general questions about life,
letters and so on. The school secretary would come in and he
would say when she left, 'What is the colour of Mrs Hibbard's
eyes?' I remember that (curiously, because we were all deeply in
love with Mrs Hibbard) none of us knew the answer. There he
was, mathematically defective but with a great natural passion
for literature, which of course he was accordingly never invited
to teach. He used to give us free use of his private library at
home. He used to bring us books in a perfectly natural way. He
talked about books with joy and pleasure, and also when it was
necessary—and it turned out to be often necessary—talked
abusively about books. He had a lovely habit as he came un-

*These extracts are taken from an informal closing talk which drew to-
gether different strands at a conference.

242

gowned into Assembly—because, as you know, lawn tennis and a profound passion for literature don't earn you gowns—he had a habit, as he passed between the rows of boys, of tossing a book into your lap as he went by with some murmur of: 'Sh—you'll love this,' or 'Sh—you'll hate this,' or best of all, 'Don't let anybody see that! Keep it quiet!' I remember one of the books he told me to keep quiet about was *Tess of the D'Urbervilles,* and I am eternally grateful, though it was already half a century too late to keep quiet about that. But what a sense of conspiracy he knew how to generate! Pedagogically he was an immensely ingenious man, though in fact in pedagogy he might have rated very low indeed. How simple was all that he did, and how good it was to be made part of his life as a reader! How influential to have this utterly natural exhibition by a grown-up, with whom you were constantly in contact, of the quality of a true reader who displayed before us, quite naturally, all the responses to books, rage as well as deep appreciation. How simple! Because indeed, *that's all.*

Of course, teachers have to ask themselves questions about books and methods; but in the end I believe it is an utterly simple thing—we accept ourselves the natural benefits of reading, using the word benefits in all its richest senses, and from that acceptance we develop and draw out of it naturally those intuitions that tell us what to do about literature in education. And this, I believe, is really fundamentally our task: to become as sensitive as possible to the whole nature of literature, and to join that with our other professional task of becoming as sensitive as possible to the nature of human beings, and in our case especially young human beings. I believe that this is what, at heart, it is all about: it is about simply delighting in the existence of literature and using the energies that arise out of that delight in a natural way.

If the habit of reading does not grow, it seems to me that this is not due to some ineptitude of literature, but rather because, by being too teacherly (perhaps, as a teacher, I may use that term), we have allowed the excitement to disperse, the delight and humour and so on that are all important. We might have missed the point about William Mayne, for instance. You have to walk into one of his books sideways—it's an excellent exercise in being a crab, down to having your eyes on stalks. The books he writes are mysterious, oblique books, the relief of reading which lies in the holiday they give you from the common effort in which we are normally engaged to make a sort of stodgy continuity out of the events and ideas and perceptions in which we are involved. William Mayne, I think, is one of the few pure wits who have ever written for children. We should be careful about analysing and using such work until the excitement and delight of it are fully experienced and absorbed.

The nature of literature is such that teachers' treatment of it in schools will succeed only if the treatment reflects some sense of, as it were, a delicate, shielded mystery. For that, when the talking is done and all the questions are asked, is the inner character of literary creation itself. Ultimately what we have to do is to bring literature and children together. And in bringing about this union, one of the most important skills that we who are concerned with children and literature can cultivate is that of reading aloud. Again, it is simple. Again, *that's all.* I remember with gratitude one of the first headmasters I worked with when I taught in secondary modern schools in London. He was one of those prowling headmasters, always nervously believing that something negligent was occurring somewhere. He also believed very firmly that reading aloud is a soft option, both for children and for teachers, and that it should be reserved for the last afternoon of term and then only if the class has been absolutely saint-like throughout the whole year. So, having discovered myself that the only really positive thing I knew about my boys was that they were starved of words and language, and that perhaps the most important thing I could do was simply to read to them, I had to read to them without appearing to do so. And because he had this prowling habit and used to look through the glass panel in the door, I mastered the habit of appearing to be conducting a purely formal, dreary lesson of the kind that he thought was proper, with a piece of chalk and so on, and I would have a book on the desk and picked up the habit of being able to read two or three sentences at a time, or take them and store them in my head and walk away from the book and deliver them. It still seems to me one of the gifts of reading aloud that teachers should cultivate anyway. I have noticed that you go into a classroom sometimes and there is a teacher reading an excellent book, reading to his reluctant readers, wondering perhaps why they are not very much drawn by what he is reading. But what he is doing is simply standing there with his eyes on the book. He has not even mastered the art of looking at his listeners, which we know is essential if we are to hold the attention of anyone. He has his eyes on the book and is reading in a monotone—a teacher's monotone. The simple fact is that reading aloud is of the utmost importance—a truth that through its very simplicity and obviousness is sometimes in danger of being forgotten.

Certainly I believe the discussion of particular books is important, so long as analysis of books and discussion of the use of the books is always subordinated to the desire to take in and understand and feel a whole book as a whole book, as an ultimately unanalysable whole. It is clear that this is what the writers, who must be taken to be the greatest experts on their own work, desire us to feel about their books. If we have to examine them, they want us ultimately to withdraw from that examination. They want us first not to examine but to take in and, after our examination, again to apprehend the work as a whole. If we do this, then our children may do it; and fewer of them will carry away from school, as so many of them now do, the notion that a book is something that has constantly to be taken to pieces to find out how it works, or why it does not. But joy, I think, joy and delight excuse and justify much analysis. Of course we *talk* about books, and in doing so make more acute those intuitions and sensitivities about books that we need to take into the classroom.

When one sees the problem of creating readers at grass roots level, one realizes various things. One realizes that we can in our professional way overlook the fact that literature itself is so magnificent that very often all it really requires is excitement on our part to cause reading to take place. I think reluctant readers create reluctant readers, shy readers create reluctant readers, and insofar as the school can at all influence this matter—and some of the roots of the problem, I think lie outside the schools—it must be through the exhibition in ourselves, the teachers, of what a true reader is—an excited person, whose responses to books are many and varied and complicated.

From *Children's literature in education*, No. 2, July 1970